A

ROSE
BLOOMS

ROSE RYBACHEK

a ROSE BLOOMS

An Autobiography

LARGE PRINT

LitPrime
"Your story is our priority"

LitPrime Solutions
21250 Hawthorne Blvd
Suite 500, Torrance, CA 90503
www.litprime.com
Phone: 1-800-981-9893

Published by LitPrime Solutions   04/06/2023

ISBN: 979-8-88703-175-0(sc)
ISBN: 979-8-88703-176-7(hc)
ISBN: 979-8-88703-177-4(e)

Library of Congress Control Number: 2023902937

ACKNOWLEDGEMENTS

Bringing a book from your memory into a written document is a long, laborious process, even if it is a labor of love. It could not be done without the support of family and friends, and the encouragement they offer.

I would like to thank my kids, Sue, Sallie and Cyndi for their support. Also, my sister and brother, Henry and Debbie, for their assistance. My friend Joy has been a pillar of encouragement and help, and I thank her for everything she did for me. But, most of all, I thank my creator, who has given me a most wonderful life to write about.

Rose Rybachek

Other books by this author:

CONTENTS

INTRODUCING MY PARENTS

*D*orothy Ebner Lilley was born June 20, 1916 on her parents' homestead in Living Springs, Montana. Dorothy was the seventh child born to Lester and Anna Lilley, who would have five more children after Dorothy's birth. She could trace her family history back to Peter Lilley, who became the father of Walter Lilley in about 1764 in Pennsylvania. Another of Dorothy's ancestors came over with King George's army, and fought on the side of England. After the Revolutionary War, this ancestor stayed and married into the Lilley Family.

She grew up on the homestead and attended school in Buffalo, Montana. After she graduated as valedictorian in 1934, Dorothy went to normal school in Lewistown, which was a 2-year school to train elementary teachers. Her older sister Edna enrolled at the same time. Upon completing two years of school,

Dorothy got a job teaching school at a small country school.

FREDRICK VERNON BLOOM WAS born on January 14, 1909, in Beaver Creek, Montana. He could trace his family tree back to 1752 when John Peter Blum Jr. (later changed to Bloom) came to America on a ship at the tender age of three. John Peter Bloom (Blum) Sr. fought for the Americans in the Revolutionary War.

Fred grew up in the Roundup, Montana area, and in his early twenties, he worked with his father in Yellowstone Park. Fred was quite a dashing young man. He liked fast cars, faster women, drinking and dancing the night away. Fred was known for his hair-trigger temper. He could fly off the handle quicker than a person could blink. Usually, his temper would burn out as rapidly as it occurred, but once in a while, he would stew for days over some perceived slight.

For a while, Fred dated one of Mom's older sisters, who was quite the swinger herself. One day when he took her home, her younger sister (Dorothy) was there. Fred fell for Dorothy like a ton of bricks. He invited her to go out with him several times before she finally accepted. She was shy, timid, and concerned about his reputation.

Fred was a gentleman when he was with Dorothy. He took her dancing and to box socials (a fund-raising affair at which box lunches are auctioned to the highest bidder). At a box social, he always bid the highest on her box of goodies. He asked her several times to marry him, but she always turned him down. In desperation, he promised that if she would marry him, he would settle down. Finally, she agreed, and they were married in Lewistown, Montana on January 2, 1937.

Some people claimed that the Lilley Bloomed upon that marriage. Which may have been true. Anyway, these are my parents, Fred and Dorothy Bloom.

Remember Groucho Marx and his famous statement that "I must confess, I was born at a very early age?" Well, I must confess that my adventures of life began *before* I was born!

SECTION I

The Early Years

KEEPING OUR GUARDIAN ANGELS BUSY

This all happened on St. Patrick's Day in 1938. Mom and Dad had been married for a little over a year. They decided to go to Roundup, Montana to visit with his sister Eddie and her family. They had dinner with the Haleys and then took in a dance. An unseasonably late snow storm descended on Roundup, and my prospective parents decided to go home to Buffalo (about a hundred miles) instead of spending the night with Eddie, as planned.

They had been married for 15 months and were expecting their first child, me. I heard this story many times while I was growing up, and this is how it was told to me. Their trip was going smoothly until… Bang! Everything became a blank.

Shaking his head, my dad slowly opened his eyes. Where was he? Snow pelted the windshield as he slowly turned his head. He realized he was bent over the wheel of his 1933 three-window Ford Coupe. He could hear steam seeping from the hood of his car, and there was a dark object embedded into the front and passenger side of his car. What was going on?

Then the nightmare of what had happened slowly seeped into his consciousness. He remembered the oncoming headlights; how he'd done everything he could to avoid a collision; how he'd dived into the ditch. He remembered the horror as the headlights kept getting larger and larger, and then hearing the screech of tearing metal. Then nothing.

Upon coming to, he glanced over to his right where he had last seen his six-month pregnant wife, Dorothy. The door was open. Dorothy was gone.

"Dorothy?" he tentatively asked. Nothing. Louder now, "Dorothy?" Still nothing.

Slowly the details of the last few minutes entered his tortured brain. Some idiot had been driving on the wrong side of the road, in a blinding snowstorm, and had hit him head-on. His wife was missing, and probably dead. White-hot anger raced through him, and he uttered, "I'm going to kill the son-of-a-bitch. He killed my wife!"

He struggled to get out of the car, but his door was jammed. As his anger grew, so did his strength, but with a super-human burst of strength, he shoved the door open with a loud screech. He staggered to his feet and raced around the back of the car as fast as he could go, intending to find the driver who was responsible for the death of his wife and unborn child. What his intentions were, once he got his hands on the driver, would probably have put him in jail for years.

As he neared the cab of the other car, he heard a tiny, weak voice, "Fred? Fred?"

"Dorothy?" he called back incredulously. It sounded like her, but, where was she?

Forgetting all about revenge for the moment, he turned to find the source of the voice. Was it just his imagination? No, it surely was Dorothy. She must not be dead, since she kept asking for him. And, to the best of his muddled thinking, if she were really dead, she probably could not talk.

As she continued to call, he carefully followed the sound of her voice. Aha! She was imprisoned between the two cars. He tried to reach her, but the passenger door of his car was crumpled, and she was lying on the ground between the two cars. He could teeter the other car away from the door, but he could not hold that car away and grab Dorothy at the same time. He needed help. What to do? The only one who could possibly help was the driver of the other car.

He hastened back to the cab of the wrecked car, and there he found the driver, drunk as a skunk and singing, "Twinkle, Twinkle, Little Star." And, he was laughing.

"I'll 'twinkle' you, you drunk!" Dad yelled, as he grabbed him by the scruff of his neck, hauled him out of the cab of his old Chevy, and pinned him against the door.

"Grab hold of that car frame, and pull as hard as you can!" Dad yelled. And, surprisingly, the drunk did as he was told. The car teetered away from the crumpled door and Dad gingerly crawled under the debris, grabbed hold of Mom, and dragged her out from under the wreckage.

"Are you okay?" Dad asked.

"I think so," Mom replied. "I saw those headlights coming, and the next thing I knew, I was lying on the ground, and it was cold. I'm glad it's almost quit snowing now, or I'd be freezing… My winter coat is in the car!"

Fortunately, another car came by and stopped. "Can I give you a ride into Lewistown?" the driver asked.

"Please do," my Dad replied. "I think we'd better go to the hospital right away, and make sure that my wife hasn't been hurt by that drunken SOB," Dad replied. He settled Mom in the backseat and crawled into the backseat next to her.

Upon arriving at the hospital, the doctor examined my Mom. "She has a few cuts and bruises, but I don't see anything that would warrant keeping her in the hospital, and the baby's heartbeat is strong and healthy," he said.

It was fortunate that my Dad had an aunt and uncle living in Lewistown, so Mom had a comfy place to stay while Dad and his uncle drove the 10 miles back to inspect the scene of the accident.

The Chevy was gone, but the Ford remained. My parents never did find out what happened to the drunk! Dad and Uncle Clair pulled Dad's Ford into Lewistown, and Dad worked on it for a couple of days. A hammer straightened the door, although it never did latch correctly again. In a couple of days Mom and Dad were on their way home to Buffalo, about 30 miles down the road. I, of course, remember nothing of the accident.

It was a miracle that both Mom and the six-month fetus (me) survived the nasty wreck. Our Guardian Angels were looking out for us then, and I suspect that I've been keeping mine busy ever since.

BARELY STARTING OUT

For over a decade my Dad worked for a construction company that was developing Yellowstone National Park. As you probably know, Yellowstone Park was established in 1872, as the first national park in the United States, and is widely believed to be the first national park in the world. The Old Faithful Inn was built in 1903-1904 but was remodeled in 1927. My Dad worked on some of the outside work of the remodel, plus he built retention walls for that construction.

Over the years he worked at various sites within the Park, including Mammoth Hot Springs, West Thumb Canyon, and Yellowstone Canyon. He helped construct roads, but building retaining walls was his specialty. In 1936 when the Yellowstone Park Company expanded the Old Faithful Inn to add the Bear Pit Lounge and Restaurant, he was called back to work on that project.

After he and Mom got married, they moved to

the Park in the spring of that year. Mom had never experienced anything remotely as interesting as life in the Park. The Park Service provided permanent tent frames, which included a wooden floor. All she and Dad had to do was pitch their tent over the frame, and they had a home. They could easily move their tent from one frame to another, depending on where Dad was working. It was a nomadic life, but Mom loved it. She cooked, while Dad worked, and she kept the tent ready to move at a moment's notice. Mom met many of the other wives and enjoyed her first year as a wife.

Mom and Dad spent their winter at a coal mine near Buffalo with my future Grandma and Grandpa, Dad's mother and father. The guys dug and sold coal during the winter months. Grandpa Bloom could have worked all year at a coal mine in Roundup if he had wanted to, but he preferred to spend his winters in Buffalo. The coal mine was high on a hill, and at the bottom of the hill lived their landlords, Albert and Dorothy Dover. When spring arrived, Grandma and Grandpa, and Mom and Dad packed up and went their separate ways, Grandpa and Grandma to Roundup and Mom and Dad back to Yellowstone.

When Mom and Dad returned to Yellowstone Park in the spring of 1938, everything was different. Mom was expecting!

Mom and Dorothy (the wife of the owner of the coal mine) had become very good friends and after Mom and Dad left for the summer, Dorothy and Mom corresponded by letters. One day in late April, Dad handed Mom a letter from Dorothy. She immediately ripped it open as Dad headed back to the truck to return to work. She ran out to catch him as he drove away. "Fred, Fred!" Mom yelled. "Dorothy is expecting about the same time I am! Isn't that wonderful? Maybe I can stay with her in Lewistown until our babies are born."

"I don't much like the idea of two pregnant women trying to take care of each other," Dad replied. "I'll take you to Lewistown the middle of May. You can stay with Uncle Clair and Aunt Ruth until the baby is born, and then, when you're ready to travel, we can all come back to the Park."

"I don't much care for that idea," Mom replied. "I don't want to be in Lewistown giving birth, while you're in the Park!"

"I can't just quit my job," Dad said. "Any other suggestions?"

Not being able to come up with anything better, Mom was soon packed off to stay with the relatives. However, my parents did have another important discussion (at least to me!) before the big move. What to name the baby!

"If it's a boy, I want to call him Richard Vernon, after my Uncle Richard, and Vernon is my middle name," my Dad told Mom. "If it's a girl, I want to call her Rose Lee, after my two favorite aunts." (Dad always was pretty forceful when it came to naming his offspring.)

"Fred, I don't mind the Richard Vernon," Mom replied. "But Rose Lee is so choppy, and it sounds like some dance hall dame, I think we should call her Rosalie Ann since my mother's middle name is Anna. That sounds a lot better to me than Rose Lee!"

"Okay, you win this time," Dad said.

June 18 dawned, and Mom was in labor. The relatives hustled her off to the hospital. She was disappointed to find that she was there before her friend Dorothy, but she was happy to deliver a healthy eight-pound baby. Me! I had arrived, safe and sound. Rosalie Ann Bloom had arrived, (although most of my life I have been known as Rose, so Rose Bloomed on that day).

In those days, it was customary to keep women in the hospital after childbirth for a week. On the sixth day after I arrived, Dorothy Dover finally showed up. She also gave birth to a healthy baby girl, who was a couple of pounds lighter than I was. The good friends were reunited for a day and their offspring, my nearly twin and I, have been good friends ever since.

After discharge, Mom spent a month staying with the relatives, before Dad felt comfortable coming to get her to spend the last few months at Yellowstone. Finally, the day arrived that he came, and before long, his coupe was parked in front of a tent house in Yellowstone National Park, and they were busy unloading all the things they thought they'd need to sustain a new baby in a summer camp.

They stashed me, sound asleep, on the rear seat of the coupe, while they hauled things into the tent house. They were putting things away, when they heard me let out a horrendous scream from the car.

"I wonder what her problem is now," Mom said. "I just fed her, and she should be sleeping. Guess I better go check on her," she said, as she made her way to the door.

"Oh, no!" she exclaimed. "Fred, come here, quick. What can we do?"

As Dad looked out the door of the tent house, all he could see was the posterior of a very large black bear filling the entire open door of the coupe. The bear continued gingerly backing out the door. In its mouth was a lunch box that had been sitting on the back-window shelf of the coupe. The bear stood right over the squalling baby before it landed on the ground on all fours. Upon seeing Mom and Dad staring at it, it turned and made its way out of the campsite, taking the lunch pail.

Mom raced to where I was hollering for all I was worth, fists waving, and red in the face. She gingerly picked me up. "I think she's just fine," Mom said, as she unwrapped me. "That bear fur probably tickled her face, as he crawled up to get the lunch box and woke her up."

They never did get the lunch box back. But I was safe and unharmed.

SLIPP'N AROUND

*W*e spent the rest of that summer living in various tent houses in Yellowstone Park, while I grew and stayed healthy. When fall arrived, it was time to move back to the mine cabin near Buffalo. Mom was happy to be back with her good friend Dorothy plus Grandma Lilley and all my aunts and uncles.

The first time Dorothy and Mom got together after the move, Dorothy exclaimed, "Where's Rosie's hair?"

"Well, she doesn't have any," Mom replied. "But it's really easy to keep her head clean. I just wash it like her face. I think it must be hard to keep Maralyn's hair clean. I've gotten so used to no hair, that babies look strange to me when they have hair! Maralyn has a wonderful head of hair, and I love the barrettes you've put in it."

For some reason, I continued to be as bald as a "cue-ball" for several years. I, of course, don't have any memories of living at the mine cabin. It does seem as though I was quite active. For the next 75 years, my Mom complained about one little incident that happened when I was about 10 months old.

Mom bought fresh eggs, milk, and cream from the Dovers. Their oldest boy, Colin, delivered. One day he made his delivery of a dozen eggs and a quart of whipping cream. My Mom had "fenced" me into a corner of the room, using chairs laid down on their sides and cardboard boxes filled with books for weight, to keep the chairs from tipping over.

"Mrs. Bloom," Colin said. "I'd like to show you this strange looking plant I found on my way here. Do you know what it is?"

Mom set the eggs and cream down on the table and went outside with Colin, where she examined the plant.

"Why, I believe it's a crocus!" she said. "I bet if you plant it in your yard, you'll have a beautiful flower blooming in a week or so."

"Thanks," Colin replied. "I'll do that." Gathering up his plant, he headed down the hill to his house.

When Mom entered the cabin, she found a mess. While she was gone, I'd climbed up on one of the overturned chairs and dumped the eggs and cream on the floor of the cabin. Not being content with that, I'd gotten down from the chair. When she came back in, I was slipping and sliding around in the mixture of broken eggs and cream. I was giggling, and as happy as could be. Not one egg was left intact… I had gotten them all. The cream… well, I had more cream on me than the floor did. I was having a wonderful time, but my pleasure was short lived. Soon I was sitting in a tub of warm water, listening to Mom as she grumbled under her breath. She was not a happy camper as she cleaned up the mess.

Paper towels had not been invented yet, so cleanup was quite a chore. Plus, she had no eggs or cream for cooking. However, one good thing came from the episode. She was careful where she set down the next delivery, and I never again had the opportunity to take a bath for my complexion.

BEEHIVE BEAUTICIAN

*L*ife continued in the same fashion for the next couple of years. We spent our summers in Yellowstone Park and our winters at the mine cabin near Buffalo. When I was three, my Dad came home from buying supplies in Lewistown and declared. "I ran into this guy in town that has a farm for rent near Beehive, and I rented it. We'll be moving there instead of going to the Park this year."

"Beehive? Where is that?" Mom asked in a stunned voice.

"Well," Dad said, "it's in Southwest Montana, near the Stillwater River. This farm has 120 acres, but most of it's just pasture land. It isn't far from the Stillwater, and there's great fishing. And, we will look right at the mountains. I bet we can get a deer every year, and maybe even a cougar or two."

"You actually rented a farm?" Mom replied, still stunned. "We both grew up on farms, but I think there's a big difference between growing up on a farm and operating one. Have you ever run a farm on your own?"

"Well, no, but what's there to know? We'll have a few cows to milk and raise some sheep and pigs. According to the guy, there are hayfields and some acres that we can plant to grain. He says there's an old tractor that might need some work but runs. I've worked as a mechanic all my life, so that should be simple. And, he says there's some haying equipment, and even an old plow. It'll be a good life."

Soon all our belongings were moved to Beehive, and we were farmers. For the first year on the farm, Dad enjoyed the challenge of being a farmer. He bought a couple of milk cows; a few beef cows, chickens, pigs, geese, and some sheep. He was busy during the summer putting up hay and growing grain to feed the livestock. Mom spent most of her time in the kitchen making delicious meals, which I enjoyed. There is nothing like the smell of fresh-baked bread as it comes out of the oven. If I pleaded with Mom enough when she was making the bread, she'd give me a bite of the delicious bread dough. I liked it plain, but when I was lucky enough to get the end from a cinnamon roll, I thought I was in heaven.

It was a highlight of my day when I was allowed to go out to feed the chickens with Mom and help with the chores. Gathering eggs was the most fun, although once in a while I'd drop one, and that made a mess.

Summer was spent with both Mom and Dad working hard on the farm, and I loved every minute of being a farmer. Towards fall, Dad acquired a black and tan hound that he named Old Leed. That dog did love to hunt. Dad often went hunting with him during the winter, and they usually came home with something to show for their effort. Old Leed particularly loved chasing coyotes, but Dad seldom had a chance to shoot them. They did bring home a lot of rabbits, which were delicious when Mom cooked them. The next summer rolled around and Dad got busy with farm work. One day when Dad was occupied with putting up hay and didn't have the time to go hunting, Old Leed disappeared! He was gone for nearly a week, and my folks thought he had probably met with a horrible end. They were very surprised when he showed up, but it wasn't long before he disappeared again. After a week or so, he was back. Every time he disappeared, Mom and Dad thought a bear or wolf had caught him, but he always turned up. He weighed about 90 pounds, so it would take a good-sized predator to do him harm.

A few months later they started hearing rumors in the neighborhood of a dog running amok and even attacking deer. One day when Old Leed disappeared, Dad went hunting for him. He found him, gorging on a fawn. Dad and Mom didn't want him hunting deer by himself, so from then on, they tried to keep him locked in the house or barn. He wasn't happy being a prisoner, but most of the time he put up with it. His options were few since he never quite learned the art of unlocking doors.

Old Leed was my friend. He would follow me around and never once ran over me, even though he was a lot bigger than I was. I even rode on his back once in a while, trying to talk him into being a pony. One day Old Leed and I were in the living room, when Mom heard him crying and whining. She ran in to investigate and found Old Leed lying on the floor with me astraddle of him. I had his ears pulled over the top of his head, and I was trying to pin them together with a large safety pin. I actually had the pin stuck through one of his ears but was having trouble trying to get it through the other one, and often he'd shake his head while crying.

"What are you doing?" Mom shouted at me.

"His ears were dragging on the ground, so I'm trying to keep them clean," I replied.

"Well, stop it," she said. "You're hurting him!"

"I don't want to hurt him. I just want to keep his ears clean from being on the ground."

That was the end of my career as a beautician. Mom took away my safety pin and I never saw it again.

BEEHIVE EXPLOITS

*M*y memory of farm life in Beehive is rather sketchy, since I was not very old. But a few occurrences stand out. The kitchen was rather large and had an old icebox on one side; a gas stove stood on the opposite wall; the third wall had a double sink (it actually had running water piped to the sink); and there was a wood stove on the fourth wall with a hallway leading towards the rest of the house. The center of the kitchen held a large table, surrounded by eight chairs.

I was sitting on my Dad's lap at the kitchen table one morning as Mom was starting to cook breakfast. Suddenly it got very dark in the room.

"Do you hear that thunder?" Mom asked. "Should we go out and try to get the baby chickens indoors?"

"I think the hens will take care of them," Dad replied. "You go ahead and get breakfast on the table, and we'll eat. Hopefully, the storm will blow over by the time we're finished. That is, if there is a storm; it could just be making a lot of noise."

Mom put the bacon on the gas stove to cook. She was making her way across the room to the ice box to get the eggs, when we all heard a loud ping, followed by a horrendously loud boom. Lightning jumped from the wall mounted telephone, and streaked around the kitchen, first to the sink, then the stove, and back to the icebox. Mom stood there, with a stunned look on her face.

I immediately started howling at the top of my lungs, and Dad just sat there stupefied. If Mom had still been standing near the stove, she would have been hit by the lightning. That picture is as clear in my mind as the day it happened.

ANOTHER EPISODE INVOLVED PIGLETS. Dad and Mom were very happy to have a mother pig and were doubly happy when she gave birth to 10 little piglets. They were so cute! They lived with their mother in an old run-down barn, where Dad had built a nice pigpen for them all.

"Come help me," Dad hollered in the door one morning. "Those little pigs are running all over."

Those little suckers were fast and darted around,

almost as speedy as the lightning had been. Dad tried to trick them by putting some grain in a bucket and rattling it, but they would have nothing to do with that! Then, one of them scurried under the fence, and went running down the road. This road was not a high-speed highway, or it wasn't supposed to be, but we did have a few neighbors that acted like they were practicing for the Indy 500 when driving by.

Mom yelled at me, "Stay in the barnyard. Don't come out on the road!"

Of course, staying off the road was just what I didn't do. I raced out the gate, onto the road, and grabbed a passing piglet. They were as slippery as ice, and it soon managed to get away, and run twice as fast as it had been going. Piglets were everywhere, even on the road instead of in the barnyard where they belonged. One of them even made it into the open door of the house!

The little piglets soon wore themselves out and started falling asleep. Before long, we had all 10 of them rounded up and put safely back in the repaired pen with their mother, including the one we found sacked out in the living room of our house. Fortunately, none of our neighbors had chosen that particular time to drive down the road. Another tragedy averted.

ANOTHER EPISODE I RECALL when living near Beehive involved driving. I was three years old at the time and thought I could drive as well as anyone. At least, I had convinced my Dad that I was a good driver, even though my legs were not long enough to reach the pedals. When he was driving around the farm, he often let me sit on his lap and steer the truck.

This particular day, we had been out in a harvested grain field and I was driving the truck. Dad spotted one of our neighbors walking down the road.

Dad stopped the truck, rolled down the window, and hollered, "Want a ride? "We can give you a lift up to our place."

"Sure," the neighbor replied. "It's pretty hot out today, hotter than I thought it was, and I could use a drink of water, too."

I was still sitting on Dad's lap in the steering position. The neighbor crawled through the fence and got into the truck, Dad put the truck in gear, and we started towards home. Boy, was I proud of being able to show off my driving skills! Although both of the guys were so busy talking, they didn't pay much attention to my accomplishment.

"Now, you be careful, and don't hit the gate," Dad warned me when there was a lull in the conversation.

This was like waving a red flag in front of a bull. Dad and the neighbor were talking a mile a minute, not paying a bit of attention to where we were going, and I was steering directly towards the gate post. I didn't want to say anything, but... I was in trouble! No matter what I did, the truck would not turn. It was headed for the gate post. Visions of the truck sitting on top of the post flashed through my brain. However, I was too petrified to even utter a sound. I was helpless!

Fortunately, when we were still about six feet from the gatepost, Dad noticed our path and grabbed the steering wheel. It was an easy task for him to maneuver around the gate post. I was saved.

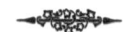

THE ONE THING I learned at an early age was that when Dad was listening to the news on the radio, I had to be quiet or I would be in a lot of trouble. I was walking across the kitchen floor one night, tiptoeing along so I didn't get in trouble, when Dad yelled,

"Jesus Christ, did you hear what those ##%%##%%## Japanese did?"

"Well, no, I wasn't listening," Mom replied. "What happened?"

"They've bombed Pearl Harbor, and sunk a bunch of ships. I wonder what Roosevelt is going to do about it?"

He didn't have long to wonder, since he spent the following day glued to the radio. I was tired of tiptoeing around, and wishing something would happen soon, and it did!

"They did it," he shouted one evening. "The U.S. declared war on those bastards. I wish I was younger; I'd enlist to help fight them!"

"I sure hope this war doesn't drag on for a long time," Mom told him. I'm worried with what is happening in Germany. It probably won't be long, and we'll be at war with them, too."

Mom was right, and just a few days later, Germany was our enemy.

THE HAIRLESS WONDER

*M*y hair continued its reluctance to grow and it was worrisome to Mom. She could envision me entering high school, bald as an egg. So, she determined to act.

She scoured all the books she could find regarding childhood baldness. She was so worried; she even asked our family doctor. "Doc, is there anything I can do to make her hair grow? It's embarrassing having a little girl without hair!"

He laughed and said, "Don't worry, her hair WILL grow when it's darned well ready to grow. She'll end up with a head of hair that's the envy of all those kids that laugh at her now!"

Notwithstanding what the good doctor told her; she continued her research. She was excited when she read something in Good Housekeeping, touting the miraculous powers of some nasty tasting concoction for growing hair. Nothing would do but that she had to place an order for some, and I'm sure you can guess who got the pleasure of being on the receiving end.

"Ooh," I said after she gave me the first spoonful. "That tastes like chicken poo!"

"How do you know what chicken poo tastes like?" she asked. "Have you ever eaten any?"

"Well, no, but it stinks, and this stuff tastes just like chicken poo smells. I don't want any more!"

From then on, when I would see her coming towards me with the bottle and spoon, I ran as fast as I could, looking for a hiding place. However, hiding NEVER WORKED, and I would be forced to down another teaspoon.

This went on for an indefinite period of time, and still my hair refused to grow. Finally, Mom gave up on the concoction, and we were both happier.

My lack of hair never bothered me. But in nearly every picture taken of me at that time, I am wearing a bonnet. I can't complain, since they were usually stylish bonnets, colorful and with some sort of flower in the material. However, it does show how embarrassed she was, due to my lack of hair.

Finally, when I was almost four, a little fuzz started growing. Unfortunately, it was very light in color and didn't show up like my Mom would have liked. I'm surprised she didn't dye it, but she restrained herself from that.

One of her brothers, my Uncle John, was quite a comedian. Every time we saw him, he'd ask me, "Where is your hair?"

I would proudly pull my short fuzz up on top of my head, and reply, "Dere it is!" He always got quite a chuckle out of that.

I was nearly five by the time most of my head was covered in hair. It was still light colored and looked like a very short haircut, but at least I finally had hair.

A BREAK-NECK DASH

My dad soon tired of farming in the Beehive area, so he negotiated to lease a farm near Buffalo. Thus, when I was almost five and my Mom was pregnant with my brother, Dickie, we were on the move again.

I really didn't mind leaving the farm at Beehive, but I was sad when Dad gave away Old Leed. He said he'd found a man that needed a good coyote dog, and this man would give Old Leed a good home. I really missed that old hound, even if his ears were still dragging on the ground.

My recollections of the place near Buffalo are a bit more detailed. My brother Dickie was a colicky baby, and the adults were tired and grumpy for months after he was born. At least, it seemed that way to me. I was afraid to ask for anything, and I wasn't sure I even liked poor Dickie. Life had been much more peaceful when it was just Mom, Dad, and me, although Grandma Bloom seemed to have become an almost permanent fixture in our family. She was rather nice. She sewed and would make me pretty dresses.

The roof of the farmhouse leaked every time it rained. Our floor looked like Tin Pan Alley, with pans everywhere to catch the drips. Each pan had a different sound when the water splashed into it, and I found myself dancing to the "music." I could really rock and roll to this music, and probably could have taught Elvis a move or two. This didn't go over very well with the tired adults. All three were quite grouchy!

One day, after we'd been there about six months or so, my Mom said to me, "Rosie, how would you like a pony? When I was a teenager, I had a pony and I think he's still alive. He must be about 35 years old, but if you'd like, we can see if we can bring him here."

"Do you mean it?" I asked. "I've always wanted a pony. I promise that I won't ever dance to the rain drops again, if I can just have a pony."

About a week later, down the dirt driveway came a strange looking vehicle. It was pulled by a white truck, and in it was the most beautiful pony I'd ever seen. Well, I may have been a bit prejudiced, since poor old Monty was pretty sway-backed, and his eyes looked rheumy, but he was to be mine.

The grownups got him unloaded from the trailer and led him into the barn, where a bale of hay was waiting. I didn't want to leave his side and had to be forcibly dragged in for dinner. I did snag an apple and was soon out trying to get him to eat it. I suspect his teeth were not all that good, and, even though he made a valiant effort, he couldn't get a bite out of it. Not to be deterred, I bit off a hunk, and gave it to him. *We* enjoyed his apple.

The next day, I asked Mom, "Can I ride him, please, Mom? Pretty please?"

"As soon as I get your brother down for a nap, we'll see about saddling him," Mom replied.

I hovered nearby, hoping and praying that Dickie would finish his dinner and have a long nap. He *finally* finished and was soon sound asleep. Hurray!

Mom helped me get the bridle and the saddle on Monty, but he still would not leave the barnyard. No matter how much I kicked him in the side, he just stood there, with me perched on his back. Mom soon had to leave me and go back into the house to start supper. She just left me sitting there in the middle of the corral on Monty. I was so happy to have a horse of my own, but how to make him move?

I finally devised a plan. I got off him and led him out of the barnyard and up a hill to the far end of the pasture. Then, I put the reins around his neck and made a grab for the saddle. I was lucky to catch the horn and stirrup on my first try, because old Monty took off like a house on fire. I was clinging to the saddle horn and praying for all I was worth.

I could see the barn door looming. Would Monty slow down? It didn't look like he had any intentions of slowing. As we neared the door at a breakneck pace, I ducked down and managed to keep from braining myself on the top of the door. Monty came to a sliding stop, and stood there, with his sides heaving. I was shook-up, too, although thoroughly excited. What a wild ride I'd just had, and it was the first time I'd ever been on horseback without an adult holding me! I felt like a real cowboy!

My Mom, who had been watching out the window, came racing into the barn.

"Are you all right?" she asked. She had seen our mad dash and thought I was a goner!

"I'm fine, Mom," I said. "Can I go again?"

"No. You better let Monty catch his breath and rest. He isn't young enough to be racing around like that."

So, from that day forward, I looked forward to sunny days. I would lead Monty to the top of the hill, and we'd come racing back. One trip a day was about all that Monty could handle, but I really looked forward to that trip. Monty made the whole move from Beehive worthwhile for me.

BIG BAD WOLF AND TOUGH CHEWING

*D*ickie finally got over the colic and was beginning to look and act like a real little human. He was crawling all over the place, and I was actually beginning to like having a baby brother.

"Can I take Dickie for a ride in the wagon?" I asked Mom one morning. "The sun's shining, and I'm sure he'd like to go with me."

"I don't see why not," she replied. "I'll wrap him up in a big old blanket, and we can pack pillows around him. Just be careful you don't go too fast. We don't want him to fall out."

She got him loaded in the wagon, and I carefully pulled the little red wagon up and down the road in front of the house. I noticed that Mom was standing by the window, keeping an eagle eye on my activities. I did feel a bit self-conscious, but was very careful not to go too fast or hit any big bumps. After a while, she was no longer looking out the window, and I felt relief.

Soon, I tired of just going up and down the road. I

decided I'd pull him to the top of a nearby hill. Maybe he would like a change of scenery, and I knew I would.

We had just reached the top of the hill when I looked down the other side, and standing there, as bold as could be, was a white wolf. Not only was there a white one, but behind it was a yellow colored one, and it looked like a black one was in the bushes to the side of the road.

My Dad had just been talking about how Montana had offered a big reward to anyone that shot the last remaining wolves in Montana. And there they were!

Dropping the wagon tongue, I raced back down the hill, yelling at the top of my lungs. "Dad, Dad, get your gun! Wolves!"

Dad came out of the barn with a pitchfork, looking skeptically at me.

"Are you sure?" he asked.

"Yes, yes, come quick!" I hollered. "Dickie and I saw them."

"Dickie?" he asked. "Where is Dickie?"

"Oh," I gasped. "I left him at the top of the hill in the wagon!"

"You run in the house and tell Mom to get my gun," he said. "I'll go rescue Dickie and see if I can get a shot off at them."

So, Dad took off in one direction, and I in the

other. Mom grabbed his gun, which luckily was where it belonged in the gun rack. She also grabbed a box of shells and ran out the door. I meekly followed, with visions of an empty wagon waiting for Dad when he got up the hill. Do wolves eat little boys? Wasn't it a wolf that huffed and puffed and blew a house in? Little boys might be on their menu.

Fortunately, as I neared the top of the hill, I could see that Dickie was still in the wagon. As I reached Dad, I looked around, but there were no wolves to be seen. They had vanished.

Dad asked, "Just where did you see the wolves?"

I pointed out the spot, and sure enough, Dad found tracks in the area where the wolves had been. He got his truck and went looking for them, but never laid his eyes on them.

A few days later, we heard on the radio that the entire pack had been eliminated nearly 40 miles from where we lived. No bounty for us.

It was just a few days later when our neighbor drove up in his beat-up old pickup. He got out of the cab, reached back inside and pulled two dead roosters from his pickup. They still had the feathers on them and were pretty gruesome looking.

He marched up to Mom, holding the two roosters

by their necks, shoved them at her and said, "Fred says he likes 'em boiled."

"Well, thank you," Mom replied, and under her breath she muttered, "I think!"

The neighbor said nary a word, just turned around, climbed back into his truck, and lumbered off down the road.

Mom was pretty bewildered as to what should be the next step with the gift. She heated up some water, scalded them, plucked them, and then cleaned them. She decided that there was more chicken there than she needed for one meal, since they were large roosters. So, she kept some of the meatier pieces to fry. The fried chicken looked and smelled so delicious! We could hardly wait to sink our teeth into it. The problem was, that we couldn't even sink a fork into it. It was beyond tough!

The next day, she boiled the reminder of the chicken. She added noodles and dumplings, and the aroma was wonderful, once again. However, even though she'd boiled the chicken for four hours, it was just as tough as it had been fried! The noodles and dumplings were delicious.

The following day, she boiled all the chicken, the fried and the boiled, for eight hours. Surely that would tenderize it, but it was still too tough to chew. Back to boiling the following day. Another eight hours, and the chicken was looking pale and water soaked, but was still impossible to chew.

"I give up!" Mom said. "That chicken is never going to get edible. I don't think even the pigs can eat it."

I saw her heading for the pasture with a shovel. She returned empty handed, and that was the last of the tough chicken.

THE STINKER

"How would you like to move into Buffalo?" my Dad asked Mom one morning, as we all finished breakfast. "this farm is not paying the bills, and it isn't even winter! I heard about a good deal on a truck. It's a 1936 two-and-one-half ton Dodge with a box on it, so it's only eight years old. I'm sure I can make enough money to pay for it. I can haul cattle to Billings this fall, and coal from the mines in Roundup to folks around here. With rationing going on because of that war, we need all the extra cash we can get!"

"Oh, no, Dad!" I hollered. "What about Monty? I don't want to give him up!"

"You can't ride him this winter anyway," Dad told me. "He can go back to Aunt Mary's, and you can still visit when the weather is nice."

"But," I wailed. "That isn't the same as having Monty right out in the barn. I can't give him carrots or brush him all the time!"

Despite my protests, we soon packed up and sure

enough, that darned old weird looking horse trailer showed up and hauled Monty back to Aunt Mary's. Dad loaded all our boxes into his big old truck, and we moved. The only fun part was that Dad let me ride along with him as he drove our belongings into Buffalo, and afterwards, he would let me ride with him once in a while when he took a load of cattle to Billings. I felt like a queen perched up in that big old truck.

That spring Dad came home with a big grin on his face. "I heard the guy that's been delivering the mail out of town is quitting and moving to Lewistown. I think I'll apply. Do you think you could deliver the mail when I'm out with the truck?" he asked Mom.

"I don't see why not," Mom replied. "Gramma Bloom can watch Dickie, and Rosie, unless she goes with you or me. It should work."

Dad got the contract, and it was hard to decide who I wanted to go with when there was a conflict. Mom often would let me put mail in the box, and that was fun. Dad would let me wave to folks as we passed by, and that was fun, also; and, once in a while, he'd stop and have coffee with a friend of his, and I'd get to listen as they told some tall tales.

My grandparents (Mom's parents) owned a hotel in Buffalo. They turned one end of the hotel into a grocery store. My grandpa not only sold groceries, but he sold ice. On a hot summer day there was nothing more pleasant than to creep into his sawdust filled ice room (with huge squares of ice melting) and cool off. Almost everyone had an icebox to keep their food cold; ice boxes were dependent upon a ready supply of ice; thus, several times a day, my grandpa would have to go into his cold storage room for ice.

I settled right into living in town. There were several kids there that were about my age and in a year or so, I'd be going to school. I couldn't wait for that!

In addition to Dad's freighting business, he also built a box on the back of his pickup and got the contract to use that as a school bus. Once in a while, he would let me ride with him on his route. Of course, I always wanted to ride in the back with the kids he picked up, but I was relegated to the front seat.

In the fall, my Dad also set out a few traps. Furs were bringing a reasonable price, and he needed the money. He would often check his traps before he started the school bus route.

One school day, I begged and pleaded to be allowed to go with him. He finally let me if I promised to mind. And, as luck would have it, it was one day that he was going to stop by an abandoned school-building to check his traps.

"Now, you stay in the bus," Dad said to me.

"Okay," I replied, "but I do need to go to the bathroom."

"There's an outdoor toilet over there by the trees," Dad said. "You can go there, but then come right back to the truck."

I made my way to the toilet and accomplished my business. I was gingerly making my way back to the truck when I heard Dad let out a yell. Wow, if something had scared him, I'd better hurry back to the safety of the bus! What might it be?

I ran to the bus and locked the doors, thinking he might have found some sort of monster. Soon I saw him emerge from behind the house. In his hand, he had a most gorgeous, but dead, skunk. While the skunk was good-looking, the odor that wafted from the two of them was anything but.

Dad peeled off his clothes, all except for his long-handled underwear (thank goodness), and left them and the skunk, behind the steps of the abandoned house. He then got behind the wheel of the bus, but the odor was enough to make my eyes water. Dad was in a quandary. He needed to pick up the kids, but he smelled awful! And, he was nearly nude!

"I guess I'll get the kids," Dad said. "Hopefully, the odor won't get into the back of the bus."

Off we went, and soon had the bus full of kids, although I could hear them grumbling about the odor.

We arrived at school, and every one of the kids getting off the bus had red, weepy eyes from the odor. When they tried to enter the school, the superintendent took one whiff of them and sent them back outside.

"You kids can't come to school today," he said. "Go on back home, and don't come back until I can't smell you."

It took about a week before Dad managed to get the bus aired out enough to quit stinking. And the kids were happy about their vacation, although I did hear there were some protests from their parents.

SKIPPER'S WILD RIDE

The summer passed quickly, with only a couple of exciting events that I recall. The first one was the acquisition of a dog. My Dad was always partial to housecats, so we had several. However, in the spring of that year, we acquired a dog named Skipper. He was a black, white, and brown, Heinz 57 variety, with a tail that curled over his back. He was a good companion, although he would sometimes get into things he shouldn't.

My Dad had always wanted a Jeep, so that summer, he bought himself one. It had a metal cab that was flat on top and Skipper liked to jump up on the roof and ride. The wind would whip his ears straight back and he loved it. He was *very* adept at sticking to the roof, although whoever was driving would usually slow down for the corners so he wouldn't be tossed off.

I was playing in the backyard one day when I heard a small airplane passing overhead, and it was very low.

Mom came racing out of the house to look at it. The engine was sputtering and it kept getting lower and lower. Soon, it passed from view behind a small hill. Suddenly, there was dead silence!

"I think that plane just crashed!" Mom exclaimed. "Let's go see if we can help. Gramma Bloom, you keep your eye on Dickie, will you?"

"Sure," Gramma Bloom replied. "Just be careful!"

We raced for the Jeep and took off with a lurch. Mom sped up the road, toward the spot where the plane had disappeared. As we neared the top of the hill that it had vanished behind, we noticed several vehicles racing in the same direction.

When we topped the hill, there was the airplane sitting on its wheels in a plowed field. Mom slammed on the brakes, and we heard, "Screech!"

Skipper came sliding over the windshield and landed on the hood. He must have heard Mom say, "Let's go," before we left home and decided to go with us! We hadn't heard him before we stopped, and it was a miracle that he'd managed to cling to the roof of the Jeep on that wild ride.

Fortunately, the pilot and his passenger were not hurt and a few days later they took off and flew back to where they'd come from.

Skipper was none the worse for his wild ride, and every time the Jeep left the yard, he would still jump on the roof… That is unless we caught him and made him stay home.

SAVING THE DAY

The second exciting event of that summer occurred towards the end of August.

"Why don't you go play with the kids," Mom said to me. "When I went to get the mail, I think I saw the McKinley family coming into town, and they let their kids off at that vacant lot. You need to get to know them, some are about your age, and you'll soon be going to school with them."

"Do I have to?" I asked. "I'm busy trying to get a new dress on my doll. Gramma Bloom made it for me, and I think my doll will look really nice in her new dress."

"You can do that the next time it rains, but for now, I think you better go play," Mom replied, as she scooted me out the door.

I made my way down the street and was quite surprised to find not only the McKinley clan, but several of my other friends playing with a baseball in the field.

"Can I play with you?" I timidly asked. I didn't know the McKinley kids, and there seemed to be a bunch of them, from a toddler all the way up to one that was almost as old as I was. I was the oldest of the bunch!

"Sure," one of the older McKinley boys said. "I'm Lester, and this is my sister, Karen. There is Kenny, and the little one is Nancy."

I got into line, and soon we were all tossing the ball back and forth, and playing an exhilarated game of catch. I was having a lot of fun, when I noticed a train speeding down the track. It made its way rapidly through town, tooting its horn, but didn't slow or stop. We all paused our game to watch the train. A few minutes later, I noticed that the grass alongside the railroad track had caught fire. The smoke was rolling, and I was afraid. I was sure that the McKinley kids, since they didn't live near the railroad tracks, had never seen a fire set by the train. And, what would happen if the fire spread?

"You kids had better come with me," I told them. Soon I had a flock of eight young kids trailing me. I headed out of town, following the creek. Surely, the fire couldn't catch us if we stayed near the water.

It was hard walking along the streambed with the rocks and downed trees to climb over and around and I kept having to encourage the littler kids to keep up. I surely didn't want that fire to catch us. Being a savior was hard work!

"Hurry up! Hurry up!" I kept telling the kids, they did their best to follow my pleas. A few minutes later, a couple of the younger ones started crying as they stumbled along.

"Please don't cry!" I told them. "Once the fire has burned itself out, we'll go to my Grandpa Lilley's store, and he'll give us ice cream!

That did the trick, and soon we were once again making our way along the side of the streambed. I did let them stop to rest when I got tired.

Apparently, back in town, things were not going so well. The men soon had the fire out, but the parents became concerned when the play-lot was empty, and their kids had disappeared! One of the parents went knocking door-to-door, asking if anyone had seen their kids. They soon knocked on Mom's door, asking their question.

"Well, no," Mom told them. "I haven't seen the kids for a while, but Rosie went out to play with them. I'll see if I can find them."

Mom got the keys, and started the Jeep. Soon she was scouring the town (with Skipper perched on the top of the Jeep), and upon not finding any kids, she widened her search. It wasn't long before she spotted the bright red jacket I was wearing. It was about a half-mile up the creek! She circled the area, found a gate, and made her way to where I was keeping the younger kids quiet with promises of ice cream.

"What are you doing?" Mom shouted at me? "And, why have you kidnapped the kids?"

"Kidnapped them?" I asked, in a puzzled tone. "I'm saving their life from that fire!"

Well, that wasn't the way she saw it, nor did the parents after she'd loaded up the kids and hauled them back to town. I got a lot of dirty looks before we reached our house. Once Mom had me alone, she taught me that I had made a big mistake. I never tried to save anyone from a fire from that day forward. (And it was difficult sitting down for a few days!)

SCHOOL JITTERS

The first day of school was traumatic. I had really been looking forward to going to school but as that tantalizing first-grade got closer and closer, I became more and more worried. I knew some of the kids that would be going to school but the teacher was new and just the thought of sitting in a classroom became scary.

However, no matter how much I worried, the days just kept marching along. Then, the dreaded day arrived.

"Do you want me to walk you to school?" Mom asked.

Horrors, what would the kids think if Mom walked me to school? They would think I was a baby!

"No," I quickly replied. "I know the way, and I can do it myself."

Since we lived only a couple of blocks from the school, I would not be packing a lunch but would be coming home at noon. My good friend Maralyn (whose nickname was "Pipe") had to pack her lunch. That sounded like a much better way to have lunch than having to go home, but... I had no choice! I did have some school supplies in a nifty bag that I could take with me. I bravely set off, but the closer I got to that big old brick school building, the slower my steps became.

Although I had spent some wonderful times there attending the Halloween fair and climbing the fire escape, somehow the school looked different. It had grown immensely in my imagination. The fire escape was an outside metal tube that ran up the side of the building from the ground to the second story where the junior high and high school classrooms were located. An agile person (such as me) could climb up the tube, since it was about four feet in diameter. Once you reached the top of the tube and went around the corner, there was a flat, raised area that made a good seat. I'd spent hours sitting on this seat in the dark, talking with my friends. It was also fun to slide down the fire escape and then climb back up.

I wondered if I could just make my way to the fire escape and spend the morning there. I would know when school let out for lunch since the kids would be making a lot of noise. I was giving that plan serious consideration when I heard a familiar voice.

"Hey, Rosie," my friend Pipe said. "Let's go in and get our seats. This should be fun!"

I was trapped. There was to be no sanctuary for me in the fire escape.

"Okay," I shakily replied, as I bravely marched along beside her.

There were two rooms downstairs in the school, one that housed grades one through three, and the other that housed grades four through six. Pipe seemed to know where she was going, and turned into the first room she came to. She sat down in a front row seat, so I sat right behind her. I surely didn't want to be in the front row! Soon, the desks were all full, and the teacher was behind her desk.

The teacher rapped a ruler on her desk to get everyone's attention, and then she started calling the roll. It was expected that when she said your name, you would say "here" or "present." Unfortunately for me, with the last name of Bloom, my name was read very near the beginning. I was so frightened; I could not make a sound. So, I just hung my head.

The teacher looked right at me, and said, "Rosalie Bloom, I see you there. Please stand up and tell me you are here."

I nearly died. But I did get to my feet, and at last a very tiny voice said, "here."

I was never so happy about anything in my life when she told me I could sit back down. Since Pipe's last name started with a "D," she was called soon after me and I was surprised to hear her reply with a booming voice, "Here!" How could she be so bold?

When I went home for lunch, I looked hopefully at Mom after I'd devoured my soup and sandwich and said, "Mom, I'm sick, I can't go back to school."

"You don't look sick to me," she told me. "Besides, you gobbled down that sandwich like you'd been starving. Sick people don't eat like that. Now, get yourself off to school."

I was soon trudging the long two blocks back to school. The afternoon went much better for me, and I actually started to enjoy the classes. I did well, as long as the teacher ignored me. However, I was thrilled when the school bell rang, and the day was finally over.

I attended that school for the next six years and while I got a bit more relaxed than I was on the first day, I was always shy and bashful. I excelled at the written tests, but oral ones were killers. Even though I knew the answer to questions, I would never put my hand up. The teacher might call on me!

The only time I came out of my shell was at the spelling bee's. I loved to spell, and was quite good at it.

GHOST STORIES

While school wasn't nearly as glamorous as I'd thought it would be and I was afraid to open my mouth, my free time was very enjoyable. I loved to hang out with some of the older kids and thought I was just as big and smart as they were.

The first couple of months I watched enviously as the kids played Ante-I-over. They'd toss a basketball over an old shed, hollering "Ante-I-over" when they threw it. If the ball didn't make it over the top, they'd yell, "Pig-tail" and then try again. Once the ball made it over the shed and was caught by a player on the other side, that person would sneak around the corner of the shed and try to tag one of the players from the opposing team. If they caught a player before that player made it to the other side of the shed, that player then joined the person with the ball's team. I was thrilled when I was asked to play with the other kids. It was especially exciting when it was dark out, but hard to see the ball to catch it.

"Hey, Rosie," my friend George said one day about a month after school started. "Why don't you join us tonight in a game of Ante and then we're all going to that old abandoned building and tell ghost stories."

"That sounds scary," I replied.

"Ah, come on, don't be a chicken," he said.

Call me anything but a chicken! (Unless, of course, we were in school.) For sure, I was going, providing that I could come up with a perfect excuse to tell Mom.

So, that evening after dinner, I offered to help with the dishes. While I was drying them, I casually said, "Mom, some of the kids from school are going to be playing Ante-I-over tonight over that old shed, and they've invited me to come. Can, I go, please?"

"So, who all is going?" Mom asked.

"I'm not sure, but Lois Jean is, and George, and I'm sure quite a few of the kids from school," I replied.

"Well, I guess you can go, but you need to be home by 8:30 to get ready for bed," Mom instructed.

We had a lot of fun tossing the ball and racing around the building trying to catch someone, but soon it was time to sneak into that old building. I was delighted to have six of my friends along for protection, in case it really was haunted. My parents had been very adamant about staying away from that old building!

But the other kids said they had already been there, and they were still alive, so I figured it couldn't hurt. They knew their way around. It was pitch black out, but someone had brought a flashlight. As we entered the building, I grabbed onto Lois Jean's hand. The light showed a large room, with some furniture draped in sheets, and cobwebs everywhere. We didn't stop there; we went down a long hallway, and into what must surely have been a bedroom at one time. More cobwebs, but only one draped chair. We were soon all sitting in a circle on the dirty floor. I was sure I could hear ghostly voices moaning in the attic. I was petrified but must maintain a brave front. I couldn't show fear in front of my friends!

The stories they told were all about ghosts, witches, and even a hobgoblin or two. I shivered with fear and could not think of a thing to say when they asked if I had any stories. I promised I'd have one the next time we met. All the time I was wondering what I was doing there, and what would be Mom's reaction if she caught me! That could be a horror story in itself.

It didn't take long before we were all frightened, and when we heard the lonely wail of a passing train, we bolted out of that house and raced for home. I was a few minutes late, but Mom didn't scold me too badly.

A few days later my friend George caught me at

school. "Do you want to join us playing Ante-I-over again tonight?" he asked. "If you do, could you bring a pack of your dad's cigarettes?"

"Oh, I'd love to join you, but I don't know about the cigarettes. What do you want them for?" I asked.

"We just want to use them to light the room for our storytelling," he replied. "The glow of a cigarette is quite spooky in that dark room, and it'll add to the suspense."

I racked my brain for a good story to tell. And I worried about the cigarettes. Was it really to light the spooky room? Seems like candles would be a better option. I finally made up a story about a friendly ghost that I thought would do. It wasn't nearly as scary as some of their tales had been, but then, it would make me feel brave to tell it. I had to work hard at convincing Mom that I ought to go play with the kids again that night, but she finally said I could go. As dinner ended, Dad took off for his radio and his favorite newscaster, Gabriel Heater. I noticed that he had left an opened pack of his Lucky Strikes sitting on the kitchen table. Would he miss it if I just happened to take them? I finally decided to find out so grabbed them and put them in my pocket.

I was startled by a roar from the living room. "We

did it!" Dad shouted. "The bastards have surrendered. The war is over!"

Mom went running into the living room, shouting, "Is it really over? Rationing will end soon then! And my brothers can come home!"

Rationing hadn't bothered me much, except that baked goodies had been in a much shorter supply than I thought they should be. I had watched Mom look really happy when the ration book appeared in the mail.

I was worried about all this excitement, as the pack of cigarettes was weighing heavily in my pocket. Dad didn't seem to miss his cigarettes, and soon I was outside playing Ante-I-over with the gang. I couldn't stop worrying about my story, and then… there was the matter of the cigarettes.

"Time to go," George said. And we picked up our ball and made our way to the abandoned house. The door creaked as we entered, but that didn't concern my companions, so why should it bother me? We gingerly made our way to the same room and were soon all sitting in a circle, waiting to start the stories.

"Rosie, do you have the cigarettes?" George asked.

"Yes, I have some," I replied, as I handed the package to him.

"Okay," he said. "Here is what we're going to do.

We're each going to light a cigarette, and when we have it lit, I will tell my story, then Rosie will, and we'll go around the circle that way."

I had never tried to light a cigarette, but I had watched my Dad. I knew you put the thing in your mouth and sucked, while you held a match to the end. So, I bravely lit the match and tried to get the cigarette going. It wouldn't cooperate, so I had to light another match. That time, I got a big mouthful of smoke and thought I was going to die. I was gagging, and coughing and tears were streaming down my face.

Everyone started laughing at me and I raced out of the house and headed for home. As I walked into the house, I must have looked a mess. I'm sure my eyes were red from crying.

"Rosie," Mom said. "Come here."

I slowly walked to where she was sitting.

"Have you been smoking?" she asked. "You smell bad, and you've burned off all your eyelashes."

"Mom, we were just going to use the cigarettes for light," I replied. "Really, that isn't smoking."

"Why did you need a light when you're playing Ante-I-over?"

I was in a pickle. I started crying, and the whole story came tumbling out. That was the last time I was allowed to play Ante-I-over with the gang and it was some time before I could sit down comfortably after Mom got through with me. Not only did she put a stop to my playing; but she also told the other moms, and the ghost stories in the abandoned house ended once and for all.

LESSONS

I really thought that school would be a lot more fun that it was turning out to be. I was in the third grade, and I enjoyed reading and spelling. I still didn't much care for it when the teacher asked me to say something. I really enjoyed the weekends, though. Usually on Saturday night, there was a movie in the Community Center. Mom would give me enough money to get in the door, but she was stingy with money for the popcorn and soda. I sat in school one Monday, trying to figure out how I could earn some money before the weekend. There was a Gene Autrey movie coming, and it was in color! I just had to have popcorn.

Then, it struck me. I could teach the kids how to see in the dark and charge them for their lessons!

When the teacher left the room, I went to a couple of the town kids, and told them, "I'm having a class on how to see in the dark on Friday night. It only costs a nickel for the first class. It really is neat to be able to see in the dark, can you come?"

"Can you really see in the dark?" my friend George asked. "I'd give almost anything to be able to do that. Sure, I'll get into my piggy bank, and I'll see you on Friday. Where and when do we meet?"

"Let's meet at the bottom of the hill that has the B on it." I told him. "We should meet there just about the time it gets dark. We can't learn to see in the dark if it isn't dark!" (The B stood for Buffalo, and was made out of whitewashed rocks, and sat near the top on a nice, rounded hill not far from town.)

I secretly contacted several other of the town kids, and before long, I had promises from about a dozen of them that they'd be there on Friday.

Friday rolled around, and I decided that I needed to dress the part of a teacher. So, I made myself a pointed hat, sort of like what I thought a witch might wear. I dressed all in black, and was waiting for the group to arrive. Ten of the kids showed up, and each had their nickel, except for one boy. He could only round up three-cents. So, I told him he could stay for part of the class.

We started climbing the hill, and once we reached the B, which was so much brighter than the grass, I had my class set down in a circle around the B, and hold hands.

"Now, close your eyes really tight. Just scrunch them tightly shut. Then, repeat after me three times, "I can see in the dark, I can see in the dark, I can see in the dark!"

The chorus rang out, and I felt very proud of my accomplishment. The kids were learning.

"Now, very slowly open your eyes, and you should be able to see just a little bit. It's going to take several lessons before you can see as well as I can. You have to have patience," I told them.

"I can't see anything," one of the boys said. "Are you sure this works?"

"Of course, I'm sure it works. I've been seeing in the dark now for over a year!" I confidently told him. "It will happen to you, too!"

There was some grumbling about the success of their lessons, but they all went home, and I was 48-cents richer. I did enjoy my popcorn and even a coke at the movie.

The next Monday in school, I told my friends, "Lesson Number 2 will be Friday night. Be sure to bring your nickel. You probably will only need another four or five lessons."

I was disappointed when it was time for my class,

and only five showed. Once again, we sat around the B, scrunched up our eyes, and intoned the magic words. There was more griping once their eyes were open this time than there had been last time.

"Remember, you have to have patience," I told them.

That Saturday, I could only afford the popcorn. But it was very tasty.

When the following Monday rolled around, I once again advertised the class, trying to get new folks interested, but apparently the word had spread that no one had been successful in learning to see in the dark. Friday came, and I was the only one waiting at the foot of the hill. My stint as a teacher had come to an end, and the movies were not as enjoyable without refreshments.

A SAD DAY

School was over for the year, and I had survived! Summer was marching on, with ball games and other activities. One scorching hot Saturday in late August, I wanted to go swimming. I begged and pleaded to no avail. Mom was being very hard-nosed about the whole thing.

So, I decided I'd join the gang that was playing baseball. There was a vacant field near our house, which drew baseball players when it wasn't too hot. Once in a while, there were enough players to form teams, but usually everyone played workup. With workup, a person had to start out in the outfield.

I had worked my way up to third base, when I spotted someone walking a cocker spaniel down the sidewalk. I abandoned my post, which made several of the players angry but the person behind me was happy. I raced off to see the dog. It was the most darling dog I'd seen in a long time, and that dog and I bonded immediately. The person walking the dog asked me if I'd like to have the dog! Wow, what a question!

I raced home and asked Mom if I could have the dog. We still had Skipper, but surely, we could have two dogs. Mom was still being a hard-nose about everything, but I persuaded her to go out and look at the dog.

"Isn't he beautiful?" I cried.

"He is rather cute," Mom admitted. However, if you get him, you'll have to be responsible for feeding him and picking up after him."

"I can do that," I said. "Does that mean I can have him?"

"Well, why don't we try it for a week, and if all goes well, you can keep him."

I was elated. I completely forgot about the game, which went on quite well without me. I brushed my dog, and spent hours petting him. He didn't eat much but I made sure he always had a ready supply of pancakes or whatever I could find to feed him.

A few days later, school started for the year, and I had to leave my dog at home when I was in class. I really enjoyed the weekends, when I could play with him. However, when Monday arrived, I had to go back to the dreaded school and leave my dog. When

I went home for lunch, I found my Gramma Bloom home alone. My dog was gone.

"Where is my dog?" I asked. "And, where are Mom and Dad and Dickie? Where is lunch?"

"Your dog is back with his owners," Gramma Bloom replied. "Dickie was playing with him and he jumped up and bit off the end of Dickie's nose. Your Mom and Dad have taken Dickie to the doctor in Lewistown. I don't know when they'll be home, but I've made you a sandwich."

I was one unhappy little girl. "I can't eat this sandwich," I sobbed. "I don't want to go back to school, either."

Grandma Bloom was very persuasive. So back to school I went. When I got home that evening, everyone was at home except for my cocker spaniel. Dickie had a big bandage over his nose and it looked like they'd doused his nose in iodine. It was a weird yellowish color. Mom had to change the bandage every day, and Dickie would holler loudly when she removed the adhesive tape.

Dickie's nose must have gotten an infection, because it developed an awful odor. Mom and Dad took him back to the doctor numerous times but it didn't seem like there was anything that could be done. It took many months before his nose started healing. Poor

Dickie, he really did look odd with the end of his nose missing.

It was in late May when Dickie came down with a high fever. Then he started coughing, and soon his eyes were swollen and red. "My throat hurts," he croaked.

Mom got the flashlight and made him open wide. "I see some little white spots in your mouth," Mom said. "I think you've gotten the measles."

He was not the only one around with measles, but fortunately for me, I'd already had them. Dickie became sicker and sicker, so finally Mom and Dad rushed him to the doctor. They put him right in the hospital.

The doctor decided that Dickie needed a blood transfusion. He tested both Mom and Dad's blood to see if either of them was compatible. He determined that Dad and Dickie had the same type of blood, so they used Dad's blood. Shortly after receiving the blood, Dickie died. My dad always thought that the doctor had mixed up the blood-typing, and that it was Mom's blood he should have been given. There was no way to prove that hypothesis and it would not have brought Dickie back to life, even if it could be proven. Mom always said that the reason Dickie got measles in the first place was because of the dog bite. This was a sad day.

HORSE TEETH

*D*uring my time in Buffalo, Pipe continued to be my best friend. She and I were born so close together that we were almost twins. I really looked forward to the times when I could visit her at her farm. She had two older brothers who still lived at home, plus her parents. I got to visit often.

She and I were budding actresses and when I was visiting, we would often put on shows for her parents and siblings. For our work, they usually gave us a few pennies which we then buried in our treasure trove. We'd often change the burial ground of our trove, thinking that spies might be watching. We had nearly 50 cents in it the last time I remember seeing it. I wonder if it is still buried in that old can somewhere near the creek?

One of her brothers found an orphaned baby deer and they raised it, using a bottle to feed it. For some reason, that deer (Bambi) never did like me. Bambi continued to grow and was very friendly to the family, just not me!

When Bambi was a year old, she took to visiting with the local deer. When she was a two-year old, she had twins. She still didn't like me.

I was visiting one day when Pipe said, "One of the horses died last winter, up towards where you used to live. I think we should go there and pull its teeth. We could bury the teeth with our treasure trove, what do you think?"

"That sounds exciting," I replied, "But what about Bambi? She doesn't like me and chases me every time she sees me!"

"I bet if you dress up in some of those old clothes that we use for our shows, she wouldn't recognize you." Pipe replied.

"Well, let's try it then." I said. We proceeded to pick out a long dress, some high heels, and a large hat. I slightly resembled one of those "ladies of the night."

"I'll get us some drinking water, and you go into the shed and see if you can find some pliers," Pipe ordered. "We'll need them to pull the teeth. While I'm about it, I'll see what I can find for a snack. It's hot out, and a long way up the hill. We might get hungry."

I found the pliers with no problem. While I was

about it, I picked up a chisel and a hammer. We put all our supplies in the little red wagon and headed up the hill.

Bambi didn't show herself as we made our way to the carcass, which, by the way, was quite smelly. We were happy we'd remembered the tools, since they worked very well at removing teeth. It was hard work separating the teeth from the jawbone, but we ended up with a nice collection of them.

We had a drink of water, but the smell from the rotting horse had removed any appetite we might have had, so we decided just to head on back down the hill. We might be ready for our snack when we reached the yard.

We put our horse's teeth into a container in the wagon and started home. We hadn't gone far when Bambi spotted us and came at me with blood in her eye. I took off running, losing the heels in the first bound. As I ran, I could hear the deer panting behind me, which spurred me to greater effort. Soon, I was headed for the four-strand barbed wire fence, so I gathered up the skirt as well as I could, running all out, and sailed over that fence with little room to spare. Fortunately, Bambi decided she didn't want to try the fence, so she turned, and sedately walked away.

Pipe gathered up all the belongings I'd strewn

along the hillside and placed them in the wagon. There were the shoes, and of course, the hat. Plus, a set of beads that I'd put around my neck. How it got off, I'll never know.

I collapsed on the yard side of the fence, and I was lying there gasping for breath, when Pipe's mom raced up to me. She'd seen the whole race from the kitchen window and just knew that I was going to smack into that fence. She was amazed that I wasn't hurt. It is very surprising what adrenalin will do for a person. No more adventures on that trip, but we had our horse teeth!

GOAT MILK IS TASTY

I went racing into the house one morning, yelling, "Mom, Mom, come quick! There's a lot of shooting going on up by Grandma Lilley's house."

Mom came out the door, wiping her hands on her apron and we both ran towards the hotel.

When we arrived in the yard, we found Margaret (Mom's youngest sister) with a .22 rifle in her hands. Margaret worked in Great Falls but was visiting for the weekend.

Tied by one leg to a post in the middle of the yard, was a chicken. The chicken was on a long tether and was running around in circles as fast as it could. As we neared, we saw Margaret draw a bead on the chicken, and let off another round. The chicken continued to circle.

"What in the world are you doing?" Mom asked.

"Well, I told our mother that I'd get a chicken for dinner, but I just couldn't bring myself to chop off her head with the axe. So, I figured I'd just shoot her but she won't stand still!"

"Good grief," Mom replied. "For heaven's sake, get the axe and I'll take care of the chicken for you. You're scaring her half to death, not to mention what you're doing to the neighbors."

Mom soon had the chicken and its head parted, and we headed back home. We stopped to visit with a neighbor who was outside watering her little garden.

"What was all the shooting about?" she asked.

"Would you believe my silly sister was trying to shoot a chicken instead of just chopping off its head?" Mom replied.

We visited for a while, then Mom went inside to finish her dishes and I meandered over to another neighbor's place. These neighbors had just bought some goats and I noticed they were running free. In fact, they were keeping the grass short on the vacant lot we used to play baseball on. Besides, they were busy adding some unwanted fertilizer to our ball field.

I was quite excited when I ran into Pipe. She was in town for a short while as her Mom had some shopping to do.

"Come look at the goats," I said. "Look at that big white one… she seems awfully friendly."

Between the two of us, we decided maybe we

ought to milk that goat. In our no doubt less than perfect guesstimate, she looked like she was ready to be milked. We caught her and then realized we had no container to put the milk in. What to do?

"You stand there with your mouth open," I said to Pipe. "I'll squirt milk in it."

Well, that chore was easier said than done. Oh, I squirted all right, but hitting her mouth was very hard. I soon had Pipe plastered with goat milk.

"It really is good, what little I've been able to taste," Pipe said. "Why don't you stand there with your mouth open, and I'll squirt some for you."

I obediently stood there with my mouth open, and Pipe began to squirt. She wasn't any better at hitting my mouth than I'd been at hitting hers. Soon we both looked a little like drowned rats.

It wasn't long before I noticed Pipe's mother headed our way. We quickly turned the goat loose, but that pesky goat would not leave us. We had no way to hide the evidence of what we'd been doing.

"What have you girls been up to," Pipe's mother yelled at us. "Look at you, you're both all wet."

We didn't want to admit that we'd been trying to milk the goat. That might be construed as stealing, since we hadn't asked permission. However, it was patently obvious what we'd been up to. All we could do was hang our heads in shame.

The next thing we knew, Pipe's mother had each of us by an arm and was marching us towards my house. Soon, our mothers were busy whaling away at our back sides. We never milked the goat again.

WHAT ABOUT GEORGE?

$\mathcal{M}$om's mother, Anna (Grandma Lilley) and her dad, Lester (Grandpa Lilley), had moved to Montana from Pennsylvania. I don't recall any of Grandpa's relatives visiting, but Grandma Lilley had a sister and a sister-in-law that came on the train to visit at different times. Aunt Verna was a jolly lady and visited several times. She had been married to Grandma Lilley's brother Henry, who had died in 1937. When she wasn't visiting, she wrote letters. Her trademark was to put a postscript on the letter, "Kiss the Baby around the Neck for Aunt Verna." I always thought that was hilarious.

When she visited, it was great fun. She liked to play games, and often the table would be cluttered with dominoes. She was my favorite.

Then, there was Aunt Eva. She was Grandma Lilley's sister. She never married and had taken care of her parents in their later years. She must have had a hard life, because she was quite bitter and never cracked a smile. My Uncle Phil (who was only five years older than I) and I used to sneak into Aunt Eva's room when she was gone, and search for candy. She usually had a whole drawer full and didn't seem to miss a piece or two. We always thought it was quite selfish of her not to share anyway, so we didn't feel bad about helping ourselves.

Her one redeeming trait was that when she wasn't visiting, she sent boxes of goodies to Grandma Lilley and sometimes we all got to share.

Then, there was the bum. I had never heard of him. He hadn't written any letters or sent packages. One day I was playing outside, and I saw this bum get off the train. In those days, it was fairly common to see someone covered with soot and ashes riding the rails of the box cars. They usually didn't get off in Buffalo. If they did, they just hovered around until the train was ready to leave and got back on the rails. This one boldly walked down the sidewalk, headed for the hotel.

"Mom, Mom, come quick," I hollered, through the door. "That bum is headed for Grandma Lilley's."

Mom came to the door and sure enough, there he was making his way towards the hotel.

"We better follow along and see what he wants." Mom said.

We fell in about a half-block behind him and we all headed towards the hotel.

We saw him knock on the door before we got there, and then Grandma Lilley opened the door. She stood there talking to him but we were not close enough to hear what they were saying. Soon, however, he entered the house, and she shut the door behind him.

"Let's hurry," Mom said. "No telling what that bum is up to."

We ran the rest of the way and knocked on the door.

Grandma Lilley opened the door and seemed surprised to see us, but said, "Come in, I want you to meet my brother George."

We were shocked, to say the least. We had never heard of a brother George. Besides, brother George was a bum? He had a thick beard, unkept hair, and smelled like he hadn't seen bathwater for months. This was my Great-Uncle George?

"I've sent Phillip out to get some water and put it on the stove to heat," Grandma Lilley said. "I think some of Lester's clothes will fit him. Once he's cleaned up and shaved, he will look (and smell) a lot better." (I added the "and smell.")

Mom decided we probably should go back home. We really were not needed there, but I was very sad not to get to stick around and watch what was going on. We did go back later that evening, and the transformation was amazing. Uncle George looked like a real person and he actually joked and was human. He had been across the country several times, riding the rails, and had some hilarious stories to tell.

We enjoyed chatting with Uncle George. Phillip and I listened raptly to his stories. We were glad it was summertime, so we could spend our waking time with him. He seemed to be a jolly soul and soon got a job painting a house for a neighbor. On the fifth day of his visit, he didn't come down from his room for breakfast. When Grandma Lilley went to call him, he didn't answer. He had died in his sleep.

Now, what to do? My parents were not well off nor were my grandparents. Neither could afford to bury him, let alone pay to ship him back to Pennsylvania. Uncle George did not have a cent on him when he arrived and had not earned much with his painting job. Mom, Grandma Lilley, and my aunt Margaret spent hours trying to devise a telegram that they could send to Aunt Eva, or Aunt Verna, or someone else back in Pennsylvania. I don't know who they finally decided should receive it, since I had to go to bed before they had it ready to go.

They wanted to make the telegram concise, to

save costs but they needed to know if anyone in Pennsylvania wanted to pay for the cost of returning the body. The telegram ended up something like this.

"George dead. Will you pay shipping costs?"

They were very disappointed when the answer came back. "No."

This really left them in a quandary. They talked to the coroner in Lewistown and were told that if someone died without family to bury them, they could be buried in a pauper's grave in Lewistown. They didn't want this for Uncle George, but none of them had enough money for burial. So, Uncle George was buried in a pauper's grave. They always felt guilty about not being able to afford a proper burial plot.

THE FAMILY GROWS

*L*ife was comfortable and fun in Buffalo. When I didn't have chores to do, there seemed to always be someone that I could play with. Next door to us was a big hole in the ground that had been a basement, but the house had burned down many years before we moved into our house. The basement was just a hole dug in the dirt, but it made an excellent place to play with our trucks. We could build roads from the bottom of the wall to the top, and many of the town kids spent lots of enjoyable hours playing with trucks. This was perhaps not the most feminine of games but one that I really enjoyed.

One of my favorite times was May 1. This was May Day, and we had a tradition of picking flowers and giving them to some of the older people in the town. We spent several days before May 1 making paper baskets with large handles. Mom gave us a ride to the fields where we found shooting stars, yellow bells, and bluebells. We'd pick a large bunch of flowers.

Mom would always get her pick of the flowers for her bouquet, and we'd keep some for Grandma Lilley and Gramma Bloom. Then, we'd separate the rest of the flowers into small bouquets, wrap the stems in a rag to keep them wet, and put them into our baskets.

We stealthily took our baskets to somebody's house. It was hard to decide who we should give our baskets to, but we usually chose an elderly person of at least thirty, that we reckoned was over the hill. We hung the basket full of flowers on her door knob, knocked on the door, and ran to hide. She usually answered the door, found the flowers and yelled out, "Thank you." Then we were off to the next house. We spread flowers and May Day wishes all over the town of Buffalo.

Summer was spent playing workup on our vacant field, fishing for Shiners (small fish) in the streams nearby, bike riding, and visiting with my cousins and Uncle Phil. Vacation Bible School was always a highlight, and I got to see Pipe every day then. Plus, since it was summer, I often got to go to her place to spend the night, and vice-versa.

By this time, they had installed a telephone system in Buffalo and Pipe's Aunt Bessie ran the telephone exchange. It was fun to hang around and watch her as she answered a call and then plugged that jack into the right hole. Our phone alert was one long, and one short ring. Often, when a phone rang, you could hear people picking up their phones all along the line. Party lines were great if you were a gossip but were the pits if you wanted to keep a secret.

Then, of course, it was back to school. I still had a problem with shyness but was getting better. After all, I knew all the kids. I thought that my life would only get better.

I will never forget the day that Mom took me aside and said. "How would you like to have a baby brother or sister?"

"Are you kidding me?" I asked. "I'm pretty happy just the way we are! Aren't we a nice family? Why would you even consider another kid?"

"Well, brace yourself. We will have another baby in a few months."

After I got over the shock, I was torn between being very excited at the thought and thinking about how my brother Dickie had been so sickly with the colic, and how none of us got any rest. Would the new baby be like that? Were all babies like that? Had I been like that? I was about to find out.

My sister Elizabeth (Betty) was born mid-December 1949. Mom made the cutest little announcement and she let me help her. She made a pink flower and attached it to a card that read, "Another little Bloom has been added to our bouquet." I wished it were not December so we could have had real flowers, but the ones mom made were cute.

Before the baby, Mom asked me one day, "What do you think we should name this baby?"

"I don't know, how do you decide what to name babies? Don't they come with a name?" I replied.

"Well, no," Mom said. "When you were born, Dad wanted to name you Rose Lee for a couple of his aunts. I didn't much like that name. It sounded choppy so I compromised, and we called you Rosalie Ann, with the Ann being named after my mother."

"Well, how about naming a girl after Aunt Ruth, and a boy after Uncle Clair?" I asked.

"I don't much like either name," Mom said. "I think we should name a girl Linda Marie, and a boy William John. Linda was my best friend in school, and my sister's middle name is Maria. William and John are both my brothers."

"Sounds good to me," I replied. "I can't wait for Linda or William to arrive."

This was a great plan, with one flaw. We forgot to include Dad.

I was very excited when Dad came home after taking Mom to the hospital and told me that I had a sister. I was so thrilled to welcome Linda home.

However, when Mom and the baby came home, I was shocked to find that her name was not Linda but was Elizabeth Pearl! My Dad had decided to name her after his aunts, so Elizabeth Pearl joined our household. She did not have the colic, so I was relieved on that score. In fact, she was cute, and I was happy to welcome her into the household.

MOVIN' ON

*L*ife continued on at a sprightly pace, with my new sister to keep us on our toes. For Christmas that year, my parents gave me a radio of my own. I listened to many exciting stories, such as The Lone Ranger, The Green Hornet and Sargent Preston of the Yukon. There were comedies, such as Red Skelton, Amos and Andy and Charlie McCarthy. There were music shows, like Bing Crosby, Guy Lombardo, and Les Brown and his band of Renown. I spent many happy hours with my radio.

Mom started a library in the house, and I was allowed to read the books. A new shipment of books arrived once a month. Usually by the time the month was up, I had read all the books in that shipment. I was sort of unhappy when someone checked one out, because that slowed me down.

My Dad loved pancakes so almost every morning Mom would cook pancakes for him. I slept upstairs in the house, and the odor of frying pancakes would waft upstairs. I got to the point that I could not look at another pancake, let alone try to eat one. For many years afterwards, the smell of a pancake cooking would turn my stomach. Little did I know at the time that I would do the same to my kids in the future, who tired greatly from daily pancakes.

I also loved to run and anytime I could find someone to race with me, I was off. I was very fast and usually managed to win, although the older kids could outrun me. I was very happy when the school went to its first track meet in a nearby town. We got to ride the bus and by this time, we had a regular bus. Dad's pickup had been retired.

I never lost a race when running in my age range. I also loved the Hop, Skip and Jump, and excelled at that. I had a whole collection of blue ribbons by the time I was finished with the sixth grade.

I was still bashful in school, but since I knew all the kids, it was getting so I wasn't afraid to put up my hand when the teacher asked a question and I enjoyed the spelling bees. I did quite well at them, too, although, I must confess that the word "tongue" tripped me up when I was in the sixth grade.

I will never forget the night I came home from playing workup and found Dad home early. Usually he was gone with his truck and I didn't see him, except for breakfast.

He and Mom were sitting at the kitchen table, drinking a cup of coffee. I thought Mom looked rather green around the gills, sort of like she had when Uncle George passed away.

"Guess what!" Dad said to me. "We're moving. I've rented a farm near Denton, and this summer we'll get all our stuff hauled over there. There's a small house and you can sleep upstairs. Once we get settled, you can even have a horse!"

"Moving?" I muttered. "Moving from here? I thought we'd stay here forever. A horse? You mean, I can have a horse of my own?" I was conflicted!

"It's been hard to get work lately," Dad said, although it seemed to me like he was always gone with his truck hauling something. Why would he say such a thing?

He continued, "I need to get over there and get a crop planted this spring so we'll have some money this fall. There's a field that will be just right to grow wheat. Later we can get some cows and a horse or two."

"You mean, I'll have to start my seventh grade in a new school?" I asked.

"I think there's a country school about two miles from the house," Dad replied. "I don't know how many students go there, but I heard they have a great teacher. You'll do fine." I cried myself to sleep that night. I didn't know if I was sad that I was moving, or happy that Dad had promised me a horse.

SECTION II

The Teen Years

DAD FULFILLS A PROMISE

True to his word, Dad immediately started packing when school was out for the summer. It took a long time to get everything we owned the 70 plus miles to the farmhouse near Denton. Not only did we have to move all the belongings, but also Skipper and several cats. The farmhouse was about 10 miles from Denton, and our nearest neighbors were at least a mile away.

It was exciting getting settled in our new house, but I did miss my friends. Besides, my wonderful radio would not work… no electricity! So, I read everything I could get my hands on.

During some of our moving trips we drove past the Pleasant Valley school. It was a tiny, white schoolhouse. Once Dad stopped in the yard, and I got to look into the windows. There were several desks all lined up, with a large desk at the front of the room. I particularly liked the large blackboard, but the wood stove was a concern. Would we have to haul wood to keep warm?

"What do you think of your new school?" Dad asked after my inspection tour.

"Isn't it kind of small?" I replied. "How many kids do you think can fit in it? How far is it from home?"

"I think about two miles, or maybe a little more," Dad replied. "I have no idea how many kids go there."

"It seemed a lot farther than that," I told him. "Do you think I'm going to have to walk? Gramma Bloom told me she had to walk five miles! I don't think they have a bus."

"I don't think you'll have to walk. I don't know how you'll get there, but probably Mom or I will drive you," Dad told me.

I always loved to drive (even after my early experience in Beehive!), and on some of our long trips between the two houses, my Dad allowed me to drive his truck. This was a two-and-a-half-ton truck with a grain box on the back. I was now 12 years old and figured I was an adult.

I also enjoyed reading, and somehow my parents obtained a Montana driver's License Manual that was supposed to answer any questions I might have about driving. I did enjoy studying and was sure I was about as good a driver as they were.

"I wonder how old a person has to be to get a driving permit," Mom said one day. "I think I'll check into it. It sure would be nice if Rosie could drive herself." Wow, wouldn't that be something?

So, the next time we were in Lewistown, Mom stopped by the courthouse.

"We can issue a Conditional permit to a resident that is 12 years of age, if they can pass the driving test," the clerk told my Mom.

"When can we take the test?" Mom asked.

"The examiner isn't busy this afternoon if you want to do it then. She would have to take a written test, and if she passes that, then the examiner will take her for a test drive."

"We'll be back then," Mom told him.

After we left his office, I became worried. "Mom, I don't know if I'm ready to take a test! I read through the manual you and Dad found, but I was just reading, I wasn't studying! What if I fail?"

"What have you got to lose?" Mom told me. "If you don't pass it this time, I'm sure with a bit more studying, you'll pass it the next time we're in town!

I took the test, and, even though I missed two questions, it was enough to pass. Then, I got terribly nervous as I waited for the examiner to finish his lunch. They would not let Mom come with me for the driving test, it was just the examiner and me. Funny how a person's confidence can wane when faced with a test!

I had not practiced parallel parking, so I hoped that this would not be part of my driving test. Fortunately for me, it wasn't. The examiner just had me drive to the corner, make a right turn, then another right and another, and we were back where we started. I had passed.

They gave me my Conditional Driver's License, with the restrictions that I could drive only between my home and Denton, between the hours of 6:00 a.m. and 6:00 p.m.

I was as proud as punch on the first day of school when I drove the Jeep into the schoolyard and parked it near the teacher's vehicle. I felt as mature as my mom.

I was sort of surprised when I opened the school door, to find there were only three other students, two boys and one girl. The two boys were in third grade, and the girl was in fifth. That left me, a seventh grader, as the "senior" student.

I really enjoyed going to this school. Our teacher came from a Norwegian family and would often bring some Norwegian treats. Their cookies were out of this world. She would let me help with teaching the younger kids. I thought I would no doubt become a teacher when I grew up. She was my idol.

The best part of all was that she had a saddle horse for sale. I was so excited when my Dad came to talk to her about the horse. Her name was Ginger, and she was a three-year-old, brown in color, and had been trained as a cow-horse. She stood 18 hands tall, a little over five feet. Before long, arrangements were made to deliver her to our house. That was one of the happiest days of my life.

BEWARE OF MOVING BUCKETS

I had a wonderful time with Ginger. She was a bit flighty, and she didn't like men, so she and my Dad had a somewhat rocky relationship. Every time he saddled her, she tried to bite him; and every time he tried to sit in the saddle, she would buck as hard as she could, trying to unseat him. After a few altercations between the two of them, Dad decided that I could not ride her with a saddle, even though Ginger was very docile with me. I went everywhere riding bareback.

Dad purchased a dozen Hereford cows. They were registered, and he was hoping to raise a prize-winning bull. The ranch Dad leased was approximately 1,100 acres, and it had only one fence across the middle, separating it into two huge pastures. As he was buying the Herefords, he also bought a couple of milk cows. It was my job to ride Ginger every evening to bring the milk cows home for milking. They would spend the night in the corral, get milked again in the morning, and then spend the day wandering in one pasture, or the other.

Sometimes when I went looking for them at night, they were easy to spot in their large pasture. Once in a while when I went looking for them, they were already headed home. The majority of the time they were in hiding. I thoroughly enjoyed riding Ginger around and exploring, while searching for the milk cows. The entire property was hilly and honeycombed with numerous hiding places. I found several nearly round sandstone rocks that had weathered into strange shapes. One site had a massive, smooth sandstone drop that looked very similar to places where early settlers may have driven buffalo over to slaughter them. I was always finding something new and exciting. My imagination ran wild.

Once the milk cows were home, we treated them to some delectable cubes that they loved. These cubes were vegetable-based protein cubes that substituted for hay. We hoped this would make them want to return every evening. It worked only once in a while; often they would hide in the oddest places. We finally put a bell on old Blackie, since she was the leader. The other milk cow was a Guernsey, so we called her Guernsey. She was much younger than Blackie, and not quite as smart at hiding.

Several times I spotted the cows as I headed in their direction. Then, I would see old Blackie make a beeline for some willows, and stand perfectly still, so her bell wouldn't ring. There were other times when I just couldn't find them, and it would take me hours to round them up. Many are the times it was after dark when I got home.

We kept Ginger on a picket line near the house. We had a stake that we'd drive into the ground, so it was quickly moved, and she could graze on lush grass every day. We also hauled water to her, since the spring was a mile away.

One day when I went to get her for my nightly milk cow hunt, I noticed that her water bucket was empty. I decided that I would ride her back to the house, taking the bucket with me, and then it would be handy to refill. I devised an ingenious plan that involved attaching a rope to the bucket, and once I was on her, pulling the bucket up to me. My idea was to catch it and haul it home. That way, I wouldn't have to walk back leading her and carrying the bucket.

I leaped on her back, with the rope in my hand. However, I had not taken into account that the sight of a bucket slowly making its way toward her was not something she could handle. She took one look at the slowly approaching bucket and lit out as fast as she could go. Which was very fast indeed!

Unfortunately, when I'd leaped on her back, I had landed on top of the rope... so I couldn't let it go, and that bucket came bouncing along behind us, making all sorts of racket. Which spurred Ginger on to faster speed.

Mom happened to be looking out the window and saw us fly over the hill at breakneck speed. She jumped in the Jeep, thinking she would find me lying broken on the ground.

I hung on for dear life and kept trying to get off the rope. I finally succeeded, but when I did, I lost my seat and went flying.

As Mom came over the hill in the jeep, I was just getting the dirt and grass brushed off, and Ginger was still running at top speed.

"What in the world happened?" Mom hollered out the Jeep window. "Are you all right?"

"I don't want to talk about it. We need to get some oats and see if we can catch Ginger. It's going to be dark soon, and I need to find the cows. I'm fine, just my pride hurt. Here, grab onto this bucket, will you please?" I said as I handed her the badly beat-up bucket.

We did finally catch Ginger. She had run all the

way to the perimeter fence. She was standing there, blowing hard. She was a little bit skittish when I approach her, but the grain did the trick, and I was soon mounted again, and on the way to bring home the milk cows.

I learned a valuable lesson, though. Moving buckets and skittish horses don't mix.

CROPPY

"Rosie," my Dad said one morning. "We're going to visit your Aunt Eddie in Checkerboard tomorrow. Dal will take care of the milk cows, so you can turn Ginger loose, and she'll be fine until we get back. We should be gone only a week or so."

Checkerboard was a small settlement, located near the Bair Dam between White Sulphur Springs and Harlowton. I always loved visiting there. My aunt and uncle were continually doing exciting things. That year, they were cutting firewood to sell to the local farmers and keeping very busy. We planned to do some fishing in the dam and took Dad's aluminum boat with us.

"I just can't get along with Rosie's horse, Ginger," my Dad said to Aunt Eddie, as they visited the first night we arrived.

"I'm losing my patience with her bucking every time I try to ride her. I really need a horse I can ride to herd those cows. Calving season is coming next spring, and I need to watch them closely."

"I know a guy that has a pony for sale," Eddie told him. "She's a descendent from one of those Indian ponies that Chief Joseph traded to the settlers back in the late 1800s when he made his break for Canada. I guess he swapped ponies for food. This is one from that line."

Dad went to look at the pony. She was nearly 12 years old, and the tops of her ears had been frozen off. She stood only 13 hands high, just a little over four feet. But the price was right, and so Dad bought her.

That cut our fishing trip short since Dad had to go back to the ranch near Denton to get his truck, put the stock rack on it, and get ready to haul our new pony home. Her ears were just little stubs, so we named her "Croppy."

I'm sure it looked a little strange when Dad and I went riding together. He had a saddle and was on the short horse, with his feet nearly dragging on the ground. I was perched atop a tall horse without a saddle. But we managed.

Ginger loved to herd cows. When I tried to make one go where I wanted, all I had to do was point her in the right direction and hold on. Croppy, on the other hand, mostly plodded along.

After Croppy entered the picture, I usually rode her instead of Ginger, unless Dad was going to come with me. It was much easier to jump on Croppy since she was so much shorter. However, she was devious. One time, I grabbed her by the mane and swung myself up on her back. She side-stepped. I went clear over her and landed on my backside in the dirt.

There was another time when I was riding her to check on the fence. I found a staple that was missing from the lower strand of barbed wire. We stopped. I got off her, got the hammer, and as I bent down to drive a new staple in, Croppy butted me with her head. This sent me flying through the barbed wire fence. Fortunately, I wasn't sliced to ribbons.

Then, there was the time that I was taking three-year-old Betty for a ride on Croppy. I was riding Croppy without a saddle. I finally got her motivated to trot, and then actually a gallop. As we neared a mud puddle, Croppy put on the brakes, and Betty and I slid right over her head, landing smack dab in the mud puddle. Betty howled, and I felt like howling, too! We ended up walking home, covered in mud and leading Croppy. We muttered under our breaths all the way back.

OINKY

It was about a mile from our place to the neighbors, if we took the steep route. Otherwise, we could go around, but it was about three miles that way, so we usually opted for the steep hill. This was some hill, almost straight up and down, with a little curve at the top. It wasn't too bad when it was dry, but when it rained and got slippery, it was one scary hill.

Once you got down the hill, you had to cross a large wheat field. This field was an excellent producer of wheat, but it was sheer torture trying to get a large combine down the hill to harvest it, and then back up to continue the harvest. We had to chain a cat to the back of the combine to hold it back, to keep the combine from running over the cat that was pulling it when we took it down, and it took a large cat to pull it back up.

These neighbors lived right on the Judith River. On a hot day, there was nothing that I liked better than to go there and swim in a pool in the river. We still had Skipper, and he would often go with us, riding on top of the Jeep. He really had to be lucky going down the steep hill, but he usually managed to stay on top.

We did notice that when we went swimming, Skipper never got into the water. He would get close enough for a drink, but he never even waded.

One day my Dad said, "I'm going to toss Skipper in the river and make him swim! Come watch!"

He picked up Skipper, who was squirming and howling, and gave a hefty toss. Skipper started paddling with all four feet, but he just couldn't swim. He was vertical in the water, and down he went, entirely under the water. His head then popped out of the water, and he was wild-eyed and flailing away with his front feet. As he went under for the third time, Dad waded out and grabbed him. He hauled him to shore, where Skipper lay panting. I don't recall Skipper ever going to the swimming hole with us again. When the jeep headed in that direction, he bailed off and remained at home.

It was a hot day in June and we were all, except Skipper, at the old swimming hole, when our neighbor stopped to chat.

"Say Fred," he said. "I had a sow die yesterday, and she left quite a few orphan piglets. I'm feeding a couple of them but can't take care of that many. Would you like to try to raise one?"

"I would," I piped up. "I'd be happy to feed it with a bottle. Can I have one?"

"Sure, stop on your way home and pick one up."

Dad looked a little shocked, but he finally agreed that I could try my hand at raising the orphan.

I could hardly wait for everyone to get out of the water, but finally, we were all ready to leave. We stopped, and I picked out a colored one; it had black, tan and white on it. I held it all the way home. It was hard to come up with a name for my piglet, but after a lot of thought, I settled on "Oinky." Very original, eh?

I had to feed Oinky every two hours for the first few weeks of her life. I set an alarm that woke me; I got up, heated some milk in the bottle and fed her. Keeping her warm was another problem, but she seemed to be okay with a blanket over her box. Then, of course, there was the necessary cleaning. I had no idea a tiny little piglet could produce so much waste. She was worse than my baby sister had been!

However, Oinky survived and grew. In a few weeks, she was able to move into the barn. Dad built her a pen, and she was a contented pig.

When Oinky was about a year old, I talked to the neighbor about breeding her. I thought that raising a litter of piglets would be great fun. He was agreeable, for the pick of the litter. So, Oinky went for a ride. It was almost four months later when I went out to feed her one morning and found that she'd delivered a litter of 10 piglets during the night. I was delighted to be almost a grandmother.

The piglets grew and prospered. I often checked the price of pigs as advertised in a newspaper, trying to decide just when I should sell them. It was a bittersweet day when Dad hauled the piglets off to market. He did give me half of the money they brought. Dad thought he deserved the other half for providing food for them. Upon reflection, I have come to believe he was right, but I wasn't so sure at the time!

FINGER FOOD

"We need to move the cows from the pasture they're in now and into the other pasture," my Dad said one morning. "I want you and your mother to catch Ginger. She shouldn't be hard to catch since she hangs around Croppy all the time. We both need a horse to keep the cattle in line."

This was exciting news to me. I loved working with the cows. They all had calves, ranging in age from a couple of weeks old to a month old. I was ready to go immediately.

"We can't go until I get Betty bathed," Mom said. "It will be about an hour, and we can take the Jeep. I might even let you drive, going."

I had Croppy picketed in a luscious looking patch of grass. She and Ginger were enjoying their breakfast. I could hardly wait until Mom was ready to go. I got a rope and some cow cubes. Both horses loved the cubes we fed the cows. I was sure that would entice

Ginger to come close so I could put the rope around her neck.

Finally, Mom was ready, and we set off in the Jeep. Neither horse was nervous when the Jeep stopped near them.

I walked towards Ginger, with a cube in one hand, and the rope in my other hand. She seemed interested in the cube and snatched it out of the palm of my hand but didn't stick around long enough for me to get the loop around her neck. So, I got another cube and put it in the middle of my hand. I needed to be a bit faster the next time she grabbed the cube.

She walked towards me, with her head stretched out as far as it would go. I expected her to do like she had the last time, snatch the cube, and back up. I was ready for her this time.

What I wasn't ready for was for her to take a bite out of my middle finger, but that's what she did. She bit so hard; she nearly severed the end of my finger. I screamed and jumped backward. Ginger took off running and ran to the other end of the pasture. Mom took one look at my wound and decided we needed to go home to tend the wound.

Ginger was free that day, and the cattle remained in their pasture. The next day, I led Croppy into the barn and Ginger obediently followed. I got the barn door closed, and she was captured. From then on, we left her halter on so she was easier to catch.

Dad and I got the cattle moved without any problems. For many years, I had a scarred fingerprint. I always said I had to be very careful not to do something illegal, since my print was very distinctive. It finally healed, and today it looks like a regular fingerprint. However, I am still afraid to do anything illegal.

LIGHTNING STRIKES

*E*lectricity had arrived at our farmhouse. It was so fascinating to see the crews come in, plant the poles, and then string the wire. However, my Dad had gotten into a quarrel with the landlady about who would pay to connect us to the electricity; neither was willing, so all we got out of it were the poles and wires marching across the fields, headed to the neighbors.

We all had our various chores to do around the farm. Mine usually consisted of feeding my pigs in the morning plus feeding and watering the chickens, geese and ducks. We had to keep our eyes open for rattlesnakes, and Dad found and dispatched several in our yard.

Betty was growing and was walking all over the place. We had one mean drake duck. He was so mean, he chased the geese off their nests, and their eggs didn't hatch. One day, he came after Betty, and while he only grabbed her by her shirt-tail, he scared her a lot. A few days later, he came after me. I turned around, grabbed him by the neck, hauled him to the chopping block, and we had duck for dinner that night.

Another of my chores was to keep tabs on Betty, so she didn't go wandering around outside, since we feared the snakes. It got boiling hot in the house during those scorching summer days. Without electricity, we didn't even have a fan, let alone air conditioning. Mom would open all the windows and the doors to try to keep the house livable, but still, it got sweltering inside.

I brought in the chicken eggs early one morning, and unbeknownst to me, a feather had come in with the eggs. Betty took one look at that feather, let a scream out of her that would have waked the dead, and bolted for the living room. What caused that? Was she afraid of feathers?

"Bring me that feather," Mom said. "Maybe we've found a secret to keeping Betty from wandering!"

I took the feather into the living room, and Betty screamed, backing up and trying to get away. From that day forward, all we had to do was anchor a feather in the doorway, and she was a captive. In later years, I wondered if the duck had instilled a fear of feathers in her?

Of course, I still had the job of rounding up the milk cows in the evening. One day it was looking like it could rain at any moment, so I hurried to find the cows. I was lucky that they were not far from home, and I got them into the corral.

I took Croppy to her picket line and had just gotten her tied to the lightweight chain on the picket when the heavens opened, and water came pouring out. I raced towards the house as fast as I could run. I was just going under the powerlines, when… the next thing I knew, I was flat on the ground and very befuddled. I jumped up and started running, but soon realized I was running in the wrong direction. I corrected that error, made a U-turn, and streaked towards the house in the downpour.

Mom was looking out at the downpour and saw the lightning strike the powerline as I ran under it. She was stunned to see me laid out on the ground and was just getting ready to see if I had been killed when she saw me jump up and run in the wrong direction. She was happy when she saw me suddenly make a sharp turn and come towards the house.

Before I got to the house, I was shocked to find Croppy racing past me. She had gotten loose and was headed for the barn. Before I went into the house, I let her in the barn. Ginger had vanished.

It took me quite a while to calm down, but dry, warm clothes helped. I still felt strange, but soon even that feeling passed.

Dad had been working in a field a few miles away and had witnessed the lightning bolt as it struck. He said that it had three-prongs. He figured that one had struck near Croppy, one had hit the power line over my head, and he had no idea where the third-prong had landed.

The next day, when Dad went to check on the cattle, he found that one of the cows had apparently been hit by lightning. It hadn't been as lucky as Croppy or me and was dead. It was too bad we hadn't found it earlier so we could have salvaged the meat.

LION BAIT

"Aunt Eddie and Uncle Alvin are coming to visit us tomorrow, and they're bringing your Grandpa Bloom with them," Mom said to me one day. "I think they're also bringing the three boys. You don't get to visit with your cousins very often, so enjoy their visit! This will be the first time you've met your Grandpa Bloom, that you can remember."

I was very excited. My aunt and uncle and cousins were planning on spending the night with us. They had a pickup with a cover over the box which was almost like a modern-day camper. They had built in a stove for cooking and had a table and some seats, plus the beds for sleeping. They didn't have a bathroom. That was fine; neither did we! Grandpa Bloom would stay in our house.

I could hardly wait for them to arrive and kept watching closely when any car would top the hill on the main road, about a mile from our house. Soon one slowed down and stopped at the gate. They were near!

Mom had decided that with extra mouths to feed, she needed to bake bread. She had it mixed and was waiting for it to rise.

It really was great to see my cousins. Bud was five years older than I; Bobbie was two years older; and Gene was five years younger. I really worshipped Bud and Bob, but I lorded it over baby Gene!

Grandpa Bloom was also interesting. He had a shock of white hair, and he had a strange odor that I didn't much like. He actually talked to me, and told me he'd been to Alaska, and enjoyed it, but didn't want to spend another winter there. Alaska sounded like some far, exotic place to me! He also brought a little booklet that he said was a Family Tree. It listed many Blooms that I had never heard of, but he told me they were all relatives. He said the first Bloom had come over on a ship from Germany in 1752, and I was in awe. He left the booklet with us, and I was ecstatic. But he still had that odor, even if he did seem nice.

Mom told me, "Your Grandpa Bloom has ulcers, and he can only eat a few different kinds of food. If he eats anything else, he gets terrific gas, and has to belch!" So, that was what the odor was all about.

The adults were talking a mile a minute, and Dad mentioned that our neighbors had gotten their electricity connected. "They seem awfully happy to have constant power and not have to use the windmill to charge all those batteries."

"What do you suppose they're going to do with their windmill?" Uncle Alvin asked.

"I have no idea, but I bet they'd be willing to sell it. Do you know anyone that might want it?"

"Well, sure, it would come in mighty handy at that house near Checkerboard. We don't have commercial power yet. How far away do they live?"

"Not far, we could run down and visit them if you'd like."

"Rosie," Mom said, "would you watch the bread for me, and when it rises past the top of the pan, just punch it down again? I'll be back before you have to do anything else with it."

"Sure, I'll be happy to," I replied. "I think Bud, Bob, and Gene are going to stay here with me, so I'll have plenty of company."

The rest of them got into the Jeep and headed down our steep hill to the river. I was a tour guide, and showed my cousins my pigs. I proudly gave them a tour of the whole surrounding area.

"There's a spring about a half-mile away that we haul water from for everything but drinking," I told them. "It's an alkali spring, so the water has a rather foul taste, but it's neat to see it come out of those rocks. It is cool!"

"I'd sure like to see that," Bob said, "how do you get there?"

"Well, it isn't that far, we could walk if you like. We just have to watch for snakes." I completely forgot about the bread as I proudly led my cousins towards the spring.

We walked along, talking and looking at things. We picked some gooseberries, which hadn't quite ripened yet. They were terribly sour and puckered us right up. They still tasted pretty good. Then, we decided we were thirsty, so we made our way to the spring and had a drink of the cold water. Although it was quite strong with that alkali, it sure tasted good on that hot day.

"I don't feel so good," Gene whined, shortly after we'd settled in the shade next to the spring. "I need to go home."

"Oh, come on, you baby," Bud replied. "What's wrong with you?"

"I just feel sick to my stomach," Gene replied. He did look a little pale and drawn.

"Okay, let's go," Bob said. We started on our walk home. We hadn't gotten very far when Gene barfed.

Apparently, the green gooseberries and the alkali water really hadn't agreed with him.

We arrived back at the house and told Gene to hurry in the house and lie down, which he was more than happy to do. When we walked into the house, I could smell bread.

"Oh, good grief," I moaned. "I completely forgot the bread."

I opened the oven, and the bread had risen way over the top of the pan. It had fallen, and there was a massive hole in the middle. It was hanging off the pan and spread across the oven floor. I carefully removed the part that was touching the oven, only to find that it was embedded with pieces of rust, and who knows what else. The rest of the dough seemed to go back into the pan nicely. The batch of bread was a whole lot smaller than it had started out and I had a whole glob of contaminated bread dough that I needed to do something with.

"Any suggestions?" I asked my cousins.

"Well, you could wrap it up in an old rag, and we could go hang it in a tree," Bud replied. "It'd be fun to explore in a different direction. Maybe the sun would bake it, and you'd have an emergency stash of bread if you ever needed it."

I grabbed an old rag and proceeded to wrap up the blob.

"Are you feeling any better, Gene?" I asked.

"I think so," he replied. "If you don't go too fast, I think I can keep up."

We set off, with Bob carrying the package of bread dough. Gene felt better the farther we walked. We came to a thick stand of trees and decided that was the place to hang the dough.

"I'll climb up the tree," Bud offered. "I see a dandy notch in that limb where our package would fit nicely."

He proceeded to climb the tree and stashed the bundle. Then, we decided to explore just a bit further. We came out on a ridge and were looking across a coulee to another ridge, when Skipper took off barking. He raced down the hill, across the dry creek, and up the hill on the other side. We wondered what he was chasing since he usually wasn't much of a hunting dog.

"Look, isn't that a mountain lion?" Bob asked. "Look how he's toying with Skipper. The cat runs at him, and when Skipper jumps back, he'll turn and run for a short distance. Then he stops and does it all over again. I think we better go home; that mountain lion may get tired of chasing the dog and come after us. All I have is my pocket knife for protection."

We mostly ran all the way home and were happy

to see Skipper catch up to us as we neared the house. The folks were back home, and Mom had put her bread into loaves. She did grumble about why her batch didn't make as much bread as it usually did, but she never questioned me. I didn't volunteer any information.

Dad was very interested in the mountain lion, so he and Uncle Alvin got the gun and went back to where we'd seen the cat. Bud went with them to show them exactly where. Upon close inspection of the site, they found that when we were making tracks for the house, the mountain lion had been making tracks behind us. We never knew how close he may have come to us, but his tracks were on top of ours and followed us nearly all the way home.

I never did go check on that blob of bread dough but have wondered for many years whatever happened to it. Did the birds enjoy it? Or, perhaps did the mountain lion have a feast?

A TOM CAT?

$\mathcal{G}$oing to school was actually fun in that little one-room schoolhouse. We got to have plays and musical presentations for almost every holiday. I'll never forget the first Halloween I spent after starting school there. We had practiced for our performance, and being the oldest, I was the star performer. Mom, Dad, Gramma Bloom, and Betty were proudly sitting in the audience. Betty was three years old, and talking quite plainly, except that she had her C's and T's mixed up.

We had an intermission, and I noticed that Mom and Dad got up and moved seats… I wondered why? They had front row seats, why would they move to the back of the room?

When the performance and refreshments were over, we got in the car and started to go home when Mom burst out laughing.

"What happened?" I asked.

"Betty," Mom chuckled, "We were sitting there watching the program. Betty stood up on my lap, took one look at the lady sitting behind me, and started yelling, 'Com Tat, Com Tat!' Mrs. J. is quite intimidating looking, but I never thought of her as a Tom Cat before! Mrs. J. didn't know what Betty was calling her, so she smiled and seemed very honored that Betty had noticed her. I couldn't stand it, so we moved."

From then on, every time I saw Mrs. J, I couldn't help thinking of Betty calling her a Tom Cat. I'm sure Mrs. J thought I was the friendliest soul alive, since every time I saw her, I broke out in a massive grin.

My Dad's youngest brother, Les, had started a band several years before I went to school in Pleasant Valley. Les played the saxophone; their brother Claude played a differently pitched saxophone; and when they could get her, my Aunt Eddie played the piano. They came to our school several times and played for dances. These were always well attended, and I got a big head from my relationship with the orchestra.

At the end of school, we had a concert on a Friday night, followed by a dance on Saturday night. Mostly, all four of us students played a recorder for the concert, but I played the piano for several of the songs. After all, I had taken lessons while living in Buffalo.

We also sang songs and the first year, I had a solo. I was pretty nervous, but I finally got "My Bonnie

Lies Over the Ocean" belted out. It might have had a rocky start, but it ended on a loud note.

The dances were a big hit, and I enjoyed having the family visit us in our farmhouse. I was eagerly looking forward to summer and being able to ride my horse when I wanted and where I wanted.

Summer was all that I'd hoped for. And, to top it all off, one day my Dad said to me, "How would you like to go pigeon hunting? There's that bridge near the school. I bet if we check it out, we can have fresh squab for dinner."

"Squab? What's that? I never heard of anything like that." I replied.

"A pigeon gets nearly fully grown before it can fly," Dad said. "If we can catch them before they fly, they are tender and delicious."

"Well, I'm game," I said. And we were off to the bridge. I never did see any water running under that bridge, and I had wondered what the purpose of it was since the road didn't go near it, but it was there. I knew that a bunch of pigeons made their nest under this bridge. When it got dark, we drove to the bridge, and using a flashlight, we caught several of the baby pigeons. Dad was right, they were delicious, and since we hadn't had fresh meat for a week or so, they were doubly appreciated.

PUFFBALL

*J*une turned very hot, although we had gotten a hard rain a few days before the heat wave. It was my birthday, and I was on my daily hunt for the milk cows. As I was riding along, I spotted something white and large on the other side of an open field. I was sure it hadn't been there the day before, so what could it be?

Croppy and I made our way over to it and imagine my surprise to find that it was a giant puffball! It was nearly two feet in diameter. I had never seen such a large puffball before. We had some that were two to three inches across, but feet? I loved the way my Mom fixed puffballs. She sliced them, dipped them in flour and fried them. It was harvest time!

I jumped off Croppy and picked the giant puffball. Then I noticed there were two smaller ones nearby. I took off my jacket and made a sling to carry them in. There was no way I could remount Croppy, so I led her home, carrying the massive package. I had learned my lesson about trying to pull something towards a horse with a rope!

"Look what I have, Mom!" I shouted as I burst through the door. "This is my birthday present!"

"Where in the world did you get those?" Mom asked. "I've never seen anything like them! Let's get them cooked before they start to spoil.

Unfortunately, I had gotten side-tracked, so I still had to go look for the cows. Which meant I had a good excuse for not helping. Besides, it was my birthday. I finally found the sneaky cows and got them home in time for dinner. The puffballs were delicious. We could hardly eat them all, but, since puffballs don't keep very well, we gave it our best shot. We were stuffed.

We needed to haul water, so the next day, Dad and I hooked up the trailer to the tractor and were off. It looked like another rain storm coming, but we thought we had time to get the water and get home before it arrived.

We got the water and were on our way up the steep hill when we suddenly heard a loud clap of thunder. Knowing that lightning doesn't usually strike a vehicle on rubber tires, we continued on. The next minute, it began to hail. These were not regular sized hailstones; they were giants. One about two inches in diameter hit my dad's thumb where it rested on the steering wheel. That did it! He stopped the tractor on the hill and shoved a rock behind a wheel. We both crawled under the tractor to keep from being hit on the head. The ground was soon covered with softball sized hailstones. Fortunately, no more hit us. They reminded me of my giant puffball, although they were not nearly as large.

Once the hail quit, the heavens opened, and we were in a downpour. The hailstones melted, and a creek started running down the hill.

"We need to get home," Dad said. "I hope the tractor will start. It's sitting on a slant, and I'm hoping the gas didn't drain out of it."

The tractor wasn't all that excited about starting, but it finally did. We made it home in the downpour. We both looked like we'd been swimming in our clothes when we got there, but we had our water.

Dad's thumb swelled up and was sore for a week or so, but it finally healed. All is well that ends well.

TEACHER'S PET, OR NOT

"I think I'll go teach," Mom announced one morning in early October. This came out of the blue, so-to-speak, and was quite a shock to me. I knew she had been a teacher way back in prehistoric times, but I had a tough time envisioning her being a teacher now! She was my MOM!

She had received a letter the day before from Aunt Eddie, Dad's sister. Eddie and Uncle Alvin were living in Checkerboard that winter, and they were cutting wood for a living, again.

"Eddie wrote that the teacher there at Checkerboard had a family emergency and had to leave. She won't be back this year, and the school is without a teacher. Eddie apparently talked to the School Board president, and he said he'd be willing to give me a shot at the job," Mom told us.

The next day, Mom went into Lewistown to see what would be required for her to get her teaching certificate renewed. It didn't take much, and she was granted an emergency certificate. She called the School Board president, and he was thrilled that she'd be able to teach and offered her a contract. She would leave over the weekend, move into the teacherage, and would start teaching on Monday.

That left me home alone with my Dad since Gramma Bloom would move to Checkerboard with Mom to care for Betty while Mom taught. I was a little concerned about staying with Dad, but I was a big girl now. I was in the 8th grade.

I spent three months living with my Dad. We managed to get along quite well, although he was an unusual cook. I do have to give him credit for trying. However, if he cooked potatoes, that is what we had. Boiled potatoes. If Dad fried steak, that is what we had. Steak. He didn't believe in cooking more than one thing at a time. I actually felt it necessary to lend my hand, and with my help, we almost had nutritious meals every once in a while.

I still got the cows at night, and he helped with the milking. He sometimes did handy-man work for some of our neighbors, so he wasn't always home. I think that experience is when I developed my desire to grow up to be a hermit.

Once in a while, Dad and I would travel down to Checkerboard to visit. The teacherage was a two-room house, and the sleeping arrangements were tight, but we made do. I was delighted when we went there, but when you are milking cows, it's difficult to get away for an overnight visit very often.

On one of our visits, Mom said to me, "How would you like to transfer to this school for the second half of your eighth grade? I already have one eighth grade student, and another one would not make much difference."

"Can I?" I said. "I'd love that. I miss you and Betty. And Gramma Bloom, of course."

It was all settled that after Christmas, I would move to Checkerboard. Mom, Gramma Bloom, and Betty came to our farmhouse in Denton to spend the holidays. I really was looking forward to going to a new school.

The first day of school, Mom introduced me to the rest of the students. There were only six of us, but I had a classmate. I soon found out that being the teacher's daughter was not what I'd envisioned. When it came time to do any of the "dirty" work, like cleaning the chalkboard, I got the job. Mom didn't want to show favoritism. She took that seriously!

My habit was to get my homework done during class, and I continued with that custom. However, when Mom noticed that I didn't have homework at night, she assigned me a bunch more. I felt like the unwanted stepchild! It was terrific being reunited again with Gramma Bloom and Betty. Most of the time, I was happy being with Mom, when she was being Mom and not the schoolmarm!

It was also fun living near my aunt and uncle and my three cousins. My cousins and I made many jaunts over the hills around Checkerboard. I was fascinated with the remnants of rocks that had been placed in circles around the bottoms of teepees. There were several of them in the schoolhouse yard. The story was that they were the remains of when Chief Joseph camped in the area on his historic trek to Canada. I never did determine if the stories were true or not, but they sounded good. We did have Croppy, who was supposed to be descended from one of Chief Joseph's ponies.

About the most exciting thing to happen was the annual spring track-meet, held in White Sulphur Springs. Schools from all around the area participated. Up until that time, I had never lost a race. But this time, I ran into a speedy individual at the track meet. If I hadn't slowed down to look and see how far ahead I was, I would have won handily. As it was, we tied.

I was actually happy to see summer arrive and with it the last day of school. I vowed then and there never to get caught again in a situation where my Mother was my teacher! I was happy when we packed our bags and moved back to the farm.

Mom had been asked by the School Board to return the following year. Upon investigating, she found out that she would need to go back to summer school to keep her emergency certificate. "At this time in my life," she said, "I don't want to go to school!" Her teaching career was over... for a while.

Then, there was that fateful day when Mom told me she was going to have another baby. Good grief, wasn't Betty enough?

SNAKE IN THE GRASS

I had a delightful summer. Dad and a friend of his made the decision to go into the haying business. They pooled their haying equipment and got jobs putting up hay all over Central Montana. They did the haying on shares so ended up with a lot of hay to sell.

While Dad was off haying, I was home with Mom, Gramma Bloom, and Betty most of the summer. It also meant that I was the one that did the summer-fallowing with Dad's TD6 International Crawler tractor. I loved running that machine. Every other day, I would have to fill it with diesel fuel and grease it. I had no trouble keeping up with the work, and the equipment worked well.

I still went out each evening to round up the milk cows, and it was my job to, at least once a week, count the beef cows to make sure they (and their calves) were doing okay. The summer passed quickly.

Then in August, we got a letter from Dad

suggesting that we could join him in a haying job near Checkerboard if we wanted to. Dad was not very good at writing letters, and his current location was near the small town of Martinsdale. We laughed because on his return envelope he'd written "Martinstale." But we were excited about the information in the letter.

He said the crew was getting restless and were tired of his cooking (and I didn't blame them!). He wanted Mom to cook for them on their last job of the summer. Mom made arrangements to take the milk cows, chickens and pigs to our neighbors to add to their herds and flocks, packed our belongings, and soon we were living in a tent near the hayfields.

"How would you like to drive the mower?" Dad asked me one morning.

"I'd love to," I replied. "I've always liked driving!"

"I'll pay you a dollar a day," Dad said. "After all, I'm paying the crew to work, and since one of them had to leave early, I need another hand."

I was flattered that Dad let me drive his International Cub tractor with the mower on it. I did wonder if the reason the one crew member had quit was due to Dad's cooking, or if he really had to leave early! Whatever the reason, I was thankful to him, since I now had a real job! I thoroughly enjoyed driving the mower. Once the mowing was done in a field, my job was to ride on the baler and check to make sure all the knots were tied well. If a knot wasn't perfect, the pressure of the bale would pop the string, and the bale was ruined.

I remember one memorable experience I had. We had stopped the operation for lunch and were enjoying the sandwiches and lemonade that Mom delivered. Before we started again, I decided I ought to relieve myself. Since there were no outhouses nearby, I just went over a small hill. I was squatting down and tending to business when I heard what sounded like a lot of rattles. We were in rattlesnake country! I glanced down at the ground, and the whole area seemed to be writhing! I leaped sky high, nearly fell flat by tripping on my britches that were down around my ankles and let out a scream.

Dad came running and saw what appeared to be a whole nest of rattlesnakes. He went back to the camp, got a rake and his .22 rifle, and came back to hunt snakes. He managed to find over twenty of the buggers. I had hit the mother-lode of snakes. From then on, I was much more careful as to where I wandered.

The remaining hay crew consisted of my Dad and a couple of young high-school boys that he'd hired. They were all thrilled when Mom came to do the cooking.

One of the boys, though, really had my mom worried. He ate heartily but would always leave something on his plate. She feared that he'd found a hair in whatever it was he'd left on his plate, or that something else was wrong with it. Finally, one day she asked him.

"Oh, no," he replied. "The food is excellent, and I am so glad you came to cook. My Mother taught me that it was impolite to eat everything on your plate. If you ate everything, it was showing disrespect to the cook! I would never show disrespect for your excellent cooking!"

She was happy after that and would proudly show us what he'd left that day!

HIGH SCHOOL

*W*e finished that haying job, and since it was late August, it was time to move back to the farm. Once we arrived back home, it seemed terribly lonely with our critters at the neighbors. It wasn't long before we made a pilgrimage to our neighbors to thank them for watching our livestock and collect them.

These neighbors lived in a huge old farmhouse, which was quite drafty in the winter. Eleanor, the lady of the house, showed us all into her living room; Mom sat on the couch, and I sat in a chair across the room from the couch. Eleanor squatted down at the end of the sofa and chatted with Mom.

I was quite surprised when I saw a couple of mice scurrying around under the lip of the couch, while Mom sat there calmly talking. Mom was deathly afraid of mice. She could face down a bear, but when she saw a mouse, she could go from a sit-down position to the top of a table in about half a second! I didn't want to say anything since she was holding Betty.

One of the mice ran under Eleanor's skirt, and out the other side. Eleanor just calmly looked at it and continued her conversation. I didn't know what I could do, so I kept my mouth shut and watched. Soon, the visit was over, and we all stood up to leave. Two mice raced out from under the couch but Mom was not looking in their direction, so they made their escape.

We retrieved our pigs, chickens and milk cows, from our neighbors. We also caught Croppy, and I was back doing my nightly roundup. Both horses and all the cows had done well while we were gone. The chickens and pigs were happy, and it did seem like the milk cows were glad to be in their large pasture once again. They could get back to their habit of hiding every night.

It was time to start the harvest. "You did so well with the mowing," Dad told me, "I think you can operate the combine this year."

We had a big old combine that had to be pulled with the International TD6 Dozer. "You really need to keep a sharp eye on the canvas to make sure you don't pick up a rock. Use this wheel to raise and lower the deck, and don't let the sickle gouge in the dirt. You also need to keep a close eye on the tank, and when we have it full, stop me, and we'll dump the grain into the truck. Do you think you can do all that?"

"Sure," I confidently replied. "I've been watching you, and I'm sure I can handle it."

We did have a few mishaps. One time, Dad turned too quickly and pulled the front wheel right out from under the combine. This disaster took quite a few days to fix. Another time, I got the reel too close to the ground and picked up a rock. It did some damage to the interior, so we were down for another fairly long time. I was in a bit of trouble for that one!

Dad showed Gramma Bloom one gear in the two-and-a-half-ton truck so when we had a full tank of wheat, he'd wave her over. She'd start the truck, put it in her gear and drive to wherever in the field we had stopped working. It took several dumps before the truck was loaded. I always wondered what kept Gramma Bloom from getting bored out of her mind, since mostly she was sitting in the vehicle waiting for her signal, but she never complained.

It was hot work and was particularly dusty and itchy when we were harvesting barley, but the wheat was not so bad. All in all, our harvesting went well.

When we had the truck filled with wheat, Dad usually drove it into Denton to the elevator and dumped it. Occasionally, he would have something else to do, and he would let me drive it in. I surely felt important driving that big old loaded truck to the elevator.

I was sad when the harvesting season was over since it meant that school was about to start. The year was 1953 and I would be a freshman at the high school in Denton. I was not all that excited about starting a new school, but I was very relieved that Mom would not be my teacher!

The first day of school came. I drove myself to school, parked in the parking lot, and sat in the Jeep trying to get up enough courage to go in and find my classes. I had registered the week before, so had an idea of where to go, but… one needed a bit of courage to take that first step!

I finally spotted a girl I knew walking to school. Beverly lived only a few blocks from the school, so I jumped out of the Jeep and joined her.

"Are you ready for this?" I asked.

"Sure, I'm looking forward to it. I've known all the kids since I was born. We don't usually get many new kids here," she replied.

There were 18 in my class. This was the largest class I had ever been in. Although the kids were always friendly and kind, I never did feel like I belonged. I was still timid and bashful. I never answered a question in class even when I knew the answers (which I usually did) unless the teacher specifically called on me! I did get good grades, though, and I really enjoyed the arts and crafts class.

The Seniors initiated all of us Freshmen, which was grueling. But, since I was made-up to represent a scarecrow, I did enjoy it. As long as I didn't have to be me, I was happy!

LIFE OR DEATH SITUATION

*I*t was a cold, snowy, blizzardy January morning when Dad woke me up from a sound sleep.

"I'm taking your Mom into town," he said. "The baby is coming, and we need to get going. Hopefully, we won't get stuck in a snowbank. You help your grandmother take care of Betty, and I'll be home as soon as I can."

I listened as the sound of the car engine faded into the stillness of the blizzard. I didn't envy them facing the 40-mile trip in that kind of weather.

Gramma Bloom and I waited somewhat impatiently for news. With no telephone, there was no way to keep in contact. We waited all that day, trying to keep ourselves occupied.

It was exhilarating when we finally heard the sound of an engine approaching late that night. It was Dad.

"We made it to the hospital in time, and you have a new baby brother," Dad said. "He was a large boy, weighing in at nearly thirteen pounds. We've named him Henry Edward."

Henry Edward! Not again! Mom and I had put quite a bit of time into thinking of a perfect name for the new baby, but Henry Edward was far from what we'd considered. Apparently, Dad had an Uncle Henry, and my Grandpa Lilley was named Lester Edward, so it was a family name. There went the very chic name we'd picked out, once again. I wondered if this brother would suffer from the colic as Dickie had, or if he'd be a good baby like Elizabeth had been.

I was very excited when Dad went back to Lewistown to get Mom and my baby brother. I could hardly wait for them to get home. They finally did, and he was a beautiful baby, although he wasn't exactly what you'd call tiny. I was afraid that he just might take off walking, he was so husky. He didn't have colic and was a pleasure to be around. What a good baby!

In February, the mail brought a notice that he had been the largest baby born in January at the hospital, and a multitude of prizes awaited Mom and Dad at the hospital. It was fascinating to go through the prizes, which included baby blankets, toys, and bibs.

All was going along well until in March when Henry was about two months old. He got very sick. When his temperature reached 105, Mom and Dad decided they'd better take him to the doctor.

We were in the midst of a freak late-March snow

storm. "I want you to follow me to the road in the Jeep," Dad said. "Then, you can drive over to Dal's and use their phone to call Dr. Shubert and tell him we are coming. Ask him to wait until we get there. With this storm, it may take a bit longer than usual."

They had a little trouble reaching the road, due to snow drifts. But they made it, and I watched as their tail lights receded in the drifting snow. I took the road to the neighbors' and had a somewhat rough time getting there myself. The road hadn't been traveled since the onset of the storm, and some drifts were nearly four feet deep. I had to hit them as fast as I dared, then back-up, and smack into them again, pushing snow with the front bumper of the jeep. I was thrilled when I saw the lights shining out the windows of our neighbors' house. They had electricity, and their home was well lit.

I knocked on the door, and when they answered, I rattled off, "Henry is sick, and Mom and Dad are taking him in to see the doctor. I'm supposed to call Dr. Schubert and tell him they're on their way and to wait for them. Can I use your phone?"

Fortunately, they made the call for me, since I had no idea how to go about making a call. Eleanor explained to the doctor what the problem was. He said he'd wait in his office for Mom and Dad. After all that excitement, it was time for me to go back home.

"I don't think you ought to try going home," Dal (our neighbor) said. "Surely Gramma Bloom will be fine without you."

I didn't want to complain, but our neighbors' house wasn't the cleanest in the world. Mrs. Dal was not a great housekeeper. While we had been making the phone call, I'd seen a mouse scurry across the room, race right under her skirts and out the backside. I really did NOT want to stay there! Their house must be mouse-haven!

"I really need to get home," I said. "Gramma Bloom will be worried if I don't get back. I'm sure I can make it if I hurry while the tracks are still open."

"Well, I'll follow you to make sure you get to your road," Dal replied, and he proceeded to get his winter clothes on.

He had a Jeep pickup, so it also had four-wheel drive and low range. I led the way, and he followed. When I approached a snowdrift, I would go as fast as I could to get a run for it. Since the tracks were still not completely filled in with snow, I made it through all the snowbanks without having to back up. Unfortunately, Dal wasn't as lucky as I was. The second large snowbank we came to, he got stuck. It ended up that I had to pull him out with a chain since he couldn't even back up.

We reached the turn-off to my house, which left me with only a mile to go to reach home. I said goodbye to Dal there and hoped he would make it back home himself. It had been very kind of him to follow me home.

I had no trouble with the last mile, and apparently, Dal made it back home. At least, I didn't see him come walking to the house to ask for a tow!

My Dad came home in a couple of days. He said that Henry had viral pneumonia and had almost died, but they had managed to save him with a new drug called tetracycline. He had apparently not responded to penicillin.

We were all pleased when Dad was able to go back to Lewistown in a couple of weeks and bring Mom and Henry back to our farmhouse.

The problem when they brought Henry home was that he would not eat anything but processed baby foods, and my parents were not wealthy enough to buy much. I was roped into babysitting our neighbor's three kids (which also included ironing!), and my wages went to buy baby food. I was proud to be contributing, but I did hate the babysitting; however, ironing the clothes was the worst!

TRAIL DRIVE

The roads were usually passable and allowed me to drive myself to school for most of the school year. However, the spring storms my freshman year were unusually severe. My parents didn't want me on the road by myself. They made arrangements for me to stay with one of my classmates. I was to do housework for my board and room. This family had three sons, and most of my housework involved ironing shirts. I hated that job, but since I enjoyed eating, I had to buckle down and iron. I was never so happy in my life as when the sun finally came out, the snow melted, and I could once again move back home.

I was delighted to see summer come. Dad decided not to go haying that year. After he had planted all the acreage he was allowed, he went to work for a neighbor. I still had my job of bringing home the milk cows every evening, and I enjoyed that. Plus, once in a while, I'd just go riding. I preferred riding Ginger, but my parents thought I should stick with the little

Indian pony, Croppy. I still had to ride bareback, since both parents thought a saddle was more dangerous than clinging to the bare back of a horse without a saddle horn.

I was pleased when our neighbors came to visit us early in June. "Rosie, how would you like to join us on our cattle drive?" Mr. Bud asked. "We plan to leave in a couple of weeks. We think it'll take us about four days to get from here to our place in Winnett. We'll bring your food and water, and all you'll need are your horses and a bedroll."

I looked at my Mom with pleading eyes. She would have to figure out how to get the milk cows without a horse while I was gone. I figured my Mom was very creative, and I was sure she could do it.

She thought about the request for a while and finally said, "Bud, we'll have to ask Fred what he thinks, but I think it would be an experience of a lifetime for Rosie. I suspect that she will be able to go with you."

I could hardly contain myself when Dad got home from work that evening. I didn't want to appear too excited about the possibility, but it was difficult to keep from grinning like the Cheshire Cat!

Mom asked Dad what he thought. He wrinkled

his brow and stared at me for a long time… at least, it seemed like a long time.

"So, how do you think your Mom will get the milk cows if you take both horses? Any idea what road they'll be traveling? I know they've done this in the past, so they probably know what they're doing, but I'm not sure you're old enough yet to go on a cattle drive."

My heart sank in my chest. Dad would NOT let me go! Then Mom piped up and said. "Fred, I think we should let her go. I can just keep the cows near the house, and they'll not be hard to find. We don't have to put them in that big pasture. Bud told me that this was the last year they were going to do this drive, and if she doesn't go now, she never will!"

What an advocate I had in my corner! The upshot was that I did get to go. It was actually hot work but really enjoyable. Most of the ninety miles was across the open plains, but once in a while, we had to herd the cows down a road. That was always exciting, since they were afraid of cars and would bolt every which direction when a vehicle came by. It took all four of us to keep them headed in the right direction and not let them run over any of the cars that passed us, or vice versa.

Bud, his two daughters (Hazel and Viola) and I

were the cowboys. His wife Carrie drove the team of horses pulling the supply wagon. It didn't much look like the wagons I saw in the movies. It did have a cover over it, though, and when we camped at night, they would pull out an old stove, set it up, and cook a hot meal. The family took turns guarding the herd at night to make sure nothing happened to them. I got to sleep all night!

I was almost sad to see the end of the trail approach. We arrived with most of the herd intact. We did have one cow that fell in a gopher hole when trying to escape and broke her leg. They had to shoot her, but they salvaged the meat. Fortunately, another cow adopted her calf, so the calf was well taken care of.

Once we got the herd into their new pasture, we loaded the horses up into several trucks and hauled them back to our ranches. For a while that summer, I felt like a real cowhand.

THE BIG FISH

$\mathcal{M}$om's family was very firm about celebrating the 4th of July. Usually, four or five of her brothers and sisters plus their families would meet at a predetermined creek for a large picnic lunch. For several years in a row, something had gone askew with the planning, and my Aunt Mary ended up with most of the food. The rest of the family had an awful time trying to find where she had gone.

"Mary is not getting away with the food this year," my Dad sternly stated when Mom was making plans for the big day. "She has managed to hide with the food long enough. It's going in our car this year!"

We were to meet at Yogo Canyon. Mom fixed potato salad, baked beans, and a coleslaw. We arrived at the picnic place and got the food set out on the table. Dad built a fire in the firepit to grill the hot dogs. Soon Aunt Mary and the rest of the family arrived. They also set their food out on the table. Before we could begin to eat, we were bombarded with yellow jackets.

Everyone began gathering food and stowing it in cars while they hollered back and forth as to where we should go. Soon we had vacated that spot.

We went to where we had agreed to meet only to find that Aunt Mary was nowhere to be seen. And, sure enough, she had the majority of the food once again. We were left with baked beans and a water jug.

"How did she manage to sucker us in again?" Dad ranted. "I'm going to go find her. You can stay here, and I'll be back." He jumped in the car, and spun away, showering us with gravel.

"Wow, he was mad!" Mom said. "Well, in the meantime, we have fishing poles so let's go fishing."

By this time more and more of the family were showing up, but again Aunt Mary, with most of the food, was missing.

I got my boots on, outfitted my fishing pole, and was off. I waded downstream, following my fishing fly. I went downstream for some distance, then turned around and hiked back along the bank. I didn't even get a bite, and it sounded like the rest of the family was having about the same luck.

The third time I made it downstream, I decided not to walk back along the bank. I slung my pole over my shoulder and trudged back up the creek, splashing water as I went. All of a sudden, my pole jerked, and I thought I'd snagged a rock.

I gave a mighty jerk to the pole and was quite surprised when a 24-inch rainbow trout flew through the air and hung off a tree limb. I cautiously slipped him into my pouch. I surely didn't want to let him wiggle off the hook! He had been hooked in the back. That was the biggest fish caught on that trip, and I never confessed as to how I'd managed to nab him.

When I got back with my catch, it was getting on towards lunch time. I was happy when Aunt Mary drove into the picnic area, followed closely by Dad. Apparently, she had gotten her directions mixed up and was waiting for us about 10 miles away at a different picnic area. Dad had calmed down, but we noticed he escorted her to the picnic site, keeping her in sight the whole way. Our lunch really tasted great that day.

NO MORE

Summer sped along, and I was allowed to operate the cat again and do a little summer-fallowing. When it was time to harvest, Dad quit his job with the neighbors and was no longer off to work before daylight. He decided this year I could operate the cat and tow the combine. Dad had planted a lot of oats, and they were very short. He was afraid I would pick up another rock, and he didn't want to have to fix the combine again. Once was enough! He also talked Gramma Bloom into operating the grain truck again so we could entirely fill the hopper with grain before we needed to unload into the truck.

One of our fields was very steep. I felt fortunate that we had the cat since it didn't slide like a tractor probably would in the sandy soil. I was really concerned that I might pull the front wheel out from under the combine as Dad had. This was the field where that accident had happened. I was ultra-careful. I was lucky, and all went well for me.

Gramma Bloom wasn't quite so lucky. She felt slighted that I was running the cat and Dad had still only shown her one gear in the grain truck. One day she took it upon herself to try a different gear. After numerous jumps and bucks from the truck when Gramma Bloom tried to start in that different gear, the truck finally started moving. She kept gaining speed and was soon tearing down the field, lickety-split.

Dad and I were staring after Gramma Bloom as she headed towards the edge of the field, wondering what in the world was going on. We were both relieved when we saw the brake lights come on and the truck started slowing. Just before it would have left the field for a rock-strewn pasture, Gramma Bloom brought it to a halt.

Gramma Bloom slowly climbed down from the cab of the truck and instead of coming in our direction, she started walking towards the house. Dad hollered at her, but she continued towards the house. Dad had to walk across the field to get the truck. He brought it to the combine, and we unloaded the wheat.

When we went in for lunch, Dad asked Gramma Bloom what had happened.

"I was tired of just barely moving when you wanted to dump the grain," she replied. "I saw you put the truck into that other gear, so I thought I could do it myself. It nearly broke my neck before it started to move and then it took off like a banshee. I finally remembered the brakes and managed to stop that run-away before we hit the rocks, but I'm through. I won't drive that truck anymore."

And, she didn't.

THE WRONG DEER

*B*efore long, it was time to think about going back to school. I wasn't all that excited about going, but I couldn't figure out a way to stop the calendar. Time just kept marching on, one day at a time! Soon I was in the Jeep headed for school. My rationale was that it might be better to be a sophomore, but those nasty roads in the winter loomed, and I probably would end up staying in town. More shirts!

We had an English teacher who was a dedicated alcoholic. When I stood near him in class, he reeked. Towards the end of almost every day, he locked himself in the teacher's lounge after he'd told one of his students to monitor his class. Occasionally, I got to be the monitor, so that was fun. Especially since the class was composed mostly of lowly freshmen, and I was a lofty sophomore.

I became friends with one of those lowly freshmen, and we had some great times together. I was elated during hunting season when she asked me if I'd like to go deer hunting with her and her dad. That sounded thrilling to me. I had done some hunting but never without one of my parents.

I spent the night with her and bright and early the next morning, we were in her dad's Jeep headed for the Missouri Creek Breaks. We got out of the Jeep at the first canyon we came to and loaded bullets into our rifles. Her dad strapped on his ammo-belt with extra ammunition, just in case we might need it. We crept quietly along the ridge looking for deer. Lo and behold, we spotted a large herd of them across the canyon, browsing in a beautiful clearing.

"They are a long way away, so when you shoot, aim above them. The bullet will drop by the time it reaches them," her dad whispered to us. We all three lined up on the deer and started shooting. We were hunting during an open season so we could bag either sex. I picked out a nice, fat-looking doe and sighted way over her head, as instructed.

"You got him!" her dad hollered, looking at me. But the one I was aiming for picked up her head, scented the air, and then took off running. I had no idea what he was talking about. Then he said, "He just went into that clump of bushes down in the bottom of the gully. I'll go finish him off. What a shot you made! He was a long way off."

Apparently, both Sharon and her dad had emptied their guns without hitting anything. Her dad needed to reload his gun before going to find my deer. He was quite surprised to discover that he had put his ammo-belt on upside down and not one shell remained in it. He had to borrow my gun to take care of my deer. It was a small buck, which made it easy to drag back to the Jeep. If I had hit the one I'd aimed for, it would have been much harder to retrieve.

I was actually happy that I'd missed the one I'd aimed for since I wasn't thrilled shooting at girl deer anyway. The one I'd hit was so far down the hill from the one I'd aimed at that it was out of my sight! I never confessed that little fact to my friend's dad. Many times after that I overheard him bragging about what a shot I'd made.

My parents were pleased to see me come home with the deer. While it wasn't large enough to last very long, it was delicious, and we enjoyed it thoroughly.

DEER OR DEAR?

One day we were surprised to see Aunt Valora (who was married to Dad's youngest brother Les) drive up to our farmhouse by herself. She never visited us without Uncle Les! In fact, she didn't seem to like visiting us at the farm at all. Perhaps she was addicted to indoor plumbing?

Anyway, after she enjoyed a cup of Mom's delicious coffee, she looked at my Dad and said, "Do you think my younger brother Dingie could stay with you for a while? He just got out of the service, and he needs a place to rest for a while. He could help you with some of your work to earn his board and room."

"Sure," Dad replied. "We have a separate bunkhouse that he could stay in since Gramma Bloom is visiting family in Libby. He'd be welcome."

Dwayne drove up in a maroon 1950 Ford convertible. It was the most beautiful car I'd ever seen. Dwayne, whose nickname was Dingie, was only about 10 years older than I was, and I immediately developed quite a crush on him. I wasn't the only one, though, because I suddenly had lots of friends in school, once the older girls found out he was staying at our place.

One day Dingie decided he'd drive into Lewistown and do some shopping. He took his rifle with him since it was still deer season. When he returned that night, he looked like he'd been fighting with a tiger.

"What happened to you?" my Dad asked.

"You'll never believe it," Dingie replied. "I was driving along, and I saw this nice buck in a hay field. I stopped, got out, and got my rifle. I shot him, and he dropped like a ton of bricks. Then I made a foolish mistake. I decided not to waste another bullet on him, so I walked up to him and hit him between the eyes with the stock of my gun. The stock shattered in my hands and the deer came back to life. I didn't even have my hunting knife with me since I'd left it back in the car. I had only my pocket knife. I didn't want to let him get away, so I jumped on his back, dug out my pocket knife, and finally got his throat cut. He bucked and jumped and forked me a few times with his horns. I've never had such a wild ride in my life. Anyway, come out and look at him!"

We all went to look at Dingie's trophy, and it was a dandy four-point buck. He had cleaned it and even remembered to salvage the organ meat. He gave us the liver and heart, which we enjoyed.

He took the rest of the meat to Lem's Locker and Grocery store in Denton. They offered butchering services as well as lockers to keep foods frozen. They rented these lockers, and my parents had one rented that they let him use since it was not very full at the time. Without electricity, it was impossible to keep anything frozen at home. Mom did a lot of canning, but it was convenient to have the frozen food.

About a week after bagging his deer, Dingie picked up his frozen meat and left to visit his sister, Aunt Valora. I never saw him again. However, my new best friends (the older girls in school) kept asking me about him. In the beginning, I kept hoping he would return, so I gave them non-committal answers. Soon a letter came from him to my folks, thanking them for letting him stay with us. He explained that he had a job nearer to my Aunt Valora and would not be returning.

The next time the girls asked, I told them that he had left for good, but he'd left his heart with me. I didn't explain that it was his deer heart that he'd left behind. For some reason, all my older girlfriends evaporated, and I was back to my normal routine.

LOST

*I*n the middle of the school year, the school held a talent show. My five-year old sister Betty had a magnificent singing voice. She could belt out those songs like Kate Smith. She and I worked up a rendition of Harbor Lights with me playing the piano and singing alto, while Betty sang soprano. It went very well, and we got lots of applause. We didn't win the talent show, but it was a good experience for us both.

Of course, the dreaded wintry weather came, and I was back to ironing shirts. I swore that if I ever got married, my husband would be wearing wool shirts, winter and summer! I did not want to iron!

Our school Booster Club was very supportive of the basketball team. We had an incredible team and didn't lose a game that year. We were going to the tournament in Lewistown. The Booster Club sponsored a contest to see who could write the winning cheer for our team. The winner would receive a free hotdog and soda for every game our team played. I was surprised when I won!

"Mom," I hollered as I came home. "I won the contest, and if I go to the tournament, I'll get a free hotdog and soda every time our team plays. Can I go, please, pretty please?"

"How would you get there? And, how long would you be gone?" Mom asked.

"I can ride the bus, so it wouldn't cost anything," I replied. "And, I can walk from the gym to Aunt Ruth's house, if she'd let me stay there, and I wouldn't have to pay for a hotel room. It wouldn't cost much, and I'd really like to go!"

"I suppose you can go, but only if Aunt Ruth says it's okay," Mom stressed.

My darling Aunt Ruth seemed happy to have me stay with her. The trip to Lewistown was uneventful, and I hauled my suitcase to Aunt Ruth's. Then, it was time for the first game.

I was in the bleachers watching the game and dropped my purse. I could see it under the bleachers, so I decided I would get it during halftime. When I went to get it, it was gone! That purse contained all the money Mom had given me to buy lunch at the games. I didn't want to tell Aunt Ruth that I was penniless, so I just hoped that Denton would play lots of games.

They did. They ended up in the Championship Game but lost that one. Anyway, I got enough hotdogs and sodas to keep me happy, and I didn't starve.

Mom gave me a lecture about not trusting anyone after I got home and confessed what had happened. I learned a valuable lesson then. Some people are dishonest!

THE MOUSERS

Our school was over for the year once again, and we were having a repeat of the year before. I was shocked when Mom said, "Sit down, I have something I want to talk to you about."

I was apprehensive. The last time Mom had said something like that, the announcement was that she was going teaching and then there was the time she announced that she was pregnant. What could this be?

"I wanted to tell you that I am going to have another baby." She said.

"Oh, no!" I muttered as I stared at her dumbfounded. Not again! What was going on? Would the babies never quit coming? Couldn't she see that we had a perfect family as we were? I spent the rest of the summer sulking. I was happy being the older sister to Betty, and Henry was all right, too, but another one?

When we moved from Buffalo, we brought several cats with us. They were good mousers, and we had lots of mice for them to survive on. They loved the milk, too, and often when we were milking, they would sit there staring at us until we squirted some milk into their mouths. They were pretty adept at catching it.

The problem with the cats was they kept multiplying. Soon we had 30 of them. Mom was beside herself and wanted to do something about the multitude of cats. One day she decided she would shoot them. She got some tasty meat and put it outside. She had most of the cats hungrily devouring their treat, and she got out the shotgun. She loaded the gun and aimed it at the unsuspecting cats. However, she could not bring herself to pull the trigger. She dissolved in tears, and the cats continued to enjoy their unexpected snack.

A few days later, a car drove into our yard. The man that got out was awestruck by the number of cats wandering around.

"How many cats do you have?" he asked.

"I think we have about 30," Mom replied. "Would you like some?"

"I would," he answered. "I'll take as many as you want to give me."

We were soon catching cats and putting them in bags. The man ended up taking 25 of them. Mom was happy! I often wondered if he was making Chow Mein out of them. Since that was a negative thought, I decided to picture them all luxuriating in a mousy hotel catching mice to their hearts' content.

THE CONTEST

$\mathcal{I}$ went back to school in the fall, not looking forward to nasty weather and ironing those pesky shirts again. Just because I wasn't looking forward to them didn't seem to carry much weight… they all arrived again before I was ready.

It would soon be October 1, and the first day of deer season. My Dad had a job with his truck and was spending a couple of nights away. No "First day of the Season" hunting for him!

"How would you like to go with me early tomorrow and see if we can find a deer?" Mom caught me the day before the season opened. "We're getting very low on venison in our locker, and it would be fun. Gramma Bloom will take care of Betty and Henry, and we can go before you need to leave for school."

"I'd love to," I replied. "I'll get the guns ready."

I was very excited about going with Mom the next day. In fact, I don't think I shut my eyes all night. We were very quiet early the following day, not wanting to wake Gramma Bloom or the kids. We left our house just as the sky was beginning to get light in the east. It was a beautiful fall day, although most of the leaves had already fallen. Harvest was over, but the deer often frequented the wheat fields, so we thought that would be an excellent place to start our hunt.

In the second field we checked there was a large herd of deer grazing. In amongst the does and fawns, we spotted one young buck. He had only a spike for horns, but he would be legal game.

I stopped the Jeep along the boundary fence. Mom was a bit slow getting out of the Jeep since she was pregnant. I, on the other hand, slapped on the emergency brake and leaped out. I ran to a nearby fence post, rested my rifle on it, and shot the buck. He fell right where he'd been standing, never knowing what hit him. The rest of the deer raced for cover. Perhaps they thought that Annie Oakley had arrived!

Mom and I drove to the gate and entered the field. We had very little trouble getting him cleaned and loaded on the hood of the jeep. He wasn't all that large, but he would make good eating.

We took off for Lem's Lockers and Grocery to have him cut, wrapped and frozen. We were pretty excited when we arrived, to find that we were the first to bring in a deer that season and Lem's was offering a prize for the first deer to show up. We proudly drove home with our ten-pound sack of sugar.

I had to get myself cleaned up quickly, and off to school. I was only five minutes late, but what an excuse I had!

"Want to go hunting again tomorrow?" Mom asked after I got home from school. "I still have my tag, and maybe we could bag another one. Your Dad would surely be surprised if we had two in the freezer when he got home. We could go out back of the house. I saw a nice two-point buck there just a couple of days ago; maybe he stuck around."

"Sure, I'd be happy to," I replied. I was excited to think of getting to go hunting for two days in a row.

It was just beginning to get daylight when we set off walking. We climbed up the hill and walked down the ridge. We stopped several times to see if a deer would stroll by, but we saw nothing.

We were quietly sitting in a clearing when Mom said, "Looks like some fog is rolling in. We better get ourselves back home before we get lost." About that time, the fog settled in around us, and we could barely see our hands in front of our faces. Mom jumped up and started walking in the wrong direction.

"Mom, where are you going?" I asked. "The house is back this way."

"No, it isn't!" she replied. "Remember we entered this clearing from over there? That means the house is in this direction."

"Well," I said. "I'm going this way. If you want to come, do. I set off in the direction I was sure was right.

"Okay, smarty pants," Mom told me. "I'll come with you just so we don't get split up, but when we come to the end of the ridge, we'll have to turn around and come back."

Ten minutes later, we did come to the end of the ridge. By that time, the fog was lessening, and we could see the farmhouse ahead. We had gone in the right direction. Mom was very quiet the rest of the way home.

BLOODY CHIN

"*I*'m going to need the Jeep for a few days," Dad told me in late October. "I told Eddie that I'd take some missionaries out hunting deer."

"You're going hunting with missionaries?" I replied. I was astounded by that announcement since my Dad was not a bit on the religious side. In fact, his vocabulary consisted mostly of swear words.

"Well," he said, "Eddie asked me, and I never can turn my sister down when she smiles at me! I could feel her smile in the letter!"

"Can I come with you hunting?" I asked Dad. "I'd only lose a couple of days of school, and I have everything all caught up with my homework. I know you're going to be staying at Checkerboard, but maybe I could help Aunt Eddie with the cooking?"

When I mentioned cooking, Dad got interested. I think he was afraid he might end up as the chief cook and bottle washer himself and was not all that excited about that part of his job. He agreed that I could go with him.

We drove the Jeep to Checkerboard on a Friday night and met the missionaries. There were three of them. We could just all fit in the Jeep, with two of them and me riding in the back seat. I noticed that Dad was cautious with his language, and I chuckled to myself about that. Anyway, it looked like it would be a delightful trip.

One of the missionaries was an Indian, and his name was Brother Hand. I never did know if Hand was his first or last name, because they introduced him as Brother Hand and that is what the others all called him. The other two were Caucasian, but I don't recall their names.

We planned to leave Checkerboard early Saturday morning just as it started to get daylight. Aunt Eddie and I packed some sandwiches for our hunting trip, and we all met near the Jeep at the allotted time. All three of the missionaries dressed in red and black checked outfits that looked brand new. They were very excited about their hunting trip.

We hadn't gone far into the mountains when we spotted an exceptional buck browsing. Dad stopped the Jeep and handed the gun to Brother Hand, who carefully and quietly climbed out of the Jeep.

He aimed, and *"Bang."* The deer dropped where it had been standing.

"I haven't lost my touch," Brother Hand proudly exclaimed. "I used to hunt back on the reservation but have not handled a rifle in years."

Dad got out his skinning knife and hatchet and proceeded to clean the deer. We all stood around watching. We were all astounded when Brother Hand took out a long knife from a scabbard on his belt, reached down into the carcass and sliced off a kidney. We were even more astonished when he took a big bite out of the steaming kidney, and with blood dripping off his chin and a big grin, he said, "Yum, that sure tastes good."

Both of his fellow missionaries headed for the woods, no doubt to upchuck. Dad and I were not far behind. Brother Hand contentedly continued munching on the kidney, and by the time he finished, his chin was dripping blood. He wiped it off with his shirt sleeve, and he looked like one happy guy!

We all soon came to grips with what we'd just seen, and Dad went back to cleaning the buck. We decided that we had enough hunting for that day so made our way back to Checkerboard. None of us were hungry, so we didn't even think about our delicious lunch.

The missionaries decided they would prefer to go to church on Sunday rather than go hunting. I think

Dad was about as happy with that decision as I was. We packed up our Jeep and went back to our home in Denton. I was a little disappointed in not missing school, but there wasn't much I could do about it.

However, Brother Hand made a lasting impression on me. Before I had seen him devour that kidney, I had never even thought about eating kidneys and for sure had never thought about eating them raw. It was many years before I tried cooked kidneys, and I found them delicious. But, I still have never tried them uncooked!

FROZEN

It was November, and Dad once again told me he wanted the Jeep. With the roads like they were, I would take our truck into town and stay there until he returned. He was going hunting near Judith Gap with a friend.

I drove home for the weekend and was as surprised as Mom was when we saw a sheriff's vehicle drive into the yard. The Sheriff got out of the car, walked to the passenger side, and helped a man get out of the car. He seemed to be blind, and upon closer look, it was Dad!

Mom raced out the door, with her apron flapping, yelling, "What happened? Fred, are you all right?"

"Ma'am," the Sheriff replied. "Your husband has frozen his eyes. It seems like he and his friend were hunting when that nasty storm caught them. They tried to make it out to the highway, but the Jeep wet-up on them, and wouldn't run. They were freezing to death, so they chopped a hole in the corner of the Jeep and got a fencepost to build a fire in the Jeep.

"Apparently, they took turns going out into the blizzard to get another post, but towards morning, your husband's friend got so weak that he couldn't take his turn, so your husband had to go out and get them all. The smoke in the Jeep caused his eyes to water, and when he went outside so often, they froze.

"Fortunately, the storm let up, and your husband's friend was able to get the Jeep started and drove to the gas station there in Judith Gap. Your husband has been to see the doctor in Lewistown, and he says there is a good chance that his eyesight will return, but he has to keep the patches over his eyes for at least another week."

It was really hard on Mom to take care of Dad when he couldn't see anything, but she did. I went back to school, and when I got back to the farm the next Friday, I was happy to find Dad much improved. He had been back to see the doctor in Lewistown, and his sight was returning. He still had to wear the patch for part of the time, and dark glasses the rest of the time, but he was regaining his sight.

Mom and I took off to go get the Jeep. She drove the car, and I was to bring the Jeep back home. What a mess it was! It was completely covered in soot inside, and even the windshield had to be scrubbed so I could see where I was going. We managed to get it home, got it cleaned up, and were very happy that Dad did regain his sight, though it took several weeks.

DEBBIE ARRIVES

*J*anuary and February saw a flurry of letters between my dad and our landlady. With the new baby on the way, Dad thought that we should be able to hook up to the electrical wires that ran through our yard. The poles and lines had been installed several years before by the Rural Electric Association. It was costly to install the needed connections and wiring, plus, in order to be eligible to receive electricity, you were required to sign a contract saying that you would continue to pay a minimum amount for five years. Dad thought our landlady ought to pay to install the electricity and also co-sign that she would pay the minimum charges. If we used more power than the minimum, then Dad thought he should pay. She felt that since it was Dad that wanted the electricity, he should pay all the bills.

Of course, Dad was not the one doing the writing; he was dictating his letters to Mom, who would painstakingly write down what he wanted. It took at least six tries before he was satisfied with what "he" was saying!

This argument between Dad and the landlady went on for a couple of months, but finally my Dad became so angry, he wrote and told her that he was not going to lease the property any longer. He was moving.

Not going to lease the farm? Wouldn't this require a move? His statement was quite a shock to me. I didn't want to move! What about my horse?

In spite of my protest, March saw us getting everything packed and what a job it was! We had been there for five years, and my parents had pack-rat tendencies. They had lots and lots of things. Dad hauled all the cattle, horses and pigs to the stockyard in Lewistown. It was a very sad day when Ginger and Croppy were loaded in the truck. Blacky and Guernsey were next to go. We butchered the chickens, and stored them in our locker.

Dad looked around and found a house for rent in Coffee-Creek, which was about seven miles from Denton, although in the opposite direction of our farm. The new home was a small, one-story house. It had a rather large living room where my bed and Gramma Bloom's would be, a tiny kitchen, and a small bedroom. It would be hard to get all our belongings into the little house, but Dad also found a shed out back where he could store things.

Mom was nearly nine months pregnant, and she did NOT relish making the move. She worked hard at packing things and labeling them so it would be easy for her to unpack them when she needed them. She, Betty, Henry, and Gramma Bloom went with the first load and started getting the beds made and things sorted.

Mom told me exactly what to bring on the next load, so I felt quite important going with Dad to load up. I wasn't feeling all that important, once we arrived at the farm and Dad would not pay a bit of attention to my instructions. He just started loading things willy-nilly, and soon had the truck loaded. Most of the things that were to come first remained in the house.

When we arrived back in Coffee-Creek, I took Mom aside and told her what had happened. She was not a happy camper and yelled at Dad, who just shrugged and continued unloading. Back we went for another load, and this one was also muddled.

Mom could not find anything, and her eyes started to water. To top it all off, two of my Dad's brothers picked that time to visit. In my Dad's family no one listened very carefully to what anybody else was saying. They all talked, very loudly and at the same time. But this time the brothers were all agog with the thought of a uranium discovery they were sure they could make. Dad had unloaded the truck before they arrived, but once they came, he gladly left everything for Mom to sort out.

Mom finally gave up and went to bed, but the brothers continued their "discussion." It got louder and louder, and Mom yelled out, "Be quiet!" She was getting louder and louder, too. Finally, she yelled, "It would serve you right if I went to the hospital tonight!"

That brought a moment of stunned silence. It wasn't long until the din rose again. The brothers were planning on going out with a Geiger counter and were sure they were going to strike it rich the very next day.

It wasn't long before Mom did start having labor pains and had to get Dad to take her to the hospital. Sure enough, my sister Debbie was born that morning. My uncles and Dad had to postpone their prospecting trip for another week.

The exciting thing for me was that we had electricity, and I could once again listen to my radio! I was happy to hear Pat Boone as he belted out songs, plus Bill Haley and the Comets. The most exciting of all were the songs of Elvis Presley. He was just getting started in 1955, and had a very distinctive sound.

PROSPECTING

*M*om had a restful "vacation" in the hospital. While she was gone, Gramma Bloom and I tried to sort the boxes and put things away. I was happy to have only seven miles of paved roads to go to school, rather than the 12 miles of gravel roads I had from the farm. Plus, there was a school bus, so I didn't have to drive all the time. I was near enough to school that I could attend some of the after-school functions, and I enjoyed myself. I would not have to iron shirts the next winter. I was almost happy with the move, except for the fact that we had to sell the horses, cows, and my pig. I missed all the animals, especially the horses.

Mom came home in five days with Debbie, and that little girl was so cute! I immediately forgot my misgivings about having another sibling. I loved all three! Mom was happy with the progress that Gramma Bloom and I had made with getting things unpacked. She was not so delighted when my uncles showed up again and were determined to go prospecting. Once again, they kept the whole house up with their loud "discussions" until the wee hours of the morning. When they finally wore out, they rolled sleeping bags out on the floor, and finally peace reigned.

They were up quite early the next morning, hardly wanting to wait for their breakfast.

"If you want to go in my Jeep," Dad told them, "you are going to wait for breakfast. (Gramma Bloom's idea of cooking was almost as bad as Dad's). "I've been craving pancakes ever since Dorothy went into the hospital. Gramma Bloom would only cook scrambled eggs, and I'm going to have my pancakes!"

So saying, he parked himself in a chair at the table and stared at his brothers. Slowly, they set their packs down on the floor, and each took a chair at the table. Having Mom's home cooking WAS good!

After breakfast, Les, Hump, and Dad got into the Jeep and were off prospecting. They returned that night with tales of a run-away Jeep; almost getting stuck; finding an outstanding prospect; and being told that they were trespassing, and nearly getting shot. They had an excellent day! They were all in a great mood.

Mom cooked them a venison roast for dinner, and they were very happy that she was home once again.

Les and Hump were leaving early the next morning for Libby. Their vacation was over, and although they had not struck it rich, they had enjoyed themselves.

They talked to Dad about perhaps moving to Libby and working at the sawmill. Dad was looking for some work, especially for the winter, so he said he'd take that under advisement. I was quite happy in Coffee Creek, but it was hard to make a living there.

SUMMER IN WYOMING

"*I* have a good job in Wyoming," Dad told us one day in May. "I'll be leaving in a few days. I think you can all come down after school is out. By the time you get there, I should have a house rented."

This announcement came as quite a surprise to me since I had never thought of going to Wyoming. All I knew about Wyoming was that cowboys lived there! Maybe we'd get to see a real, live one.

My Dad rented a house in Hanna, Wyoming, which was about 40 miles from Rawlins. His job with a mining company was about half-way between Hanna and Rawlins, so this was a perfect location.

Debbie was almost three months old when we packed up the car with everything we could get in it and set off for Wyoming. The car was crowded with people, since there was Mom, me, Gramma Bloom, Betty, Henry and baby Debbie. We were traveling before car seats were required. (I had never heard of a car seat, let alone seen one! We tried to hold the kids tightly when hitting bumps or making sharp turns.)

It was a long day. We didn't stop until we were in Hanna. We were all exhausted, and the kids had been sleeping the last few hours. Mom and I took turns driving, so we were doing okay. Dad had beds all set up for us, and we had brought the bedding. We had to make the beds before we could fall into them. A bed never looked so inviting!

I thoroughly enjoyed my time in Wyoming. On the weekends Dad and I would go prospecting. We saw ruts left by the pioneers in the wagon trains, and once in a while, we would discover a grave alongside one of the trails. It was always an adventure to look for minerals. Dad got very excited when he found a unique rock outcropping. He'd chip off a sample and have it assayed. He never discovered anything that was mineable, but it was thrilling.

I met my first boyfriend there. We had a fun time together. One time we went to the Hot Springs in Thermopolis and soaked in the hot water. I had no idea that I was allergic to the minerals in the water, but I must have been. I spent the next week in bed, running a high fever and feeling lousy. I never ventured to the Hot Springs again.

Another time he cooked me a steak. I always liked

my meat well-done, but this one had barely hit the frying pan before he flipped it over, and then on my plate! I hated to tell him that I couldn't eat it, but I finally asked if he'd mind if I cooked it a bit more. It was still on the rare side when I finished, but I braved a bite. I was amazed at how good it tasted and how tender it was! So, he taught me that meat did not have to be burned to a crisp to be delicious.

Summer passed all too quickly, and it was time to go back to Coffee Creek, and school. I was entering my senior year, and I was looking forward to it. However, I hated to leave my boyfriend! He suggested we run away and get married, but I thought that was not a good idea. I promised to write every day, and I mostly did.

We left Dad at his job and drove back to Coffee Creek the same way we'd come. Dad had another month of work before he could come back home. He immediately started looking for another job for the winter. I was back in school. Being a senior was fun; we got to initiate the freshmen!

THE HOMEMAKING TEST

"Are you going with us to Lewistown on Friday to take the test?" my friend Beverly asked me one morning as we headed to English class.

"What test is that?" I asked.

"Well, in Home EC yesterday, Mrs. Campbell told us about a test sponsored by Betty Crocker. I think it's a scholarship test of some kind, but it's called the Betty Crocker Homemaker of the Year, and if you win in your school and then in the state, they fly you back to Washington, D.C., for an awards ceremony or something. Besides, there's some money for scholarships involved."

"You know I never took Home Economics," I replied. "I took arts and crafts instead, and I've enjoyed learning how to do leatherwork. I don't suppose I'd stand a chance, but it would be fun. Find out if I can take the test even if I didn't take Home Ec, okay?"

Later that day in study hall, Beverly told me that Mrs. Campbell said I could go with them to take the test. We were to gather at the front door to the high school at 9:00 a.m. on Friday. Several were driving, so there would be no problem with catching a ride, and both Beverly and I managed to find a ride with one of our friends.

All 10 of the girls from the Denton High School Class of 1956 entered the gym of the Fergus High School in Lewistown together. We sat down, and soon a representative from the Betty Crocker Corporation gave a short spiel about what the requirements were. They passed out a written test and told us that the one receiving the highest score in each high school would receive a pin, and their entry would join the other school winners in competing for the state award.

There were numerous high schools represented in that room. The tests were not simple. It took several hours before we had waded through all the questions and then we were "on our own" for lunch. Beverly and I opted to eat at the local five and dime (otherwise known as Woolworth's). We were to go back to Denton in the afternoon. We had an enjoyable trip home.

Several weeks went by, and I'd forgotten about the test. But one day, we were called into a general assembly in the gym. We had no idea what it was all about, but anything to get out of class was welcome. I was shocked when the principal took the microphone and asked me to come forward. What had I done?

"I am proud to announce that you have won the honor of being the Betty Crocker Homemaker of Tomorrow for Denton High School," he said. I'm sure my face turned red, I didn't like being in the spotlight, but I did love that pin! Unfortunately, that was as far as it went, no scholarship money for me!

A TUMBLE

When we had returned to Coffee Creek from our summer in Wyoming, Mom discovered that the house next door was for rent, and the rent was only five dollars a month more than the small house we were renting. This house had a large living room and kitchen, plus it had two bedrooms upstairs. But the clincher was that it had a real, indoor bathroom! We would no longer have to use the friendly facilities of an outside outhouse! It would be the first house I'd ever lived in that had an indoor toilet. Plus, it had a bathtub.

Without consulting Dad, my Mom rented the house on the spot. We began the tedious job of trying to get all our belongings moved into the house next door. It was quite a job, but we finally were moving the last of our things when Dad arrived.

"What are you doing home early?" Mom asked. "The last letter said your last day of work would be in six weeks, instead of the month you had figured. And, I just got your letter yesterday!"

"I took Hump's advice, and checked with the sawmill in Libby," Dad replied. "The foreman called me at work yesterday, and told me he had an opening, but I'd have to be there Monday. So, I quit my job, and I'll get a few things, and be off to Libby on Sunday."

Both of Dad's brothers (Les and Hump) were living in Libby, and Dad was ecstatic to think that he would be living near them. He left Sunday morning in the car to scope out his new job. I was back in school, but there was a school bus that ran between Coffee Creek and Denton, so I mostly rode it. If I had something going on after school, I'd drive the Jeep, but usually I was on the bus.

It wasn't long before we got a letter from Dad. He said that he had no problem landing the job with the sawmill and that he had found a house to rent. He said he would be down for us in a couple of weeks.

I was devastated, thinking I would have to leave high school in my senior year to go to a new school. Gramma Bloom didn't want to move to Libby, either. She was unhappy with her sons at the moment and wanted to be independent. So, she and I hatched a plan whereby she and I would stay in Coffee Creek until I graduated. She would find a place to move to that was nearer to some of her friends, and then I would move to Libby.

I thought Mom was in a reasonably good mood one evening, so I calmly said, "Mom, Gramma Bloom and I want to stay here until I graduate. She doesn't want to move to Libby, and we think we can find a nice place for her to live. Is that okay?"

My question was met with dead silence, as Mom stared at me. Finally, she said, "Actually, I can understand why you don't want to move during your senior year of high school. I know that Gramma Bloom has expressed unhappiness with moving to Libby, but what do you think your Dad will think? We'd have to leave you the car or Jeep, and I don't know if he'd be willing to do that or not."

I had won half the battle. Mom wrote to Dad and told him our plan. By the time he arrived in the car, he had cooled off and agreed that we could do what we wanted.

It was with mixed feelings that Gramma Bloom and I watched as Mom and Dad loaded up the truck and the car, and with my three siblings, drove down the street headed for Libby. It seemed very quiet in the house when they were gone. Gramma Bloom and I continued to live in the rental home. I found a few babysitting jobs, and this time I didn't have to buy baby food with the money. Although, if I drove the Jeep much, I had to buy gas! Do expenses ever end?

We didn't have a television, but the place I was babysitting did. I was happy when I was asked to stay with the kids. That TV was amazing!

With graduation looming, Gramma Bloom and I started going out on weekends, exploring for the ideal place for her to move. We finally found a lovely home in Moore. The only drawback was that it was upstairs. It was only a block from the grocery store, though, and the rental price included all the utilities. The clincher was that she had a friend that lived just down the street.

Mom and Dad brought the truck back a month or so before graduation. "Now, you be careful driving the truck," Dad told me. "We'll be back for graduation, but you should have Gramma Bloom mostly moved by that time. We'll have to vacate this place by the end of that week. We need to get the rest of our stuff and yours loaded in the truck for the move."

Gramma Bloom still had some of her belongings stored in Buffalo at my Grandma Lilley's house. We drove the truck over one day, found them, and got them moved into Gramma Bloom's new apartment. Packing them upstairs was a chore, but we got it done.

The next Monday when I came home from school,

I found Gramma Bloom lying at the base of the stairs. "What are you doing there?" I asked.

Gramma Bloom moaned, and said, "I thought I'd bring that big rocking chair down the stairs, and it got away from me. I can't move."

I called the ambulance from our neighbor's phone, and soon they arrived with sirens blaring. I followed in the Jeep.

"Your grandmother has a broken hip," the doctor told me. "She has a nasty break, and it is doubtful if she will ever walk again."

I went to Aunt Ruth's and used her phone to call Mom and Dad. I told them the news, and they were as shocked as I was. Gramma Bloom would not be able to live alone in her new apartment. Her children, including Mom and Dad and my siblings, all came to see her in the hospital and helped move her belongings back out of the apartment in Moore. She would need to move to Libby when she was able to travel, or to Roundup to live with Aunt Eddie.

The house that Dad rented in Libby had a bedroom downstairs, and Gramma Bloom would move into that. Mom and Dad would move upstairs, and I would have a room next to theirs, with Betty and Henry.

Graduation came, and my whole extended family was there. It was a bittersweet time for me since I was happy to graduate but was sad about Gramma Bloom. Besides, Mom and Dad decided they could not have Skipper in Libby, so they gave him to a neighbor. I missed that old dog!

However, it wasn't long before we were all traveling down the road to Libby. Gramma Bloom was to come later since the guys all had jobs to go to, so we left her in the hospital. When she got out of the hospital, she spent some time with my Aunt Eddie before she was able to travel to Libby.

LIBBY

Once I arrived in Libby, the first thing on my agenda was to get a job. I checked the want ads in the newspaper, and there was an ad for a clerk at the Lincoln County Treasurer's Office. I applied and got the job. I enjoyed issuing license plates and renewing driver's licenses. I even enjoyed collecting real property taxes. In fact, they had a program where any person could pay delinquent taxes on a piece of property. You could then foreclose, and the owners had a specific time in which to pay the penalty and interest. If they didn't pay, the property became yours. I picked out a beautiful piece of bottomland and paid the taxes.

Dad and his brothers had a wonderful time being together. They often played chess or checkers. My dad was the checker champion. Uncle Les thought of himself as the chess champion. Poor Uncle Hump was mostly the loser. I had played chess in high school, and while I wasn't all that great at it, I did enjoy the game.

One day I felt brave. "Uncle Les," I said, "want to play a game of chess?"

"With your Dad?" Les replied. "I didn't think he wanted to play chess."

"No, with me!" I said. "I played some in high school, and I enjoy the game."

"Well, maybe later," he said. "I think I'll go talk with your Dad."

I was a bit depressed, but I kept after him, and he kept putting me off. I think he was under the impression that I hadn't played much, and he didn't want to waste his time playing with a complete amateur. I didn't give up. One day he capitulated, and we had our game. I caught him in a Fool's Mate, which is a simple strategy that only takes three moves to win. He was shocked about that since he wasn't looking for it. He and his brothers were so far beyond that simple maneuver that he no longer considered it. I never played with him again, although he asked me many times, no doubt hoping to get some revenge.

One day my Dad and his brothers went fishing with a spear. The water was so clear in the streams that they could see the fish swimming. They'd throw the spear, which was attached to a rope, and once they had speared a fish, they'd pull it to the boat. They thought this was great sport. That day, they ended up coming home with Les looking like he had gone swimming wearing his clothes.

"What happened?" Mom asked.

"The water was so pretty and clear, we could see the rocks on the bottom as sharp as if they were on the surface," Dad replied. "We spotted a huge old trout hovering just above a log. He was lazily moving his tail enough to keep his place in the stream. Les grabbed the spear and let fly. He'd tied the rope around his waist, but the water was much deeper than he thought it was. The next thing Hump and I knew Les was pulled head first into the creek by the rope! I'm sure that old trout is laughing his head off somewhere, but we had to come home early. Les didn't have a change of clothes with him!"

On one of their fishing trips, they forgot to pack snacks, so they stopped at a little country grocery to get some cheese and crackers. The only cheese the store had was blue cheese. They had never heard of blue cheese, but all cheese must be good, right? So, they bought 5-pounds…at a pretty hefty price.

Once they were fishing in the boat, they decided to sample their blue cheese. They were shocked when they unwrapped the block of cheese, and discovered that it looked moldy! Good grief, they couldn't have that, so they tossed it to the fish. I've often wondered what that big old fish thought of his new treat.

Then there was the time that Mom got a Guinea pig for my siblings. Henry had the pig out playing with it, when one of his friends came and asked him if he could run over next door to play. Henry didn't want to take the time to put the Guinea pig back in its cage, so he put it in the sandbox and covered it up. He was quite shocked when he returned to find a lifeless Guinea pig. What does a three-year-old know about a living, breathing animal needing oxygen?

Another day, Henry was out riding his bike on the sidewalk, when he decided he'd go to the grocery store and get a candy bar. He was gone when Mom came out of the house to check on him, so she scoured the neighborhood looking for him. Before long, he appeared, pedaling down the street without a candy bar. That was when the four-year-old learned you need money to buy candy!

I also remember the time when I was reading in my room, and I heard Mom yelling for help. I raced down the stairs and found that she was defrosting the freezer and had gotten her wet arm too close to the sidewall. Her arm was frozen there. I had to get some warm water and thaw her loose.

Life went on, and I decided that I wanted to

further my education. I turned in my notice to the Treasurer's Office, and the first of January Mom and Dad delivered me to an apartment in Spokane, Washington. I was going to business school. I was pretty excited about the move since my best friend from high school was already enrolled in a business college. She and I would share an apartment, and with the wages I'd earned all summer, I felt almost rich.

One of Mom's sisters, my Aunt Edna, lived with her husband Chet in Coeur d'Alene, Idaho. This city was only about 30 miles from Spokane, so I hoped to get to visit them often.

THE FOURTH OF JULY

I attended the business school for about three months. However, I had taken business courses in high school and done very well. I had my 100-wpm pin for shorthand, my 70-wpm pin for typing, and had passed the bookkeeping classes with straight A's, all from high school.

I was surprised when one of my business school teachers called me into the office in March and told me, "We think you should get a job. There isn't much more we can teach you, and the experience would do you good."

"You think I'm ready for a job? What kind of job do you have in mind?" I asked.

"There's a Teacher Placement Agency in this building, and they're looking for a clerk," My teacher replied. "It's just a summer hire, but they need someone to write letters to prospective clients, and to prospective schools where they have vacancies. You would not be doing much bookkeeping, but it would be a good experience. You can take some summer classes here, if you want, and can always come back full-time in the fall."

What an opportunity! Of course, I jumped at the chance. So, instead of going to class every day, I was going to work. Fortunately, work was only a couple of blocks from the apartment that Beverly and I rented. I really enjoyed my summer at the Agency. Often the four ladies who worked there would go with me to the Davenport Hotel and order a delicious pastry called Bear Paws. They came heated and slathered with butter. I had never had much pastry, except what Mom had baked, and I really enjoyed our outings.

Then there was the day that Elvis was going to perform at the Davenport Hotel. It was right across the street from where I was working, and one of the clerks in our office hollered, "Come, look! Elvis has driven up to the back door!"

We all raced to the window to get a glimpse. Soon four burly guys went to the back door of the limo and helped someone out. We couldn't see his face very well since his head was hanging low, but he was dressed in a white outfit similar to the ones we'd seen Elvis wear. The guys supported him until they all entered the building. We figured that he'd been partying too much, but it was only 10:00 a.m. We soon heard that

Elvis's evening performance had been canceled, due to illness. Hum.

Since I was making money, I decided I ought to buy myself a car. So, I went shopping. My Dad was a Dodge man, so I looked only at Dodges. I found a nice 1947 four-door sedan that I could afford, so I bought it. I was so happy to have my own transportation that I told Mom I would come to Libby and visit over the 4th of July. It turns out that Dad had moved to Great Falls for another job, and Mom was planning on going to see him there. I said I'd drive her and the kids over in my "new" car.

I drove over to Libby with no problem. We got as much as we could loaded in the car since Mom figured she would soon be moving to Great Falls and wanted to have some things there. We arrived in Great Falls at night, after an exciting trip over the "Going to the Sun" Highway. We had a wonderful 4th of July. I proudly showed my car to Dad, and of course, he had to check it all out.

"Your tires are bald," Dad said. You better get new ones before you leave here."

"Well, can you take care of that for me?" I asked. "I don't have all that much money, but if we can find a sale, I think I can swing it."

He did find a sale, but he ended up having to

purchase five new tires. Not one of the ones on the car was suitable to use as a spare, and the spare that I was carrying was utterly flat. In fact, it had no inner tube and had a few cups of water inside it. If I'd had a flat, I would have been up the creek without a paddle.

I got Mom and the kids back to Libby, and then I made it back to Spokne. It had been a great get-away.

POP THE QUESTION

*B*everly and I enjoyed having a car to get around in. We went to many USO dances and toured the countryside. We visited my Aunt and Uncle in Coeur d'Alene almost every Sunday. We often went roller-skating. I wasn't all that good at skating, but Beverly was great.

One Saturday night just four days before my 19th birthday, we decided to go roller skating to celebrate. We were just getting our skates on when the door opened, and two young, handsome airmen entered. You could tell they had been drinking since they were loud and making very witty comments, at least they must have thought they were witty as much laughing as they were doing. They got their skates and one plopped down next to me. The first words out of his mouth were, "What generation are you?"

"I don't have any idea," I answered, "What generation are you?"

"I'm second generation," he proudly proclaimed.

Just then, an announcement came over the speakers, "The next dance is going to be Crack the Whip! Grab your partners."

The airman sitting next to me asked everyone sitting in the area if they'd like to dance with him. They all turned him down. Finally, it was my turn, and I said yes. Beverly was mortified. She tried to talk me out of it, but I said I would, so he and I staggered out onto the floor. We were the last couple to enter, so ended up at the end of the line. When they cracked the whip, we would go flying. Neither of us was an expert skater, so we spent more time crashing than we did upright. One time, he fell right in front of me, and I actually jumped over him. Everyone was laughing at us.

When the humiliation was over, I asked him what his name was. He said, "Stan Rybachek."

I laughed out loud, thinking he was joking. "No one has a name like that, really, what's your name?"

He kept insisting it was Stan Rybachek. Then, he asked me if I'd like a drink. Thinking he meant to buy me a coke, I agreed. I was quite surprised when he headed for the door, and we went outside. At his car, he opened the trunk, reached in, and pulled out a beer! I had never tasted beer and wasn't about to.

So, I declined. He didn't seem to care, just opened it, and drained it in a couple of big swigs.

Back to the skating rink we went and managed to skate for a while. Time passed rapidly, and it was soon time to go home. He followed me out to my car and got into the passenger seat.

"What are you doing?" I asked.

"Ray can drive my car to your place, and Beverly can ride with him." He replied.

He handed his keys over to Ray, and with disgust written all over her face, Beverly went with Ray. They followed us to the street where I parked. Beverly got out of Ray's car and made her way into the apartment.

I sat there for a few minutes, expecting Stan (or whatever his name was) to get out of my car and into his. But he never budged. "What are you doing?" I asked.

"If you give me your phone number, I'll go home with Ray," he told me.

I didn't have anything to write my phone number on, so I rattled it off. "Now," I said, "If you leave, I'll lock the car."

"I think I'll spend the night right here, and then I'll be here when you come back to the car in the morning," he replied.

"There is no way you are going to spend the night

in my car," I told him. I walked over to his car and asked Ray if he could evict him.

"No, I can't do a thing with him when he's in this kind of a mood," Ray replied. "The best thing to do is just go and leave him. I'll wait, and I'm sure he'll soon get tired of sitting there and come on back to the barracks with me."

Beverly was fit to be tied when I got into the apartment.

"What do you think you're doing?" she ranted. "Now, they both know where we live!"

"I really liked Stan, or whatever his name is," I replied. "I'd marry him if he asked."

That shut her up, and we didn't discuss it any further.

I went out early the next morning to see about my car and was happy to find that he was gone and my car was locked. I was amazed when the phone rang later that afternoon, and it was Stan. I thought for sure he would never remember my phone number, considering the condition he was in when I left him.

He told me later that he and his buddies had been at Liberty Lake, with a keg of beer. They had fished and had a picnic but drained the keg. He had to make a run into town to get more beer, which was why he had the case in his trunk. When they decided to go home, he had been speeding on the highway. A cop turned on his red lights, and Stan outran the policeman. He ducked into the skating rink, and that's why he was there. It was the first time he'd ever gone to a skating rink. (I believe it was also the last.)

He wanted to take me to the amusement park that day, and I agreed. We had a wonderful time. He called me the next day and the next, and the next. We saw each other every day, except when he had duty that he could not get out of at the Air Force Base. I learned that he was a Staff Sergeant stationed at Geiger AFB near Spokane, doing teletype maintenance, and had recently returned from a tour of duty in Iceland. He saved his money while in Iceland and bought his 1952 Mercury. He turned this car into a hot rod, which was how he'd outrun the cops. And, his name really was Stan Rybachek.

We had been dating for about three weeks when he popped the question. True to my word, I agreed to marry him. We set a date for September 2 when I hoped my parents would be able to come. However, seeing him every day and every night took its toll, and I soon agreed to elope with him. On August 3, 1957, just seven weeks after we'd met, we headed for Coeur d'Alene, Idaho.

A NEW BEGINNING

There were lots of wedding chapels in Coeur d'Alene. We had seen them, but none of us had ever been inside one and had no idea what the requirements were. In the late morning of August 3, Stan, I, Beverly and Ray climbed into Stan's car and drove to Coeur d'Alene. We picked out a likely looking chapel and went to see what we had to do.

"Welcome to our wedding chapel," the lady gushed. "Do we have two happy couples, or one?"

Beverly and Ray looked equally shocked, but both Ray and Stan hastened to tell her only one couple!

"You need to fill out these papers," the lady said. "When you're finished, you have to take this one to the lab down the street and get a blood test. When you have done that, you can come back in about four hours, and we should have everything ready to go. Oh, by the way, you pay $25 now and $25 when you come back."

We got the papers filled out and took our blood

tests. "What should we do for four hours?" Stan asked. "We didn't bring our swimming suits, so can't go swimming."

"Well, we could go visit Aunt Edna and Uncle Chet," I piped up. "It's been over a month since Beverly and I have seen them, and since you'll be related, it probably is time to meet them."

Nobody else came up with a better suggestion, so we were off to visit. We didn't want to confess what we were up to, so we tried to keep a calm demeanor. A couple of long hours later, it was time to go for lunch, and then back to the wedding chapel. The service was short. The man was the preacher, and his wife was the musician. We were pronounced man and wife!

We went back to Spokane, dropped Beverly and Ray off at their respective places, and went for our honeymoon to Grand Coulee Dam. We had only one night and day to spend, since we had to be back to work on Monday morning. Stan was worried about getting a hotel room, so he took our marriage license in with him. He wasn't asked for it, which put him in kind of a bewildered state. But we enjoyed ourselves, including the tour of the dam on Sunday morning.

I called Mom and confessed what I'd done. She was sad to have missed our wedding ceremony, and was thinking that she would have enjoyed a trip to

Coeur d'Alene to visit with her sister. But the deed was done.

We settled into married life. We rented a basement apartment, and our landlady (Mrs. Frezon) remodeled it. She put up wallpaper and painted. It was ready for us when we got back from our honeymoon.

A NEW ASSIGNMENT

The next weekend we made a trip to Libby to visit with my uncles and their families, and to introduce Stan to them. My uncle Les had rented a bar, and was operating it. He and Hump played music at the bar a few nights a week. We went to the performance on Saturday night. By that time, I'd learned to drink beer, so Stan and I both ordered one. I was chagrined when Stan's beer came, but none for me. They brought me a coke instead. My uncle knew my age, and the drinking age in Montana was 21. I didn't quite qualify!

A few weeks later, Stan's Pa came to visit from North Dakota, and that was enjoyable. Although, that was my introduction to someone chewing "snuff." I thought it a disgusting habit!

Stan and I often went grocery shopping together, and one day I spotted a leg of lamb.

"Let's get this leg-of-lamb," I told Stan. "I love it smothered in sauerkraut."

"I hate lamb, or sheep of any kind," Stan replied. "Instead, how about we get these kidneys, and smother them in onions?"

"I've never tasted kidneys, and I had a rather bad experience with them once," I told him. "I tell you what, if you'll try my leg-of-lamb, I'll try your kidneys."

"It's a deal!" he said, so we bought both. I prepared to cook my leg-of-lamb one day, but it was so large, I decided to cut a few steaks off the bone. I froze them in a plastic bag, but forgot to label them. True to his word, Stan didn't eat much of the lamb, and said it tasted awful to him. I, on the other hand, enjoyed the kidneys when he'd cooked them.

A few days later, Stan decided to cook steak and eggs for breakfast. He had a package of venison in the freezer that he'd brought back from North Dakota on one of his trips there. I did notice, however, that instead of grabbing the venison, he'd grabbed my lamb steaks. I, of course, didn't say a word.

"Now, that is delicious steak," Stan gloated. "Don't you just love this venison?" Well, I managed to keep a straight face, and agree that it was delicious. It was only after we'd polished off the entire meal that I confessed that he'd cooked my lamb. He couldn't believe he'd tricked himself like that, but from that day forward, he enjoyed leg-of-lamb whenever we had it.

Then, Stan's brother Rodney enlisted in the Army and was being shipped overseas from Tacoma. Stan took leave, and we made a trip to Tacoma. It was the first time I'd ever seen the ocean, and I loved it. We found delicious boysenberries growing along the ditches, so we all ended up with purple mouths. Rodney had a lot of free time, and we spent it with him. It was a sad day when his ship sailed, and we had to leave that idyllic place and go back to Spokane. On the way home, we found a cornfield where they were selling gunny sacks full of sweet corn for a dollar. We filled the car, and once we got back to Spokane, I spent the time canning corn.

One weekday, I went to visit my Aunt Edna in Coeur d'Alene, and realized once I got there, that I didn't have any cash. I needed gas for the car!

"I know the clerk really well at my bank, and I'm sure she'd cash a check for you," Aunt Edna told me.

We set off in her car. I was mortified when my aunt told the clerk, "This is my niece, Mrs. Rubbercheck. She wants to cash a check!" I was surprised that the teller actually cashed the check with that introduction!

Stan was up for reenlistment in January. He'd served four years in the Air Force. "What do you think about us moving back to the farm?" he asked. "It isn't huge, and I don't think it will support Pa and us, but I'm sure he'd be happy to have us."

"I don't suppose there's any job in teletype maintenance around there," I replied. "Maybe I could get a job in a store or something,"

"Maybe it would just be better if I re-enlisted and asked to be stationed at Malmstrom AFB near Great Falls," Stan said. "That way, you'd be close to your Mom and Dad, and I like the hunting in Montana."

He reenlisted for six years and was granted Malmstrom as his new duty assignment. Before we left Spokane, we decided we should see if we could get title to the property that I'd been paying taxes on in Libby. So, I submitted the proper documents to the Treasurer's office, and the occupant had a certain amount of time in which to come up with the back taxes, interest, and penalty. We waited with bated breath and were pretty excited when a letter arrived from the Treasurer's office. We were a little disappointed that the letter contained a check, but with the interest it had earned, it had been a good investment... Although I'd rather have had title to the land!

MONTANA, HERE WE COME

"*I* picked fruit last year for some of the farmers, and I bet I could do it again this year," Stan said to me about a week after we were married. "Would you like to have some to can?"

"I helped Mom can vegetables," I replied, "But I don't know much about canning fruit. I'm willing to try."

He spent every waking moment that he wasn't on duty picking fruit. He picked cherries, plums, apricots, peaches and apples. Our Spokane landlady became a good friend. She taught me how to can fruit in the oven. We scoured the secondhand stores and thrift stores for jars. In the end, we had almost 200 quarts of canned pears, 120 jars of plums, and nearly 100 quarts of applesauce, in addition to various amounts of other fruit. We were fortunate that the Air Force would move all our belongings!

One day when we were canning, I mentioned to Mrs. Frezon that we would be leaving her around the first of January. "We are thinking of driving down the coast of California and visiting some of Stan's sisters and brothers, before we make our way to Great Falls," I told her.

"I have a sister that lives in California, and I haven't seen her in years," she replied. "I wonder if I could get a ride with you? I'd pay half of the expenses."

"That sounds like a great idea to me," I said. "I'll ask Stan, but I bet he'd be happy to have you ride along."

Stan agreed, and we set off for California one snowy day. We had not gone far from Spokane, when we nearly had an accident. A car pulled out in front of us, and with the snowy roads, the driver was having trouble getting traction. Stan managed to maneuver around him and avert an accident. We all breathed a sigh of relief.

Our first stop in California was to drop off Mrs. Frezon. She had been a model rider. I had never been to California, and it was great fun to meet some of Stan's family and enjoy the warm weather. There was no snow in California, at least where we went. Then, on to Tucson to visit with more of Stan's family.

We were planning on spending five days with them. "Want to go across the border into Nogales, Mexico?" his sister asked us.

I had not realized we were that close to Mexico and was excited at the thought.

"What do we have to do to go to Mexico?" I asked.

"Just get in the car and go," she replied. "We usually park on this side of the border and walk across, if we don't have anything we are hauling across the border."

Off we went! I was fascinated. I had also never tried tequila, and we bought a bottle with a worm in it. We thought that would be good when we got back to Montana where it was much colder. Hot toddies sounded good!

"Let's try a taco," I said to Stan. "I've never had a taco in Mexico."

So, we tried a taco, and it was anything but edible. Neither of us could choke it down. Stan's brother-in-law told us it was probably horse meat, and they didn't have refrigeration in Mexico in those days. Ugh!

It was downright cold in Arizona the few days we were there. The radio said the temperature was 42 degrees, but there was ice on the duck pond. We thought the Chamber of Commerce had influenced the weather report. They loved visitors, and if it was freezing, who would come?

We had a great visit with Stan's half-sister and family, plus his Pa. Pa was spending the winter in Tucson. He was laughing about a story that had happened to a couple of Stan's half-sisters in Mexico a few years before.

"Roy," Stan's Pa told us, "had to deliver a load of chickens to a friend in Mexico. He invited Thelma and Pauline to go with him. They wandered down the street while he was selling the chickens, and the local police picked them up for being prostitutes. They argued, but the police guy was adamant. They either had to buy a prostitute license for five dollars apiece, or face fines of $50 for being without a license. They bought the license. I thought Pauline should frame hers, but she burned it!"

We got a good chuckle out of that story, and I was happy that I had stuck close to Stan on our visit. All good things must end, and soon we were headed North. We still had some time before Stan needed to check in at the base, so we decided to go to Pa's farm in North Dakota. We had a bit of trouble going over the mountains near Denver with white-out conditions but made it. It was quite an eye opener for me when we landed at the homestead in North Dakota. Stan's dad was not a very good housekeeper, and it took us a couple of days to just get the house livable. But we did!

Stan took me around and introduced me to many of his friends. The worst thing that happened is that I came down with a terrible cold. I blamed it on the freezing cold in Arizona. They had no way of heating their house in Arizona, except using a propane oven, and I had nearly frozen. At least, the homestead had a nice wood stove! I was feeling mighty poorly, when Stan suggested that perhaps a shot of the tequila would fix me up. I was surprised when I sipped it, and it tasted like water. I thought it would probably burn all the way down, but no… it was smooth.

Stan, on the other hand, coughed every time he took a sip. I thought he was a sissy. Anyway, we enjoyed our week at the homestead, but were soon on our way to Great Falls. We stayed with my aunt until we could locate an apartment. Our belongings had been shipped from Spokane, but they were in storage. It was nice to find a suitable apartment and get our stuff delivered. We spent quite a bit of time at the second-hand stores, buying furniture and getting settled.

We had been in our new apartment for a week or so, when Stan said, "I think we ought to celebrate with a drink of that tequila. I'll be careful not to pour out the worm!"

"That sounds great," I replied. "I think I put it in that cupboard… I'll get the glasses."

Stan poured us each a small glass of the tequila, and left the worm still floating in the bottle. Why do they put a worm in the bottle anyway? Like I had in North Dakota, I took a big swig. I thought I was going to die. It burned all the way to my toes, and nearly knocked me on my keister. My cold was gone, and with it the ability to slug down tequila. I have hated tequila ever since, worm or not!

ALASKA, HERE WE COME

*J*ust before we arrived in Great Falls, Mom and Dad moved again. This time, Dad had a job on a ranch near Stanford (which was about 60 miles from Great Falls). Along with this job came a delightful two-story ranch house. There were plenty of bedrooms, and everyone in the family could have their own bedroom.

On most weekends we'd drive out and visit them. There seemed always to be some chore that needed doing, and we enjoyed our time on the ranch.

Summer disappeared, and soon it was hunting season. Dad loved to hunt, and often Stan and I were invited to go with him. One time, we had gone hunting in the mountains near Judith Gap, when Dad decided that we ought to split up. He parked the Jeep, and we all went in different directions.

We agreed to return to the Jeep in two hours; both Dad and I arrived at the allotted time, empty-handed, but there was no Stan. It wasn't long before we heard a shot. Soon Stan showed up with blood on his hands. He had bagged an elk.

"I had trouble with that old 30-30 that I got from my dad," Stan told us. "I saw this herd of elk, and when I went to shoot a nice fat looking one, the gun jammed. By the time I unjammed it, the only one in range was a little spike, but he's lying over there."

We helped him drag the small elk out and strap it on the Jeep. That was the only game we got on that trip, but Stan was as proud of his elk as if he had a trophy bull. It was tender and tasty.

Dad and Mom stayed on that farm for less than a year. Then Dad got another job farther away from Great Falls, in the town of Moccasin, and bought a three-room house. The family was back to sharing bedrooms once again. When we visited, it was the couch in the living room for us. This house was near Ackley Lake, which had trout in it, and Dad had a small, aluminum boat.

Stan and I often went fishing in Dad's boat. Mom was an excellent fish-fryer, and we enjoyed those trout.

On one of our trips, Mom said, "I'm going to go to work part-time at the grocery store. Gramma Bloom will watch Henry and Debbie while I'm gone, and Betty will be in school."

"At least you won't be teaching," I replied. "I didn't

much like it when you were my teacher, so I don't want Betty to have to suffer!"

Stan and I moved out of our apartment and into a small house in Great Falls. It had a fenced in yard, so we decided we needed a dog. We found a Cocker Spaniel mix that we fell in love with, so Ike joined our family. (Eisenhower was president at the time, and his nickname was "Ike," thus the name for our dog.) Ike enjoyed traveling, so every weekend that we were free, he would join us in visiting my parents.

Since my parents had given our dog Skipper away, they were without a dog. We decided we couldn't have that, so one day we found a Boston Bulldog mix advertised in the newspaper. We got him for my parents. He was just a tiny little puppy and cute as could be. They named him Pudge, and Pudge lived a good long life.

One day when we were fishing at the Lake, we ran into the people that my parents had given Skipper to back in Coffee Creek.

"Aren't you the folks that gave us Skipper?" the lady queried.

"Yes, how is he?" I asked.

"He passed away in his sleep a couple of years ago, but you'll never believe what he did. My two-year old daughter was outside playing and wandered too near to the bank of the canal. I was watching out the window and saw her fall into the canal. I ran out as fast as I could, but before I got there, Skipper reached out from the shore as far as he could and grabbed her dress. He dragged her back up on the bank. I loved that dog… he saved her life!"

"When we had Skipper, he was afraid of the water and wouldn't get wet! Did he ever learn to swim?"

"I don't think so. He was cautious about not getting in the water but was able to grab her dress from the shore."

We hoped that Pudge would be as heroic.

While living in Great Falls, we also spent a lot of time visiting with my Grandma Lilley. After Grandpa passed away, she'd sold the store in Buffalo and moved to Great Falls to live with my Aunt Margaret. Also, another of Mom's brothers, Bill, lived in Great Falls with his wife Edna, and their three kids. We had lots of relatives to enjoy. It was an excellent time for me.

My parents often came to Great Falls to shop, and visit. One day, Mom was driving the car and got into an accident. While it was debatable if it was her fault or not, she was in danger of losing her driver's license. They didn't have insurance on the car. Mom had 90 days in which to prove that she had insurance, or she would lose her license to drive. About the time of the accident, Stan put in for a transfer to Alaska. He thought he would enjoy the big game hunting in Alaska. We were both shocked when his orders arrived, to find that he had been assigned to Greece as an Attaché. Neither of us were excited about that!

Stan had a friend in the Air Force who had married a Japanese lady, who was not allowed in the US. Both Stan and the other guy had the same clearance and same qualifications, so Stan and the other airman applied to make a swap. It was approved, and we were going to Alaska.

"How do we get to Alaska?" I asked Stan. "Is there even a road? Or do we have to fly? I'm sure hoping we don't have to fly since I've never been on an airplane!"

"There's a road that they opened to non-military traffic about 10 years ago," Stan replied. "But, it would do you good to fly, scaredy-cat!"

Stan was to check in at Ladd Air Force Base near Fairbanks in early October. Since I was six months' pregnant at the time, I asked my OB doctor about driving to Alaska.

"With your type O-negative blood, I don't think it's a good idea," the doctor said. "In fact, I won't authorize travel. You can wait until your husband is settled and fly up."

I was crying when I reported that conversation to

Stan. "What can we do?" I wailed. "I don't want to stay here and fly up later. I don't want to fly at all! I want to come in the car!"

"Why don't we see if your parents want to come with us?" Stan replied. "I think your Dad has always talked about going to Alaska, and now with your Mom's problem with her driver's license, it might be an ideal time. And, I think your Mom or Dad probably has O-negative blood, and while I don't think you'll need a transfusion along the way, if you do, we'd have a supplier with us."

We went to visit Mom and Dad that weekend. "Guess what!" I told my parents as we came in through the door. "Stan's transfer to Alaska has been approved, and we're leaving in early September. Stan was wondering if you'd like to come with us?"

Dad got all excited, and hollered, "Mom, how would you like to go to Alaska? Dad worked on the DEW line outside of Fairbanks, and he always talked about how wonderful Alaska was. I think it would be a great experience."

"I don't know," Mom replied. "I kind of like it here in our house in Moccasin, and the kids are just about to get into school. I don't think we should go, and besides, what is the DEW Line? I don't think I ever heard you talk about it!"

"If I remember rightly," Dad replied, "it was called the Distant Early Warning Line, and was a line of radar installations stretching from Pt. Barrow all the way across the Northwest Territories. I think Dad worked in construction at several of the sites. Besides, you won't be able to drive for a year, starting the end of September. Maybe they won't know that in Alaska! I think we should go."

I think that was the winning argument, and soon we were planning our trip to Alaska. However, the weekend soon ended, and Stan and I were back in Great Falls, excited about our upcoming trip.

Stan came home one day from the base with a big grin on his face. "Do you know what my friend told me?" he asked.

"Not an idea in the world," I replied. "What did your friend tell you?"

"Well, he said there's a publication called The Milepost, and it gives information about the ALCAN Highway. You know that's the one that goes to Alaska from Dawson Creek in British Columbia. He even told me where to get a Milrpost, and I did! Look at this, isn't it something?" and he pulled a copy of a medium-sized book from behind his back.

We spent hours poring over the information in The Milepost. The more we looked, the more incredible it became that soon we would be traveling down that road.

Stan would have a month to get to Alaska, so we packed our things; shipped what we could; helped Dad get the truck ready, and we were headed for Alaska.

SECTION III

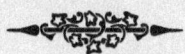

Alaska Bound

ON THE ROAD

*G*etting Dad's truck loaded was quite a chore. Mom and Dad couldn't leave the large, old piano, although I was the only one who played it, so aboard it went.

"When your Dad bought this piano, the guy he bought it from said it was the second piano to come into Montana in the 1800s, so we can't leave it," Mom told me. Besides, she planned to have the kids take piano lessons. I was surprised when they loaded the large kitchen stove, Dad's welders, and a couch, and packed them so well, they still had room for more.

Fortunately, Dad still had his 1949 two-and-a-half-ton Dodge truck with a stock-rack on it, but it was soon piled high. That truck was loaded with everything, except the kitchen sink. No room for that! He tied a tarp over the load, then hooked his Jeep on behind the truck, and he was ready to leave.

At a family meeting, I asked, "Are we planning on camping? If so, where will we carry our camping supplies? Surely there isn't room in the truck for them, and they'd be hard to get at every night. The car will be full, too!"

"I saw a small trailer for sale down the street," Stan said. "If we can get that, I can put a trailer hitch on the car at the Hobby Shop, and that will solve the problem!"

Stan bought the trailer, and we loaded that with our camping supplies. We secured Dad's aluminum boat on top of the Mercury. Two people would ride with Dad in his truck, plus the dogs, and the other four would ride in the Mercury. Dad's two cats were banned to the Jeep.

It was a warm September morning in 1958 when we set off. It was nearly 200 miles to the border crossing at Sweet Grass, Montana. Except for Stan, none of us had ever been across the Canadian border. Stan told us not to worry; everything would be A-Okay. We went to the Customs gate first in our car, with Dad following us in the truck. They asked a few questions, but since Stan had orders for Alaska, it was a cursory examination. Not so for Dad! They wondered what he had in the truck and threatened to have him unload the whole truck so they could inspect it.

We had parked on the other side of the gate, and Stan walked back to help Dad.

"Sirs," Stan told them, "Most of the items in this truck are being hauled for me, and I have these orders from the Air Force."

"Even with orders," the Customs agent said, "we have the right to inspect any suspicious vehicle."

"You can inspect it if you have to," Stan told them, "but we'll need help getting it loaded again, and it is getting on towards dark. We may have to spend the night right here."

They finally let us go. Customs sealed the rifle that Dad kept out to protect us in case of a marauding bear. Once through the border, we began looking for a parking spot. We found a nice gravel pit before we got to Lethbridge, B.C., and camped for the night.

Dad was worried that his truck was overweight. So far, he hadn't been forced to go through a weigh station.

"You kids go ahead of me, and when you see a weigh station, let me know," Dad said. "You can try to find a road around it because I sure don't want to have to leave part of our belongings behind."

We took our job seriously and also got to see parts of some of the cities we traveled through that we would not otherwise get to tour!

Dad was also worried about parking his truck in a soft spot, so every afternoon starting around 2:30

p.m., we began looking for a place to overnight. Gravel pits were our favorite.

The dogs were always happy when they could get out of the truck and run free for a while. The cats remained in the Jeep. Every day after we parked, Stan and Dad got the tent unloaded from the trailer and set it up, rain or shine. The kids and I tried to clear the bigger rocks away from where we would sleep. Sleeping on a pointed rock could become unbearable! Then, the kids and I would blow up the two air mattresses.

Stan and I had opted to use blankets instead of sleeping bags, so we had our bed to make. Mom and Dad also opted for blankets, so we had their bed to make, too, and Debbie slept with them. Only Betty and Henry had their own sleeping bags. The adults had dibs on the air mattresses.

While we worked on beds, Mom started preparing dinner. After the men had the tent erected and the heating stove set up, Mom put her two-burner Coleman gas stove on the heating stove. She used that to prepare the meal. If it was really chilly out, she would build a fire in the heating stove and put her Coleman stove on a wooden box. At each campground, we all went looking for firewood for the heating stove.

Mom had canned a lot of soup during the summer, and that soup was what we usually ate for our dinner.

Once in a while we'd stop at a store and buy a steak or some chicken. We had included a bag of potatoes, so meat and potato meals were extra special. We did get a little tired of soup, so steak nights were what we looked forward to.

Depending on the time we found a suitable stopping place, and how long it took to have dinner and do the dishes, we often had time to play some games before bedtime. Morning came early; we were up at 6:00, using a gasoline light so we could see. It was my job to get the bedding folded and ready to store while Mom cooked. Dad still insisted on having his pancakes so, we had pancakes every morning. Sometimes we had bacon or sausage to go with them, but often it was only cheese.

Once breakfast was over, and the dishes were washed, dried, and stored, we began the task of getting everything packed for the day's journey. We always tried to hurry as fast as we could, but inevitably it would take us at least four hours, so it was 10:00 when we set out. Some days we would drive for 150 miles, others less. No wonder it took us over three weeks to arrive in Fairbanks!

BRIDGE OVER THE RIVER

*W*e soon settled into our travel routine. When we got close to a town, Stan and I (in our car) scouted out the weigh stations. We usually returned to find Dad parked alongside the road, waiting for instructions. We had great success in finding our way around the towns.

We went through Calgary without a hitch. For years, I had heard of the Calgary Stampede, which was a world-famous Rodeo, Exhibition, and Festival. Unfortunately, the Stampede had already been held in July, just a couple of months before. I was hoping we would at least get to drive past the grounds, but no such luck. We found a nice bypass that took us mostly around the city.

The next large city on our route was Edmonton. As was our habit, we took the car to scout out the weigh stations, and we soon found that the only way around one was to go through the city.

When we got back to where Dad was parked, we gave him the bad news. "We just can't find a way around the weigh station, unless we go right through downtown. We'll have to cross the river twice if we go that way," Stan told my Dad.

"Well, I really don't want to have to unload anything from the truck, in case we can't pass the weight restrictions, so you go ahead, and I'll follow."

We set off on our round-about road through the city. Of course, it was difficult to stay within sight of the truck, since red lights seemed to plague us. Crossing the North Saskatchewan River was simple on our way into the city. Once we had penetrated the city, we came to a covered bridge in the center of Edmonton. Stan and I drove across the covered bridge, only to find that Dad wasn't following.

"We have to turn around, and see what's keeping him," Stan said. So, we went around the block and back across the river. There sat the truck, parked on the side of the street.

After another turn around a block, we pulled in behind the truck. Stan got out to see if he could find out what the trouble was.

"Why are you just sitting there?" he asked.

"Well, do you see how high that bridge is? I think

the stock-rack on the truck is too high, and I don't want to lose part of my load!" Dad replied.

Upon eye-balling it and even measuring with a 12-inch ruler, we decided that the clearance on the bridge was very close to the height of the stock-rack, and where the canvas covering bulged upwards, due to something under it, it probably would hit.

"So, what do we do now?" Stan asked. "Can you back the truck up with the Jeep behind, or do we need to unhook the Jeep? There's another street behind us. It's just a little way, and the traffic is light. We can no doubt find our way to another bridge from that side street."

"I think I can back it up," Dad replied. "You kids can flag down any car that comes, and one of you can let me know what the Jeep is doing since I can't see it in my rear-view mirrors."

Slowly and carefully, Dad managed to back the truck and Jeep down the street, until he could turn onto the side street. Then, the problem came as to where to go. The map showed that the street with the covered bridge was the straightest way to get back on the Highway. The map forgot to mention that it was a low covered bridge!

Once again, Stan and I went scouting. We finally found a route that would take us down a steep hill, to where another bridge crossed the river. This one was not a covered bridge, but the problem was that the road then climbed back up the hill to reach the highway. This seemed to be the only way.

We went back to where Dad was parked again and motioned for him to follow us. Down the steep hill we went, across the bridge, and then up the steep hill on the other side. Dad drove in a very low gear both ways, since going downhill he didn't want to rely too heavily on his brakes; going up, he had to gear down to get up the hill.

We were all thrilled when we were once again on the road headed North. What next adventure would lie ahead?

ANOTHER BRIDGE

We were nearly 300 miles northwest of Edmonton when we encountered a long line of traffic stopped in the road. Dad pulled the truck into the line, and we followed closely behind him. He and Stan walked up the line to see what the delay was.

When they returned, Dad said. "Apparently, we have to cross a railroad bridge. They said the bridge would open in about half an hour for traffic going our way."

"You mean, they only have a railroad bridge?" I asked. "Did they take all that equipment and supplies to Alaska over a railroad bridge?"

"Well, the guy said they had a suspension bridge over the river until last year, when it collapsed. He said it was a spectacular collapse! Since then, the railroad has been kind enough to let vehicles cross their bridge. It is a little way downstream from where the other bridge was located, and the guy said it's about 300 feet above the river, and there are no guard rails. It sounds like it could be treacherous, but it's the only way to get to Alaska, and I'm headed for Alaska."

Good grief, I was afraid of heights! Should I try to walk over? No, that would be worse than riding! What to do? I didn't want to act like a coward in front of my siblings. I know I turned a pasty white and began trembling, but I swallowed my fear as much as I could. That was about the longest half hour I've ever put in.

Dad made sure that everything was still tied down on the truck, he kicked the tires to make sure they had enough air, and we waited. I huddled in fear, trying hard to be brave, but secretly praying that something would happen to delay the crossing. It was with mixed feelings that I noticed the line of traffic slowly begin to move.

As we neared the Peace River Railroad Bridge, I could see that it was very long ways down to the river – it was very high indeed, and, as advertised, not very wide. A few planks had been added along the tracks to try to make it safer. However, when it was Dad's turn to cross, I watched in horror as part of each of his outside duals extended off the edge of the planks. That picture was burned into my brain. It's the last thing I remember seeing until I heard Stan say, "You can open your eyes now, scardy cat. We're across, and your Dad is waiting."

Sure enough, there was the truck pulled into a wide spot in the road. We had survived.

A few more miles, and we found a delightful gravel pit for our nightly stop. What a relief to have crossed the river and to be off that bridge! But, would there be more like it?

NO WAY AROUND

*W*e arrived near Dawson Creek in a downpour. As was our habit, Stan and I found the weigh station, and then we looked for a road that would bypass it. We went up one dead end after another, but there was NO bypass.

We had to go back to where Dad was parked and deliver the bad news. "There is just no way around this one," Stan told my Dad. "You're going to have to go through it."

Dad was quite crestfallen, but stoically started the truck, and went to the weigh station. He was very uneasy as the attendant told him to stop on the scale. Dad undoubtedly feared the worst and could just visualize having to start unloading his treasures. He was white as a ghost as he grimly sat waiting for the verdict. He was very shocked when the attendant just waved him on through! The truck was not over- weight after all! All those detours had been in vain! Our reconnaissance would not be needed in the future. He could just drive right on through the weigh stations.

This was the official start of the ALCAN (Alaska-Canada) Highway. Our book, The Milepost, was to be our travel Bible for the rest of our journey.

We filled all our gas tanks and spare gas cans before leaving Dawson Creek, and then we stopped for a hamburger. We thought we should celebrate. We had safely traveled a thousand miles, and had only 1,500 more to go.

The ALCAN was a gravel road, very dusty when someone passed, and very dusty for our car following Dad's truck. We lagged way behind the truck, to be able see the road enough to dodge the potholes and other hazards. We found lots of washboards on the road. (Washboards occur on unpaved roads; they are a wavy pattern in the gravel. It feels like you just ran over a series of closely-spaced speed bumps.) We also encountered mounds of gravel that had been kicked up by the larger trucks. Stan had to maneuver carefully to keep the car from dragging on some of the piles.

Shortly after we left Dawson Creek, it was time to find a spot to park for the night. It was much easier locating gravel pits after we had The Milepost, since it told us where they were. Some gravel pits were usable, and some were not.

We found a camping spot, got our camp set up, had dinner, and bedded down for the night.

It was still raining the next morning when Stan said, "I guess I'll go start the car while you ladies get breakfast cooked."

We didn't hear the car and were surprised when the tent flap lifted, and Stan stuck his head in. "The car won't start, and even with all the rain, there's a strong smell of gas near the car. I guess I must not have been as careful as I thought I was yesterday, and knocked a hole in the gas tank."

Fortunately, we had several extra cans of gas, so he poured one into the gas tank. We took off ahead of Dad and the truck, looking for a gas station. We hoped they would be able to fix the gas tank.

We found a station, and Stan was able to get the car on the hoist and take a good look at our problem.

"Look how the drain plug is bent out like that," he said. "One of those rocks must have knocked it loose."

The filling station had no way to fix the problem; their solution was to sell us some gunk in a tube that was "guaranteed" to dry as hard as the original weld had been. The only difficulty was that we needed to have a completely dry tank to use the stuff, and we had gas leaking out. We waited until Dad caught up with us.

"Fred," Stan said, "The tank is still leaking, and these guys can't fix it. I did get some gunk from them that's supposed to seal it, but I have to drive until I run out of gas. If I don't do that, maybe we can find a good gravel pit to camp in, and I can drain the tank. It says it dries in 12 hours. What do you think?"

"Well," Dad replied, "Probably driving until you run out of gas isn't a good idea. You'd probably run out in the middle of a hill or something. So, let's find a good camping spot, and drain it."

It wasn't too far until we found a suitably solid gravel pit to camp in. Stan drained the gas, and the tank dried almost immediately, once the drip stopped. He screwed the drain plug back in, tightened it as much as he could, and then used the gunk to cover the whole area completely. We should be good to go... right?

WRONG GEAR

$\mathcal{W}$e traveled on, heading north. We found several streams that had no bridges at all. We didn't know if high water had washed them out, or if the construction workers had just not gotten around to building them yet. Most of the streams were easy to cross, and there was a gravel road right to the edge of them. They all had gravel bottoms and were only a few inches deep.

Then, we arrived at one that was not so friendly. There was no nice gravel road leading to the edge of this stream. There was a field of mud. They had a bulldozer pulling vehicles across, and most of them were dragging in the mud. We parked alongside the road and watched as they pulled a vehicle across from our side, then brought another car back across.

"I believe that if you get in the Jeep and push the truck with it, we can make it across without needing a pull," Dad said to Stan. "The car is for-sure going to need to be pulled, and Rosie can drive it. They'll hook onto it when it's her turn. I'm sure we can make it. I think if you put the Jeep in second gear, four-wheel drive, and low-range until we're near the mudhole, and then drop the clutch in, we'll go right through that area lickety-split."

Stan was agreeable and went to get into the Jeep. He realized, when he looked carefully at the Jeep, that he could not see anything out the window. The entire Jeep was one big ball of mud, from all the muddy roads we'd been traveling on. Before he opened the door to get into the Jeep, Stan scraped a peephole in the mud on the windshield so he could see the back of the truck.

Remember the cats? Well, they had NOT been using their litter box, and the inside of the Jeep was a smelly mess. But Stan got in, and soon Dad was pulling him towards the thick mud. We all lined the edge of the road, watching. They slowly made their way down the muddy road. Then, Dad pushed on the accelerator of the truck and the engine began roaring. Stan let out the clutch on the Jeep, and the wheels on the Jeep started turning… backwards! Instead of having it in second gear, it was in reverse!

Once Stan pushed the clutch in, the truck started gaining speed once more. Again, Stan let out the clutch, and the whole outfit slowed, with the wheels of the Jeep turning rapidly in the wrong direction. Once again, Stan let in the clutch, and they started speeding up. They were getting closer and closer to the large mudhole.

When they slowed down that time, Dad stopped the truck, got out of it, and waded through the mud back to the Jeep.

"Will you put it in second instead of in reverse?" he calmly asked Stan. Stan was shocked and embarrassed. With all the windows of the Jeep covered in mud, he had no idea what was going on.

Dad went back to the truck, put it into gear, and that time Stan had the wheels of the Jeep turning in the right direction. They gained speed and ran through the mudhole without a hitch. They had no trouble crossing the creek and soon were parked on the road on the other side.

They watched as I gently maneuvered the car to where the dozer could attach, and we were pulled through the mudhole without a problem. We were soon on our way to Alaska once more, but poor Stan never lived down the time he had the wrong gear.

MUNCHING AT MUNCHO

"Oh, no," Stan said when he went out to start the car the next morning. "The gas is gone again!"

Apparently, the trip through the muddy creek had knocked off the gunk that he'd used to seal it. There was nothing to do except add more gunk. Fortunately, we had some extra gas in the cans, enough to get us to the next gas station. It was wise to keep those extra cans full! Our next step would be draining the tank again, and re-gunking it.

Driving through Fort Nelson, B.C. was terrific since we didn't have to scout for weigh stations anymore.

"Look, there's a laundry!" Mom shouted at us. "We are all needing some clean clothes, and maybe we can go shopping while they are drying."

Not only did they have laundry facilities, but they had a lovely public shower available for only a dollar each. A hot shower never felt so refreshing! Sponge baths are okay, but nothing beats a real, live shower!

While the laundry was drying, we found a grocery store and stocked up. Not only did we get our bread and milk replenished, but we even bought some lovely steaks for our dinner. Since the day was rapidly waning, we didn't stay long in Fort Nelson, once the laundry was finished.

Our next stop was at Muncho Lake. It was a beautiful camping spot. We arrived there in the early afternoon and were awed by the green-tinted water in the lake. The lake is very deep, cold, and delightful. We pitched our tent and enjoyed having time to take a walk and enjoy the fresh air, while the gas again drained out of the Mercury. The water in Muncho Lake is tinted green due to mineralization. It made us want to dip a line in the water and see if we could catch a fish. Before we had left Montana, we had not even thought about fishing along the way, so our fishing gear was safely stowed near the bottom of the truck. But we could dream!

Stan built a fire in the firepit, and we wrapped potatoes in tin foil, and they baked splendidly. While Mom was cooking the steaks, Stan re-gunked the car's gas tank. With full tummies, we rested well that night and thought about just staying another day in that idyllic spot, but... we decided we probably could not afford the time. While we really hated to begin the arduous task of packing up to hit the road, it was no doubt necessary. We promised ourselves we would return one day and just spend a week!

We were off, and as we rounded a turn in the road, a huge stone sheep was sedately strolling along the road. We all got out to look at that sheep, and he wasn't a bit afraid. He had a magnificent full curl on his horns. What a treat!

SMELLY MOOSE KILL

*W*ildlife was plentiful as we journeyed on the ALCAN Highway. The leaves were turning colors, and the views were spectacular. We saw herds of buffalo and caribou wandering along the road. Between Great Falls and Fairbanks, we saw so many different animals, it was hard to keep track of them. We saw: buffalo (or bison); grizzly and black bear; caribou; moose; wolves; red and cross fox; marmot; black tail and white tail deer; elk; stone, mountain and Dahl sheep; beaver; ducks, including mallards, pintails and teal; squirrels; porcupines; and birds, including crows, hawks and eagles. What an abundance of wildlife along the Highway!

As we made our way towards Watson Lake, we were thrilled with the scenery. It was exciting to leave British Columbia behind, and enter the Yukon Territory. As we drove into the town of Watson Lake, we were amazed to find a Sign Post Forest. The "forest" consisted of many signs from various cities in the world.

"Where did all these signs come from?" Mom asked the waitress in the restaurant.

"Would you believe that a homesick G.I. in 1943 started this display?" she replied. "I understand he was assigned light duty while recovering from an injury and erected a signpost from his hometown: Danville, Ill., 2,835 miles. Since that time, thousands of signs have been added to his original. They told me that today there are over 100,000. Anyone can add a sign to the forest, and lots of travelers have. Signs come in all sizes and shapes, and the forest is very impressive."

It was time to do laundry once again, and the shower felt perfect. We spent a bit of time wandering around the city and enjoyed eating a meal that we didn't have to cook. We spent the night there, parked before the "forest," with our tent nearly on the road. Our next large town would be Whitehorse, Y.T. From Whitehorse, there would only be about 600 miles left of our journey.

As we got ready to leave, Stan entered the tent, and said, "More bad news. I filled up the car last night, and this morning it is down to about half-a-tank. I just put some more gunk on it, but since it's still seeping gas, I doubt it's going to help much."

We traveled steadily and were lucky to find a suitable gravel pit for our overnight stay. It was near a very picturesque, bubbling stream. We pitched the tent, had our dinner, and off to bed. The next morning while we were getting things packed, the dogs disappeared. We called and called, but neither one of them appeared. Finally, Stan went looking for them.

"Did you find them?" I worriedly asked.

"Oh, yeah, I found them," he replied. "They were munching on a dead moose. It's been dead for some time and is very smelly. Those dogs stink! They refused to leave their feast."

He rummaged around until he found a bar of soap and a rope. He intended to scrub the dogs in the cold stream, tie them up so they could not return to their bountiful feast, and then try to get them somewhat dry before we loaded them in the car.

He returned sometime later, quite wet and bedraggled-looking himself, and he was shivering. He had both dogs on various ropes. They also seemed pretty bedraggled and wet. Stan needed to change clothes. Although he balked, we dug out a change of clothes and sent him into the bushes to make the switch. He had almost quit shivering when he emerged in dry duds.

The dogs were not very happy. They kept wanting to break free and go back to their feast! We hated to put them in the car, but it was almost noon by that time, and we needed to make a few more miles towards Whitehorse. The tent was down, and everything was packed.

So, we wrapped the two dogs in towels and put them in the truck with Dad. He said they unwrapped soon, and as he drove off, they kept looking longingly in the direction of their feast. A slight odor remained on both of them, which was not pleasant in the truck. In fact, a slight odor remained on Stan, too, which was not very pleasant in the car, either! It was a bit chilly to drive with the windows down, but self-preservation demanded that we had to. No one was happy.

NO MORE LEAK

*W*hitehorse seemed like another good place to do a load of laundry and have a shower. We found a nice Laundromat that also had showers, and we were getting set to do the laundry, when Mom asked, "Do you have any Canadian money left? I seem to have run out!"

"Well, no," I replied. "We went to that bank in Great Falls and got $400 of it, but I've spent all I had. I think Stan and Dad are out, too."

We had not counted on the high cost of gas going through Canada, and that leak surely didn't help. We didn't have anything like a credit card. We had to use cash to pay for everything. At the bank in Great Falls, we received $1.25 Canadian for every $1.00 of American money. We soon found out that if we tried to pay for anything in Canada with American money, the merchants would take an even trade… so, for every dollar we spent, we were losing a quarter!

"I think we'd better find a bank in Whitehorse

and convert some more of our American money into Canadian. We can't afford to lose that quarter every time we buy something!" I told Mom.

We found a bank all right, but their exchange rate was quite different than the one in Great Falls. They only offered $1.10 for an American dollar. Nevertheless, it was better than an even swap, so we converted what we thought would see us through. Provided, of course, we had no further problems with either vehicle.

Stan searched for a shop that might be able to weld our gas tank. He found one that had a welder, but they were not willing to do the welding. They told him that if he wanted to weld it himself, they would let him borrow their welder, but he would have to do it outside.

It wasn't long before he had the gas tank off the car, filled it with cold water, and started welding the drain plug attachment. Some of the mechanics watched as he used quite a bit of welding rod to make sure it would never leak again. That tank was heavy now, but it surely shouldn't leak!

When he finished with the last welding rod, he drained the tank and then heated it to make sure it was dry before putting gas back in. I was concerned about that part of his plan, but it worked. Soon steam was coming out from the top of the tank, and with the drain plug out, the fumes must have left, since it didn't explode. We were all relieved when the tank was once again on the car, full of gas, and no drip. It never dripped again.

We spent the night in Whitehorse. We found a beautiful park that had outhouses. That was a real treat from parking in our gravel pits!

BORDER CROSSING

*L*eaving Whitehorse was exciting since we knew that the next wide spot in the road would be Haines Junction, Yukon Territory. Had we wanted to take a side trip of about 150 miles, we could have visited Haines, Alaska. However, time was at a premium, so we had to continue on.

As we neared Destruction Bay, Mom read to us from The Milepost.

"Both Destruction Bay and Burwash Landing are located on Kluane Lake. Destruction Bay was established in 1942 by the U.S. Army as a highway construction camp. Shortly after it was constructed, a high wind almost destroyed the camp, thus its name.

"The history of Burwash Landing is much different, although they are only about 10 miles apart. Burwash Landing was first used as a summer fishing camp by the Southern Tutchone Athabascans until a trading post was built in the early 1900s by the Jacquot Brothers.

"The Jacquot Brothers were trained as chefs in France and had traveled to the Klondike in 1898 during the gold rush. They later came to the Kluane Gold Rush in 1904 and established their trading post. Burwash Landing grew during the construction of the ALCAN Highway."

After all that history, we were thrilled to see the world's largest gold pan in Burwash Landing. We spent a night on the shores of Kluane Lake, and in the morning, we could see white dots moving around on a nearby mountain. We wondered what they were, so dug out the trusty Milepost. We were excited to learn that they were Dahl sheep, and the mountain was Sheep Mountain. We drove right past the mountain.

The sheep were very close as we maneuvered around the winding road. We felt like we could reach out and touch the majestic beasts. However, we didn't have much time to spare in gazing, so soon we were on our way down the highway.

It wasn't long until we passed through Beaver Creek, just a few miles from the Alaska border. We were getting nearer and nearer to the end of our journey. We had no trouble going through Customs and were soon back in the United States of America. It felt good to not be on foreign soil any longer.

We stopped in Tok to once again do our laundry and have a refreshing shower. Then, on through Delta Junction, and Big Delta. Only a hundred miles left to journey.

WE ARE HERE!

*I*t was exciting to drive past Eielson Air Force Base, and see the warning signs, "Do Not Take Pictures." We didn't.

Soon we arrived in Fairbanks. We found a camping spot just off Farmer's Loop Road and pitched our tent. Early the next morning, September 26, 1958, Stan and I went looking for a place to rent. We bought a newspaper and read the "for rent" ads. One looked promising, so we went to talk to the agent.

"I see you have a three-bedroom house for rent," Stan told the agent. "I'm with the military, but we have my in-laws with us. We need at least a three-bedroom."

"I have a really nice three-bedroom house," the agent replied. "I can rent it to you starting October 1st if you want. We have a rule that if you rent a house, we cannot prorate the rent, so if you wanted immediate possession, I'd have to charge you a full month's rent."

We decided we could wait. We did the paperwork and paid the man.

"Would it be all right if we began unloading our stuff in the house before the 1st is here?" Stan asked.

"Sure, that would be all right, you can get moved in, but you just can't sleep in the house," he replied.

We went back to the campsite, got Dad and the truck, and started moving into the house. The kids were excited to pick out which bedroom they would have. Mom and Dad would have another one, and Stan and I got the little one!

We spent two days eating and sleeping in our tent, while methodically getting the truck unloaded, the beds set-up, and the furniture placed. All was going well, until the next night when we went to bed and the temperature started dropping. We woke in the morning shivering, with about three inches of snow on the ground. It was still snowing hard. The dogs kept running in and out and crawling into bed with us when they came in cold and wet.

This was not good! "Do you think we could move into the house, if we didn't use any lights at night, and kept the dogs quiet?" Stan asked.

"I am all for it," Mom replied. "I'm sure after this experience, everyone will be as quiet as church mice!"

So, move we did. We took our tent down in a

blinding snowstorm, packed everything in the truck and car, and moved into our new home. The blankets dried in the heated garage before it was time to use them that night. We were afraid to answer the door when the doorbell rang the next morning, even though we suspected it was a neighbor welcoming us to the neighborhood. We were happy when October 1 rolled around.

THEN AND NOW

*Y*ou have just had the "then." Fast forward 60 years, and here comes the "now."

I was enjoying lunch with the Alaska Women in Mining in the spring of 2018 when my friend Val started talking about driving down the Alaska Highway in the fall. Val owns and operates the Alaska Yukon Trails tour company.

"I haven't been down the Highway in about 15 years." I told her. "It must really have changed since then."

"Would you like to ride with me?" she asked. "I plan on leaving sometime in early October."

"That sounds like a lot of fun. I usually leave in early October, and sure… I'd love to ride with you," I told her. "I think my brother and sister could pick me up in Great Falls, while you go on to Illinois."

Well, plans changed during the summer. Val was diagnosed with breast cancer and started undergoing chemo treatments. She had to have a total of six of them, three-weeks apart. Her last chemo would be October 2. Then, I had bladder repair surgery on September 13, but my doctor released me to travel on October 7, as long as I didn't lift anything over 10 pounds. Val thought she'd be able to travel on October 7, so our new plan was in place.

We set off near daybreak on October 7. It had been a late fall in Fairbanks, and while there had been freezing temperatures for a few days, it had not snowed. We had an overcast day, but the roads were great. We enjoyed seeing some wildlife. A cow and calf moose were munching willows in the ditch (and stayed there). A couple of beautiful wolves slunk across the highway and disappeared into the trees on the side of the road.

There were a few clouds that obscured the mountain tops, but on the whole, it was a beautiful drive. We had no trouble crossing the border into Canada and saw more wildlife. A couple of beautiful white swans were lazily swimming in a pond of water, and when we were near Sheep Mountain, Yukon Territory, we saw several flocks of brilliant white Dahl sheep. I was amazed at how the roads had improved since the last time I'd been over them. Where did the frost heaves go? We found a motel in Haines Junction and settled down for the night. When my Yorkie, Tex, and I went outside about 3:30 a.m., there was just a skiff of snow on the ground. We left at daybreak and caught the storm before we reached Whitehorse. About the time we caught up to the storm, we saw two huge critters in the ditch.

"What do you think those are?" I asked Val.

"They look like buffalo," she replied. "I see that car parked right by them, so they must be harmless."

As we neared them, we could see that they were grizzly bears, and huge ones at that.

"Look at how the snow is sticking to their fur," Val remarked. "I've heard of silver-tipped grizzlies, but these really do have silver-tips! If it were me in that car, I'd be further away from them than that car is!"

The storm continued, and it wasn't long before we saw a herd of elk. The massive bull was standing guard over his harem of five. There were two babies and three cows. He was magnificent. Shortly after that, we saw an eagle that was eating away at something in the ditch. Not far from him, were about six ravens, having a fit. Apparently, they didn't want to get very close to the eagle, but they wanted their lunch, too! We also saw several flocks of geese headed south, and thought they were pretty wise to be getting out of the snowstorm.

After we left Whitehorse, it kept snowing harder

and harder, and soon the road was packed with snow, and getting quite slippery. We saw one car in the ditch upside down, and another that had just driven straight into the ditch. Soon, there was about five inches of snow on the road, making driving treacherous. Apparently, the highway department had sanded the road when it was still melting, and the sand had made gouges in the snow. It was like driving over a washboard. I wasn't sure this was good for my surgical wound, but Val was driving slowly, and there wasn't anything that could be done about the rough road.

We were hoping to make it to Toad River, but with the roads the way they were, we debated the wisdom of looking for a room in Watson Lake. We needed gas, so stopped at a gas station about 4:00 p.m. to fill the tank. Would you believe, the car decided we ought to stay since it refused to start. It wouldn't go into neutral, but all the gauges worked. Anyway, while Val was trying to figure out what to do, I set off in the five inches of snow, looking for a hotel room (fortunately, I had packed a pair of boots!). The first place wouldn't take pets, the second one was full, and the third had a room on the second floor (with no elevator) that would accept pets. I grabbed it since the hotel was filling rapidly. I hiked back to the car, and we got our luggage. It was the Canadian Thanksgiving, so no mechanic was available, but the gas station attendant said we could leave the car where it was!

It was a terrible trek back to the hotel. I found out that the wheels on suitcases don't do well in five inches of snow. Val was very weak from her chemo, and I looked back once to see her laid out in the snow. A group of six Arab gentlemen came by and offered to take our luggage to the hotel for us. God sent us angels! They wouldn't even accept a tip for their trouble! We really appreciated it. Then, we had to maneuver up the stairs, but fortunately, the hotel clerk helped us with some of our luggage.

The next morning, Val took off to see about getting her car worked on. While she was crossing the street, she fell and banged up her knee, but she did find a mechanic, and the verdict was that it was a cracked battery. They installed a new battery, and the car started. Val was exhausted, and I wasn't much better, so even though it was about noon, we decided to spend another night. The roads were still horrendous, and we were told that a semi-truck had jack-knifed just shortly after we'd gotten to town, blocking the Highway for several hours. We also heard that four cars were in ditches inside the town limits. It was an excellent decision to stay put.

We left Watson Lake at about daylight the third

morning out of Fairbanks in overcast skies, and the roads were still snow-packed. This lasted for about 100 miles before the Highway started to become bare, and soon the sun came out and the rest of the day was terrific. We'd missed a lot of beautiful scenery when we were in the storm, but after the sun came out, it looked like a Christmas Card. All the trees were covered in snow, the towering mountains had a fresh white coat, and we saw more wildlife. We saw a red fox, with his beautiful bushy tail waving, two eagles, this time sitting off to the side of the road, while the Ravens were devouring the meal, and three caribou, two cows and one calf. We saw so many buffalo, we couldn't count them all. One of the young ones decided to cross the road in front of us, so five huge ones surrounded him and escorted him across safely. We saw a doe deer with two fawns, quite a few flocks of geese and sandhill cranes. The tamarack trees were golden in amongst the green firs and pines. It was a lovely drive.

About a hundred miles before we arrived at the terminus of the Alaska Highway in Dawson Creek, we found a picturesque motel, with log cabins. We each ended up with our own cabin since they only had full-size beds and a loft. Neither of us was able to climb up the ladder to the loft.

We left the next morning, headed for Dawson. How the roads had changed. It was paved all the way, where 60 years ago, there were not even bridges across some of the streams. It was great to see open fields, with huge bales of hay still in them. Some of the fields had been grain fields, and flocks of geese were gleaning the grain. Cows and horses munched contentedly in their fields, and it was a fantastic drive into Dawson Creek. We made a quick stop in Dawson so I could stock up on pickled herring, and then headed towards Edmonton.

We found a bypass around Edmonton and stopped for the night. The third motel we stopped at would allow pets, so we were happy that Tex didn't have to sleep in the car. We had a great night, but the next morning, we had a problem with the car keys. They disappeared into thin air. Fortunately, Val had a spare set for her car, so we finally were on the road again. We enjoyed seeing lots of deer, a few elk, and a coyote. It was good to cross the border, and be in Montana. We had thought about staying the night in Great Falls, but Val was feeling good, so decided to go ahead to my brother and sister's place. Her destination had changed when she found out about her breast cancer, so she was headed for Yuma, Arizona, to continue treatment, instead of Illinois.

It did get a bit on the dark side before we reached White Sulphur Springs, and about three miles out of town, we saw this huge black object hurtle across the road in front of us. Val was able to stop before the second one came across the road. They were moose, and not small ones, either. Who would think you would have to travel 2,500 miles to have a moose nearly cause you to wreck?

We spent the night with my sister and brother, and it was time to say goodbye to Val. Henry and I unloaded all my things from Val's car, and she was off, headed south. It was the next day when it dawned on me that I'd forgotten a package. Yes, before I left Fairbanks, Sallie had given me some Christmas presents, and told me emphatically that I should not forget them in Val's car! Well, I had.

I talked to Val, and told her what I'd done. As it happened, she was about to go through Las Vegas, and Sue and Jerry were visiting there on their way to meet me in Texas, so she found them and delivered the packages. As one of my friends said, she is better than UPS. She delivers! The missing keys had a happy ending too. Val found them when she got to Arizona.

Well, time to slip backward in time to the 1960s. I hope you enjoyed the fast-forward.

SECTION IV

Alaska, The Good Life

SETTLED IN OUR OWN HOME

"What's going on here?" Mom asked as she was making the beds one morning. "I can't move this blanket, and it moved fine yesterday." We were legally living in our new home, but it had turned downright cold.

"I think the blanket's frozen to the wall," Mom continued. "Come here and look." Sure enough, there was a patch of frost on the wall, and the blanket was securely frozen in place.

"I guess we can use that portable heater to thaw it loose," Mom continued with her suggestions, "then, we'll just keep the beds away from the wall."

Dad's cats had not made the trip well in the Jeep, although he still loved them. They had forgotten everything they'd ever learned about being housebroken. So, they were banished to the garage. We had too many belongings stored in the garage anyway to use it for its intended purpose, so we covered our things with tarps, and hoped the cats would learn to use the cat box once again.

We had been in the house for nearly a month when I made a couple of apple pies. I set them out in the garage to cool, and would you believe, those darned cats ate the center out of both of the pies before knocking them to the floor, upside down!

"Dad, come and look what your nasty cats did!" I shouted. "This has to stop!"

"Well, I told you if you could find a good home for them, I'd part with them," Dad responded. "I don't know if they're ever going to learn to use the litterbox again, but if we could find a farmer that needs good mousers, I'm sure they would do just fine."

That night I talked with Stan about the cats. We decided that we could take care of the cat problem. "Dad, Stan has found a good home for your cats," I told him the next morning.

"Gosh, that was quick," he said, "but I'm happy they will be taken care of." We took care of them, all right, with a bullet apiece. The cat problem was solved. We hadn't exactly lied; they had found a good home.

Stan was working on Ladd Air Force Base and made quite a few friends. Many of the guys working there were single and lived in the barracks. They all wanted to take a trophy caribou rack home with them, but they wanted only the horns. They had no way of taking care of the meat, but it was the law that if you shot one, you had to harvest the meat. This was ideal for Stan, since he wanted the meat but wasn't interested in the horns. If he bought a nonresident hunting license before living here a year, it was costly. So, most weekends, he (in Dad's Jeep) went hunting. Our freezers were full, and Stan's friends were happy.

On December 14, our son Danny was born. Stan dropped me at the hospital but was not allowed to stay. So, he decided to go change the oil in the car. While he was doing that, he also drained the radiator and flushed it. Several hours after Danny was born, he finally appeared at the hospital.

"Where have you been?" I asked. "You told me it would only take an hour or so to service the car, and here you've been gone for at least four hours!"

"Well," he replied. "I ran into a little bad luck. I accidentally put the oil in the radiator, and when I put the antifreeze in the transmission, I realized my mistake. So, I had to flush the whole engine out to make sure I didn't have antifreeze in the transmission." I guess becoming a new dad was traumatic for him!

I was very concerned when I brought Danny home because he had a dark blob on the end of his nose.

"Mom," I said. "Is that a birthmark right on the end of his nose?"

She laughed and replied, "No, it isn't. Danny is so strong that he's made a blood blister on the end of his nose from turning his head so often." What a relief that was!

Hunting season ended, and Stan was without his weekend hunting trips. As the winter weather grew colder, we found that playing pinochle was a good substitute for hunting. Mom got part-time jobs babysitting for some of our neighbors, and I was busy with tending to Danny. In our spare time, the pinochle cards were kept busy.

Betty and Henry were enrolled in school, and poor little Debbie felt left out. She told us one day she wanted to go to school.

"I'm big enough and smart enough, I'm just not old enough," she said. She was right, she wasn't old enough. The next year she could attend school with the other two.

One of Stan's co-workers, Bob, wanted to bring his wife to Alaska but said he needed a sponsor. Since we were settled into our rented house, Stan volunteered. We met Dee as she got off the airplane in February, 1959. It was around 40 degrees below zero. She threatened to turn around and go back to

Pennsylvania but decided to stick around. That was the beginning of our friendship that lasted until her death.

As the winter waned, Stan and I started looking for a home to buy, as did my parents. Stan found one at Twelve Mile Village on the Richardson Highway. This was about half- way between Ladd AFB where he worked, and Eielson AFB. It was near the village of North Pole. We moved into our two-room home the first part of June.

Mom and Dad found a lot they liked on the Piledriver Slough and bought a couple of Quonset huts to use for their home. They used part of one for a garage and put the rest on the front of the original one, so they had room to build a bathroom and a washroom. We gave up our quarters in Island Homes and moved. We were about 12 miles apart.

Stan immediately started building an addition to our two-room house and spent most of the summer getting that ready to move into. He added a kitchen and two bedrooms to the original house, plus remodeled the bathroom. He also built a brick fireplace in the living room. This was his first experience as a brick-layer, but Dad gave him many hints. It was a beautiful fireplace.

We met our neighbors and enjoyed many card

parties at their houses, and at ours. It was a relief to Stan when he had been in Alaska a year and could get a resident hunting license. He spent the whole moose season hunting and brought back a nice bull. It was good to have the freezer loaded again.

FIRST CARIBOU HUNT

*N*ovember saw a turn in the temperatures. Instead of freezing at night, it turned a balmy 35 degrees. I was baking bread one morning when Stan walked in the door.

"How'd you like to go caribou hunting with me this weekend?" he asked. "I hear the caribou are migrating in the 40-mile country, and the weather is spring-like. We could take the car and run up there on Friday night. We'd have to sleep in the car since we wouldn't have room to take a tent, but we might just get a caribou."

"I'd have to get my hunting license," I replied. "But I'm sure that Mom would watch Danny, and I've never seen a live caribou, except on our trip here. It sounds like fun."

I got my hunting license, and Mom agreed to watch Danny. Yippee! Friday night after Stan came home from work, we loaded the car with our sleeping bags, enough food for the weekend, guns and ammo, and four extra gas cans; and were off.

It was a long drive in the dark, and I would have preferred to go during the day since we were missing all the scenery. The first 200 plus miles of our trip was over the Alaska Highway. We turned off the Alaska Highway at Tetlin Junction and onto the Taylor Highway. This was all new territory. We found a sign that warned, "Road Closed, Travel at your own Risk!" Disregarding the sign, we went about 60 miles before we decided it was time to stop and get some rest. We had just passed the nearly-ghost-town of Chicken, Alaska, and found a wide spot in the road.

I decided to be nice, so I said, "Do you want to stretch out in the back seat? You're taller than I am so you might be comfier." I fully expected Stan to be a perfect gentleman, and tell me to take the back seat.

"Thanks, I'll do it," he replied. Where was my perfect gentleman? Sound asleep and snoring in the back seat! But I was tired, and actually slept well curled up in the front seat, dreaming of caribou.

When the sun came up, it was time to move. We figured we had another hundred miles to go before we needed to worry about crossing the border into Canada. We lit our one-burner gas stove and made some coffee to go with the cold sandwiches we'd packed. We filled our thermos, so we had coffee to drink as we hunted. We were soon on the road again. It was delightful to be able to see the scenery, as we climbed up hills, went around switchbacks, and looked for caribou. We found some tracks but no caribou. We did find an old picturesque cabin near the highway, so we stopped and took pictures of it.

Night fell, and we still had not seen a caribou. We decided to camp near the old cabin, dug out our gas stove, and heated up some soup to go with our sandwiches. We would have to leave fairly early the next day, to get back to North Pole, since Stan had to go to work Monday morning. We went to bed early and had a restful night. He didn't even ask if I wanted the back seat, and I was happily curled up like a pretzel in the front.

We were up early the next morning before it was daylight, so we used the lights from the car to make our coffee. We were surprised to see that it was snowing. Huge flakes were falling from the sky. They were beautiful! Another cold sandwich, and as it began to get daylight, we started hunting in earnest.

We wanted to make it as far as Eagle, which is only a few miles from the Canadian Border. The higher we climbed, the harder it snowed. We finally passed through Eagle and found where the road forked, one went on, and the other went to what we thought must be an airport.

We decided to drink the last of the coffee from our thermos, and just watch the snow as it came lazily floating down. It was beginning to pile up on the road, and we knew that we needed to be moving towards civilization pretty soon. After all, we were traveling at our own risk! As I was taking my last sip of coffee, Stan said, "Do you see something moving on the runway? It looks like the whole ground is moving."

I peered through the falling snow and could barely see what he was talking about. It did look like the whole ground was moving. "I think we should drive down there and see what's going on," Stan said.

He started the car, and when the defrosters began their work, we took off in the direction of the unknown mass. As we neared it, we began to see individual caribou. It was a mass migration of what appeared to be thousands of caribou! Stan drove right down the runway smack dab into the middle of the herd. We jumped out, grabbed our guns and started firing. After several shots, Stan yelled, "Stop! We don't want to get too many. We're only allowed three apiece. We better see how many we have!"

We carefully made our way through the herd and

counted the caribou that we had downed. We had five! With our limited room in the car, that was enough!

It wasn't long until the herd disappeared in the falling snow. We set to work cleaning our caribou and loading them. We ended up strapping two of the caribou on top of the car, but the other three fit in the trunk. We made fast tracks out of there, as the snow kept piling up. The car was dragging as we made our way from the runway back onto the highway.

We could not make very good time, as the road was covered in snow, and it was hard to see the ditches. We were happy when we reached the crest and began to descend down the mountain towards home. The lower in altitude we dropped, the less it was snowing. Soon we felt safe in pulling off to the side of the road and unloading our caribou so they could properly cool. As we sat there waiting, a bunny jumped out of the bushes and sat in the middle of the road. Stan shot it with his 30.06 rifle.

He cleaned the bunny, and I got out the tin foil. We used our gas stove to roast the rabbit in the tin foil. We didn't have any salt, but there were a few potato chips left from our lunch, so we crumbled them around the bunny as it roasted. The aroma was tantalizing, especially since I'd miscalculated, and we had eaten our last sandwiches for breakfast. The rabbit was as tasty as it smelled.

When we decided the caribou were cold enough that they wouldn't spoil, we loaded them once again and gingerly made our way down the road to the Alaska Highway. It was after midnight when we arrived back at our home in North Pole, but we had enough meat to share with Mom and Dad, and our freezers were overflowing. It was my first caribou hunt, but not my last!

THE SAGA OF LITTLE SWEDE

*W*inter passed, and I found myself pregnant again, with the baby due in August. Stan came home one day, all excited, "I think we ought to go fishing at Little Swede Lake," he announced. "Frank just told me that the ice went out, and they're catching a lot of rainbow trout. It's a couple miles or so off the Denali Highway near the Tangle Lakes, and we have to walk in, so we can't take the boat into the Lake, but Frank says you don't need a boat. He says the fish almost jump out of the water to get on your line! Your Dad and Mom can go with us, and I'm sure Danny is old enough for his first fishing trip!"

We talked to Dad and Mom, and they were excited to think of a fishing trip. After further discussion, we decided that taking our 18-month old Danny would not be a good idea, so we asked our good friend Dee if she would watch him. She was more than willing.

We packed as light as we could for the trek in to the lake, with dried foods and the minimum in sleeping bags and tents. We were concerned about a bear, so we packed along a couple of handguns. Stan and I drove our car, and Mom and Dad drove Dad's Jeep, with Betty, Henry, and Debbie changing vehicles at every stop. We had the boat tied to the top of the car, in its customary place for traveling, just in case we found a lake to fish in. We were off early Friday morning.

"We better stop at Big Delta," I told Stan. "These kids eat snacks like an elephant scarfing up peanuts, and we are almost out already."

"Sure," Stan replied. "I could use a chunk of beef jerky myself, and I think I just saw the last disappear down Betty's throat!"

We arrived in Big Delta and replenished our snacks. A few miles down the road, we came to Delta Junction, and continued on the Richardson Highway towards Paxson. We were amazed to see Donnelly Dome rising out of the tundra.

Then, Black Rapids Glacier was so near, we could have chipped ice off it to fill our coolers but didn't. Rainbow Ridge was another sight that brought us to a stop to just stare. What beautiful colors in the soil! Summit Lake was another beauty. Here was this lake at the summit of a mountain pass, how had that come to be? Nearly 200 miles after we left North Pole, we arrived at Paxson Lodge.

This was where we would part company with the Richardson Highway and drive west towards our goal, Little Swede Lake. We filled the cars with gas and had a sandwich beside an overgrown landing strip. It felt good to get out of the vehicles and stretch our legs.

Back in the cars, we headed down the winding, gravel covered Denali Highway, towards the Lake. Frank had told Stan that we could leave our cars near the trailhead and that we would have no problem seeing the spot where the trail left the Highway. However, we somehow missed it and ended up at the Tangle Lakes. They looked awfully inviting to go fishing in, especially with the boat, but we stubbornly decided that we would hike into Little Swede. That was our goal. Back we went and found the right parking area.

Stan loaded his backpack with a five-gallon can of drinking water and a few other items. Betty and Henry were given small packs to carry, including their sleeping bags. We distributed the rest of the supplies among Mom, Dad and myself.

Frank had told Stan that it was an easy hike into the Lake. What he forgot to warn him was that the last part of the trip was a very steep hill, going down. That meant that on our way back, we would have to climb up this steep hill! The trail was not a smooth walking trail at all, but wound around the clumps of tundra, and scrub pine. Not a very good path for any of us, let alone a pregnant woman, and a five-year-old girl. My sister Debbie was just five years old.

It took us a long time to make the trek, and we battled mosquitoes all the way. The large, clumsy ones drove us nuts buzzing around our heads. However, we finally arrived, worn to a frazzle. Stan set up the small pup-tents and got the sleeping bags rolled out. I crashed on one of the sleeping bags and didn't wake up for a couple of hours. It was nice to wake up to the smell of frying fish! While I was napping, Stan and Mom had caught several rainbow trout. Dad had not fished since he remembered that he had forgotten to buy a fishing license!

"That dinner was delicious," I told Mom. I hope we can catch another mess of fish for breakfast! You cooked them to perfection, and I loved the way you fried those potatoes. Maybe we won't have to eat all that dehydrated stuff!"

We sat around the campfire and enjoyed sitting in the smoke, which kept the mosquitoes at bay. We were all tired, so off to bed early. The next morning, I set up my fishing pole along the edge of the lake and tried to keep my eye on it, as I made pancakes for breakfast. No, we hadn't gotten up early enough to have a mess of fish to fry! A couple of times, it looked like I might have a bite, so I asked Dad if he'd check the bait. One time, the bait was gone, and the other time it was intact.

We were just settling down to eat our breakfast when a gentleman in uniform strode into our camp.

"Can I see your fishing licenses?" he asked. We sort of thought that a "Good morning" might have been more appropriate, but that wasn't what we got!

We had six poles set up along the lake. Betty, Henry, and Debbie, were not old enough to require a license. Mom, Stan, and I, had our licenses, but Dad had no fishing license nor fishing pole. However, the Fish and Game officer said to him, "I saw you handling a fishing pole, and you don't have a license. I could run you in for that, but if you go back to Paxson and get a license, I'll let you off this time."

Dad meekly nodded his head, and the Game Warden departed. Dad was so upset; he completely lost his appetite and couldn't finish his breakfast. As soon as our meal was over, Dad got on his boots and took off for the two-mile hike back to the jeep, and a trip back to Paxson. It was many hours before he returned. In the meantime, we had caught enough trout for our dinner.

We had a repeat of the evening, sitting around the campfire, and enjoying the stars, although it didn't seem as though there were as many out as there had been the night before, and the moon was hiding in the mist. We didn't let it worry us one bit and made another early night of it.

Imagine our surprise when we woke up the next morning to about six inches of new, wet snow on the ground, and more coming down every minute. We were soon soaked, and the temperature kept dropping. We decided we needed to get out of there as quickly as we could, so we packed up our sleeping bags, our tent, and the remains of our food. We just dumped the water, since there was no use packing it back to the car.

Poor Debbie had an awful time trying to climb the hill in all the new snow. Before long, she was sitting down in the snow, and bawling her eyes out. Mom had a load, and couldn't carry her, nor could any of the rest of us, so Mom stood her up, and gently pushed her in the right direction. They slowly made their way up the hill, with Mom gently pushing with her boot every few steps, and with Debbie roaring at the top of her lungs.

When we got to the top of the hill, and the going got much easier, Debbie soon started walking without additional help. As we neared the car and Jeep, it quit snowing, and the sun came out. Before long, the snow was melting, and it turned out to be a pleasant day. We decided that instead of going home, we would set up camp along the banks of the Tangle Lakes. We hung our belongings on every possible hanger and soon were dry and comfortable. We even went fishing and caught a few graylings for our evening meal. Life was good again.

SAND ISN'T TASTY

Our fishing trip ended uneventfully, as did our return trip home. Stan planted a delightful garden. He was busy digging in the dirt when I noticed that he was headed directly for this quaint little building that we used for storage.

"What are your plans when you get to the building?" I asked. "Well, I'm planning on hooking onto it with your Dad's Jeep, and pulling it out of the way!" he replied -- and, he did.

In August of 1960, our daughter Suzie was born. She was a very well-behaved baby, and we were very proud of our family.

Stan and Bob were close friends, and both loved to hunt and fish, so it wasn't out of the ordinary when the two men hatched plans for a caribou hunting trip. The unusual part this year was that they invited Dee and me to go along with them. We figured they just needed someone to do the cooking. They were planning on going to the Taylor Highway, but this time, it would be before the road was closed for the winter.

We got everything packed, and I sweet-talked Mom into taking care of Danny and Suzie for a few days. This time, we would leave on a Thursday, and return on a Monday. We packed what we thought would be a surplus of food, plus our sleeping bags. We decided to take Bob's car this time, and he would pull our trailer. It was with high hopes that we left after work on Thursday and headed for the Taylor Highway. Since Stan and I had hunted there the year before, we remembered that picturesque old cabin that sat near the highway and thought we might be able to camp in it, so we had not brought any tents along.

We arrived at the cabin fairly early on Friday morning and were lucky that no one had claimed the cabin. It took a bit of cleaning, but we found a broom in the corner and were able to sweep out the dirt and droppings from various animals. There was only one drawback. It had a big hole in one corner of the floor that had evidently led to a tiny under-the-floor room used to keep things cool. There was no cover for this hole. Bob was especially worried that someone might fall down the hole, and we could see water in the bottom. We didn't think the hole was all that deep, but no one bothered to get a stick and see just how deep it was.

The cabin had only one small window, but it had a door that we could keep open so the sunlight would pour in when there was sunlight. By the time we had the cabin livable, the sun had disappeared in a cloud, and it looked like it could start snowing at any minute. There were a couple of barrels in the cabin that we stood on end. We set our gas stove on one and used the other for a worktable. The guys went hunting, while Dee and I tried to make the place more sanitary.

Soon it started to snow, and we were concerned about the guys. Stan was the first one to return, but Bob was busy hunting. When Bob hunted -- he hunted! It was almost pitch black by the time he returned. We had the gas light lit, and hanging from the rafters, and left the door open so the light would shine out.

"Be careful of that hole!" were the first words out of Bob's mouth. We pointed out that we had spent the afternoon there and had managed to stay away from the hole.

"I don't want one of you falling in," he cautioned. "If someone broke a leg, we'd have to return to Fairbanks. I want to hunt!"

Dee and I had brought some steaks along to fry, so we hurriedly started getting dinner on the table.

We all enjoyed our dinner, and the beds were not too uncomfortable. The guys woke up the next morning to good tracking snow, so they were off hunting, while Dee and I worked around the cabin, played some games, and ventured out just a short distance looking for any small game. We did get a couple of rabbits for dinner that night. We had packed the guys' lunch, so we were not expecting to see them, and we didn't. It was nearly dark once again before they showed up. Again, the first words out of Bob's mouth were, "Be careful of that hole!"

This time, they each had a caribou, so they were quite happy with themselves. We ate our dinner and played a game of pinochle before crashing.

The next morning was a repeat of the day before. The guys came back with another couple of caribou. We saw quite a few hunters traveling on the roads, but we were pretty snug in our cabin. The guys were outside when we called them to come and eat. When they entered the cabin, Bob decided to hang his coat on a nail, and before you could say "Jack Robinson," he had fallen into the hole. You should have seen the surprised look on his face, and then it turned to a crestfallen, sheepish look. After all the times warning us, he was the one that fell. Fortunately, only his pride was hurt. We found out that the water was only about two-and-a-half feet deep! He soon had on dry clothes and enjoyed dinner.

The next morning, Stan went outside, and when he returned, he said, "It really is snowing hard. I think we need to get on the road. Even if they are still maintaining the road, if we get snowed in, it could be a week before they get us plowed out. Besides, four caribou are probably enough."

Dee and I fried the last of our potatoes, with some steak and eggs for breakfast. The guys loaded the trailer while waiting for breakfast. We almost had breakfast finished, when we heard a shot outside. This was followed by a lot of dirt and sand crashing down from the ridgepole, landing right in our breakfast!

Dee and I raced outside to see what had happened. There stood Stan, with his .357 in his hand. He was looking pretty proud of himself. "What happened?" I hollered.

"Bob bet me I couldn't hit the ridgepole with my .357, and I did!" He smugly replied.

"Well, you managed to ruin breakfast completely," I yelled at him. "Come and see what you did!"

He walked into the cabin, and there were the frying pans, smothered in dirt.

"Oh," Stan exclaimed. "I never thought about the

dirt roof when I made the shot! I'm so sorry for the sand, and breakfast smelled so good, too!"

We ended up dumping our breakfast and just heading home hungry. Poor Bob never did live down the time he'd fallen in the hole! Stan was often called "Mr. Sandman" for ruining our breakfast. It was a memorable hunting trip.

ICE BARRIER

Our winter was filled with card parties, watching Danny and Sue grow, and shoveling snow. It was a cold winter. We had found a thermometer hanging in the window of our house, but the coldest it would read was 50 degrees below zero. When the mercury in the thermometer curled into a little ball under the minus 50 and stayed there for six weeks, we decided it was time for a new thermometer.

We made a rather startling, and not very happy, discovery. When we moved that little shed during the summer, we had placed it on top of our sewer line. When our new thermometer read 70 degrees below zero in January, our sewer line froze solid. We had two small children and no way to do laundry, except to take the clothes to Mom's until we could figure out how to get the line thawed. This was before the advent of disposable diapers, so I had plenty of laundry to do. Fortunately, Danny had been potty-trained before Sue was born. But, no flushing toilet!

Driving in 70 degrees below zero temperatures was no picnic, either. Since the car had to sit outside, the bottoms of the tires froze flat. Thus, when you started to move, it really jarred your body until the tires finally rounded out. We needed to get that sewer line thawed out pronto. So, we called one of the local Pumping and Thawing businesses. They showed up with their thaw truck and put the hose down the toilet. All was progressing well until they reached the ice. Then, the forward progression of the hose stopped. When pieces of the sewer pipe started floating to the surface, we told them to stop! We didn't want to have to replace the whole sewer line when it was thawed!

One of our next-door neighbors, Malcolm Fisher, came to see what was happening. He looked the situation over, and then he told us, "I have a sewer snake and a small steam boiler. If you have any old tires lying around, you can put one around that boiler, light it on fire, and with water in the boiler part, you'll soon have a good head of steam. I have a hose, and if you wire that to the sewer snake, you can then shove it right up against that ice clog, and keep pushing, and before long, you'll have it thawed."

His suggestion worked well. It was a relief to have our plumbing system back in order. However, we were shocked when we woke up five days later, and the line was frozen again. Back to the boiler, sewer snake and hose, and before long, it was thawed again. Stan had to thaw the line a total of seven times that winter before it warmed up enough to quit freezing. He became an expert!

As the snow finally started to melt in the spring, Stan said to me, "The first order of business when the snow is gone is to move that shed. I think we can put it off to the side, and maybe use it as a playhouse for the kids."

"What a great idea," I replied. "When I was growing up, I always wanted a playhouse. I'm sure the kids will love it." And, they did!

We moved it to a different location, once again using Dad's Jeep, and from that point forward, no more frozen sewer lines. We were happy to return the boiler and sewer snake to Malcolm and be done with that project.

As June approached, Stan and Dad started speculating about going to try their luck at Little Swede Lake again. Very few lakes in Alaska had trout, and since Dad was raised in Montana where trout fishing was plentiful, he was hungry for a good mess of trout. This time, he had his fishing license before the snow melted.

They put their heads together and agreed on the

day they thought the ice would be melted off the lake. The first week in June found us headed back to Little Swede Lake. Stan and I decided that we could take both Danny and Sue with us for this trip. Stan volunteered to carry Sue to the lake, and then go back for the water and other heavy things. I was expecting another child in August.

On our way down the Richardson Highway to the Tangle Lakes, we stopped at the Black Rapids Glacier and put ice in our ice chests. We were planning on catching a lot of fish and wanted to be able to keep them cool. We were a little surprised to find a rather significant amount of ice on the water when we arrived at the Tangle Lakes. However, this did not deter us, and with high hopes, we returned to the Little Swede parking area and then hiked to the top of the hill looking down on Little Swede. Our expectations were dashed when we saw that it was completely covered in ice. There was not even a fringe of water visible. Another conference and we decided to camp at the Tangle lakes, and just fish there. We had the boat, and even if we were just catching grayling, they were a delicious fish.

Dad, Stan, and my siblings took the boat out while Mom and I got the camp setup. The fishermen started the motor and were able to get quite a distance from shore. They came back with a nice mess of fish.

After dinner, I said, "Mom, why don't you and I go fishing? The guys can take care of doing the dishes and get things ready for bed, while we catch breakfast!"

"That sounds great to me!" Mom replied. "I'll be with you in a moment, just let me get my jacket in case it gets cooler."

True to her word, Mom met me at the boat in just a few minutes. We pushed away from shore and started pulling on the rope to start the motor. That motor refused to cooperate.

"I bet there are fish near the shore," Mom said, "Why don't we just fish from here, and forget about the motor!" Using the oars, we paddled out not far from shore. We were fishing and enjoying catching a fish now and then when the wind came roaring out of the east. This was the direction of most of the ice pack on the lake. We were shocked when we noticed that the ice pack was moving in our direction.

We grabbed the oars and started rowing. We were not very coordinated, and the harder we rowed, the more circles we made instead of heading for shore. We took turns with the oars, but neither of us was able to do much except travel in circles. We glanced towards shore, only to be met with the sight of everyone gathered around a roaring campfire. Apparently, the wind wasn't bothering the fire!

Soon the ice floe caught us, and we were surrounded by ice. There was ice between us and shore, plus we were in only a small circle of water. We were still going in circles. We might as well have quit trying, and just enjoyed the spectacle of the ice slowly surrounding us.

"Do you think ice can crush a boat?" I asked Mom. "This boat's only aluminum, and not very heavy. With the ice around us, we can't even swim to shore. I know you can swim, but I'm not very good at it. That water is cold. Any suggestions?"

"The only thing I can think of is to pray. We really are in a jam, and the guys can't do much since we have the only boat!"

We bowed our heads and prayed. Then, I picked up an oar and tried to row again towards the shore, hoping to find a path through the ice, but once again, we just went in circles. We were about to give up when the wind died down. The ice between us and the shore miraculously opened, and Mom grabbed the oars. She rowed us in a straight-line right to the shore.

Needless to say, the two of us never ventured out alone in a boat again. Although I did make Stan show me the finer points of rowing, and the next time I went in a boat, I could row as well as anyone.

We spent three days at the Tangle Lakes and brought home a cooler full of fish.

THE KEY TO START AN ENGINE

*I*n 1960, the Air Force announced they were closing Ladd AFB, and it would become an army post called Fort Wainwright, named for General Jonathan Wainwright who led U.S. Forces in the Philippines in World War II. Stan immediately requested a transfer to Eielson AFB, hoping that he would be able to stay in the Fairbanks area. This transfer was granted. Shortly after Sue was born, Stan started work at Eielson. His good friend Bob also transferred with him, so they were still working together.

We were glad we had moved about halfway between the two military establishments. Stan's commute continued to be the same, only he had less traffic going south than he had when going towards town.

The hospital on Eielson was small, so most of the Air Force personnel continued to get their medical treatment at Fort Wainwright, including me.

Sallie Mae was born a few days before moose season

was to start, 1961. I had some problems with my blood pressure, so I ended up in the hospital for a week before she was born. Stan was getting antsy, since he wanted to go hunting, and moose season started on August 20. He was thrilled when she arrived, and he immediately began making plans for his hunting trip. I would be able to get out of the hospital on August 22, so Stan planned to take off early on the morning of the 23rd. He would take me to Mom's place and leave me. Already Danny and Sue had moved there. Stan had been eating his meals at Mom's.

He was a bit disappointed when he found a medium-sized bull moose on the second day of his hunting trip and had to return back home. I was happy to see him, though, and I'm sure that Mom was pleased to see us move back to our house at 12 Mile Village. Although, she was very kind and invited us to stay as long as we wanted.

We got the moose cut up, and in the freezer, and Stan went back to work. He decided to save his leave time for caribou hunting later in the fall.

Stan came home from work one evening, very excited. "Guess what," he said. "I just bought a Jeep! The guy who owned it was transferring out, and needed to get rid of it in a hurry, so I bought it. We need to get some money out of the bank, and I can get the title tomorrow."

"You bought a Jeep?" I stammered. "Dad has a perfectly good Jeep! He doesn't mind if we borrow it. Why would you buy a Jeep?"

"Well, it was a good deal," he replied. "Plus, the guy is leaving tomorrow, and if I have my own, we won't have to ask your Dad. We can go caribou hunting this weekend!"

So, we planned another hunting trip for caribou, and Mom said she'd be willing to take care of the three babies. We planned to leave on Friday night, and return on Monday. It would be the first trip we made with Stan's new Jeep. After our experience with the snowstorm and roads the year before, we thought it would be wise to go in early October.

Stan was very proud of his Jeep, although it did need some repairs. So, he had the cylinders in the engine block ground, purchased new pistons and rings, and installed them. He worked on it all day Thursday. It was getting dark when he finished tightening the last nut.

As he entered the house, he said, "Can you give me a hand? I've run the battery down trying to start the Jeep, and I don't want to take the time to recharge it.

If you can get away for a few minutes, you can pull me with the car, and I'm sure it will start."

"Well," I replied, "I can get away since the kids are at Grandma's. I'd rather you pull me, instead of me pulling you. I'm not a very good puller."

"Sure, fine," he replied. "Grab your coat and let's go. There isn't any heat in the Jeep, and it's about 10 degrees below zero outside."

I put on my boots, grabbed my parka, and got into the Jeep. He had the chain already strung out between the car and the Jeep. He climbed into the car and slowly tightened the chain between the two vehicles. I held the clutch in until he got the car going fairly fast, and then I let the clutch out. All four wheels on the Jeep locked-up, and we skidded to a stop. After a couple of tries, he came back to the Jeep.

"Will you take it out of four-wheel drive?" he asked. I hadn't realized that I had it in four-wheel drive, but I was happy to comply. Away we went again, and this time when I let out the clutch, only two wheels locked-up. He pulled me around the block several times before he once again stopped.

"Do you have the key on?" he asked. I looked down and was shocked to see the key in the off position. I hated to admit that I didn't have the key on, but the evidence was staring us in the face. By this time, it was completely dark, and I was using a flashlight to see what I was doing. Plus, my teeth were chattering!

I apologized, and he got back in the car. This time, when I let out the clutch, the Jeep took-off with a roar! I even managed not to run into the back of the car. We had succeeded and could go hunting!

The Jeep ran flawlessly, and we managed to bring home a couple of caribou. When we had turned onto the Taylor Highway, there was that sign posted by the State of Alaska that they were no longer maintaining the highway, and you would travel at your own risk. But there was very little snow, and the roads were in excellent condition. How much risk could there be?

We were happy to share the caribou with Mom and Dad and to retrieve our little family. Once again, we settled in.

BROKEN BELTS ARE TROUBLESOME

The caribou we'd brought from the Taylor Highway were a small breed, and the meat from them didn't do much towards filling the freezer.

"I think we ought to try another hunting trip down near the Denali Highway, what do you think?" Stan asked me one day. "We don't have much meat in the freezer, the weather is nice, and I have a three-day weekend. Want to try it?"

Never one to turn down a chance to go hunting, I agreed that it was an excellent idea. Mom was willing to watch our three kids again. We got things packed in the Jeep and, after work on Thursday, we headed down the highway. It was dark when we reached Paxson, but the gas station was open, so we stopped. We even went into the lodge to have a cup of coffee.

The temperature was moderate, being just above zero. We were anxious to get our tent setup, and crawl into our sleeping bags, so we finished our coffee and got into the Jeep; Stan turned on the key, pushed the starter, and -- nothing. It didn't even turn over! He checked the battery cable, but it seemed to be tight. When he checked the generator belt, he found that it was broken, and the battery had not been getting a charge.

"If we get this thing started, I think we should just go home," I said.

"No way!" Stan replied. "I've come to hunt caribou. If we park at the top of one of those long hills, we can push the Jeep to get it rolling, and you know how easily it starts when you let the clutch out, at least, when you have the key turned on!" He would have to remind me of that episode!

Stan talked the service station man into bringing his wrecker over and jumping the Jeep battery to get it started. And, we were off, looking for a long hill that we could park the Jeep on. I was happy when our headlights showed us a long, straight hill. We were lucky that there was a wide spot in the road at the top, so we could almost get the Jeep off the highway. There was a clearing not too far back that would work for our campsite. As we unloaded our tent and other camping supplies, we were happy that we had brought along a gasoline lantern, so we at least had some light.

We tromped down a trail to our campsite and shoveled the snow out of the spot we'd chosen to pitch our tent. We were getting all the tent pegs located when it dawned on us that we didn't have the center pole. Apparently, we'd left it back in North Pole. A tent without a center pole was worthless!

"I'll just take the lantern and see if I can find a spruce that will do the trick," Stan said. He grabbed the lantern, leaving me in the dark. Fortunately, a full moon had peeked out from under the clouds, and I thought there was enough light to see any predator thinking I might make a tasty snack. It wasn't long before Stan returned with a tree. He trimmed off the branches but left them about a foot long on the tree trunk. It was a little dangerous getting close to the snaggly thing, but once it was in place, those branches were convenient for hanging things on, like wet socks!

It was with relief that we crawled into our sleeping bags about midnight. We slept like logs, but somehow Stan's inner clock rang just about a half hour before daylight. I'd forgotten to bring the alarm clock, too. I was peacefully sleeping when I smelled the coffee. So, I crawled out, and we got ourselves ready to hunt.

It didn't take much effort to get the Jeep rolling down the hill, and once Stan let out the clutch, it made a couple of jumps and then fired up. "Be careful you don't let it die!" I cautioned. "We need it to run until we are on the top of another hill!"

We hunted that day but didn't see any fresh tracks. We were happy to get back to our campsite and enjoy a hot meal.

The next day it was snowing. The Jeep started like it had the day before, and we were out hunting. At least, this time, we saw a few fresh tracks. About noon, we heard some shooting. We thought we'd check that out and see what the hunters had found.

We found the spot where a vehicle had stopped, and tracks led in through the trees, but the vehicle was gone.

"I think I'll go see if I can figure out what they got," Stan said. "It could be a ptarmigan or a grouse. Or, maybe they found a lonely caribou."

Stan followed the tracks out of my sight, while I stayed with the Jeep to make sure it didn't die. He was back in about 15 minutes. "Guess what!" he said. They got a caribou, but all they took were the horns. It's still warm, so I'm going to get my knife and saw and salvage the meat. Keep the Jeep running!"

He returned in about an hour dragging the body of the caribou. We never did know who had abandoned a perfectly good caribou.

When we got back to our campsite, it was time to dismantle our tent and put everything back in the Jeep. By that time, the caribou had cooled enough that we could safely pack it in the Jeep. Our trip home was uneventful. It was a relief to get a belt for the Jeep, so we didn't have to look for a long hill to park on before shutting it off!

FLYING THE GREAT ALASKA SKIES

"How would you like to go with us next weekend?" Stan asked me one morning, as we had our breakfast. Stan's buddy Bob owned a Piper PA-20 airplane, and the two of them had been flying around Alaska almost every weekend that winter.

Bob was in the process of building a cabin on a small lake named East Kindamina, in Interior Alaska. Their routine was for Bob to load his plane with building supplies, and they would fly to his building site, unload, strap on their snowshoes, and run their trap line. They had a few sets out for lynx and wolf. Once they returned from their snowshoe trip, they'd hop back in the plane, and fly to various nearby lakes, where they had beaver sets. If time allowed, they would then fly over to West Twin Lake and go ice fishing. A nice mess of fish always tasted delicious in the wintertime. However, this was the very first time they had invited me to go with them. What was the catch?

"Why?" I asked, suspiciously. "Why ask me to go now?" I couldn't believe they'd actually asked me to go. Something must be in the wind.

"Bob has some plywood he wants to drop off at his cabin site, and then we thought we'd just go fishing. If you go with us, we can catch more fish, since we'll have three licenses, instead of two. Honest, that's all we're planning to do."

It didn't sound too "fishy" to me, so I agreed. I asked Mom if she would watch the kids while I went with the guys. As usual, she was more than willing.

Saturday morning dawned overcast and reasonably warm. It looked like a great day to be out and about. We loaded the kids in the car and dropped them at Mom's. They were ecstatic, as usual. Nothing like getting to spend the day at Grandma's house. Bob lived in Lakeview Terrace and kept his plane on the Lakeview pond on floats for summer flying, and skis for winter. For in between times, he had wheels. Since the ice was so smooth at the moment, he was using the wheels for today's trip. When we drove into a parking spot on the edge of the pond, Bob was loading his plane with a huge pile of assorted items. There was a large stack of 4x8 sheets of plywood, an extra gas can, a sleeping bag, etc. I was a bit surprised to see the airplane seats sitting on the ground next to that big pile.

"So, are those the seats?" I cautiously asked. Surely the guys didn't expect to fly without seats!

"Don't worry," Bob answered. "The seats wouldn't fit in with this load of plywood, but it isn't far to the cabin site. Stan will sit with his back against mine, to prop me up so I can reach the pedals. You can sit over on the other side, to balance us. We'll take the seats along with us so we can put them back where they belong once we get unloaded."

This didn't seem like a very sound idea to me, but Bob was an experienced pilot, and if the guys felt comfortable with it, I guessed it would be okay. While the thought did cross my mind that perhaps they only invited me to go with them for ballast, the guys were too wise to admit they may have had my weight as an ulterior motive.

Finally, the plywood, fishing poles, seats, more building supplies, and incidentals, plus the three of us and our lunch, were loaded in the plane. I had been in a plane only once before, and that had been a De Havilland Beaver, a much larger aircraft than the Piper. As I sat bracing myself on the opposite side of the top sheet of plywood, I was definitely hanging on for dear life. I, who was afraid of heights, was about to take off into the Alaskan skies in a heavily loaded airplane. How did I get myself in this predicament?

Bob started the engines, and soon we were taxiing down the lake. But the plane didn't lift off; instead, Bob hit the brakes, and we came to a screeching halt on the other side of the lake, with a sharp turn and snow flying over the windshield. I hung onto my strap for dear life. Talk about white knuckles!

"You can let me off now!" I hollered. "I think there's too much weight in here, and I'll walk back to the car."

"Sit tight," Bob said, as he goosed the engine once again. "We'll make it this time"… and again we went streaking across the lake, hell bent for leather towards our parked cars.

Once again, he applied the brakes, and we came to a screeching halt, similar to what happened on the other side of the pond. Stan, who had been sitting there quietly bracing Bob's back, finally uttered a sound.

"We'll make it this time, hang on!"

"Let me out!" I yelled. "I can't do this. I have to get out!" I clawed at the door, but before I could get out, the madman drove us up on the bank of the pond, then roared down the embankment, and across the lake again.

This time, he barely lifted off in time to clear the bank on the other side, and we were airborne. There was no escaping now!

My heartbeat had about settled down to normal, when he came in for a landing at the building site. Even with the heavy load, he was able to land calmly and sedately. It wasn't long before Bob and Stan had the plywood unloaded, along with the other building supplies they had jammed into the plane. Screwing the seats back in was a breeze. This time, we had no trouble taking off, just like the picture-perfect images I'd seen on TV, depicting bush planes in Alaska. It was good to be buckled into a seat with a seatbelt. I actually enjoyed that leg of the journey.

Another smooth landing at West Twin Lake, and we found a set of four fishing holes that someone had cut in the ice. We needed only to remove a small layer of ice before we were fishing. It was pleasant on the lake, but the fish were not cooperative. We fished for nearly an hour, with nary a bite.

"I see some friends of mine over near that point of land," Bob said. "I think we should go over and see if they are having any better luck fishing than we are." Sure enough, there were three airplanes parked over on the other side of the lake. We loaded our fishing poles, the remains of our lunch, and ourselves back in the plane, and Bob started to taxi in their direction.

"Thunk!" went the plane, and the wing on my side of the aircraft dropped onto the surface of the ice on the lake and started skidding along. Bob applied the brakes, and we came to an abrupt stop. Upon exiting the plane, we discovered that the strut had bent nearly in half. As the strut was the support that held the wheel in place, without it, the plane was in deep trouble… and so were we!

"I better get the attention of my friends," Bob said. "We need to see if they can help before they leave." So, he dug out his revolver and fired three shots into the ice of the lake. Before long, we saw two of his friends taxiing up in their planes. The third one took off, did an overflight and wiggled its wings.

"Looks like you got yourself into a pickle," one of his friends said. "I think we have room to take Rose and Stan back, but don't have room for you, Bob."

"I have some duct tape and some baling wire," Bob replied. "I think if we get a small tree, and I can straighten that strut, I can wire and tape the tree to the strut. That should give it enough strength to get home. If we just do a bit of work with the duct tape on the wing, it should be almost as good as new."

Stan grabbed the axe, and made his way to the

shore, where he managed to chop down a respectable, if small, tree. While he was gone, the guys worked at trying to straighten the strut and taping the wing. With the aid of the duct tape and baling wire, soon the plane was looking normal again, with its taped-up wing in the proper position. Stan was to ride with one of Bob's friends, and I was to ride with the other. We all watched in awe as Bob made a perfect take off, and headed for Fairbanks. The rest of us were soon following him, and at last I was delighted to see the lights of Fairbanks shining through the darkness.

However, the darkness presented another problem. The Lakeview pond had no runway lights! How could Bob see to land, let alone the rest of us, I wondered? As we neared the lake, I saw that the ice was glistening in the moonlight, just enough to make a perfect landing for all of us. We had arrived back home, safe and sound.

We were very fortunate that the strut had broken when we were just taxiing. We did offer thanks to our Guardian Angel that it had not broken when we were landing with that heavy load of plywood, or even when we made the landing at West Twin.

We had survived another Alaskan Experience.

BROKEN BRAKES

*I*t was getting to the point that I was not sure if I looked forward to Stan's harebrained schemes, or dreaded them. But sure enough, once again he came home from work with an excited look on his face. "Bob and Dee want to go caribou hunting again up the Taylor Highway," he said as he came through the door. "We can leave on Friday and should be able to spend about five days there. Do you think your Mom would watch the kids again?"

"I'm sure she would," I said. "Do you think the road is good enough? Remember that sign? They've quit maintaining it."

"I don't think it's snowed much since we were there, and it was almost bare then, so I wouldn't worry about it. If the road gets too bad, we can just turn around and come back home."

I phoned Mom to ask if she'd watch the kids again. (While we'd had phone service for a year at our house, Mom and Dad had just gotten it at their place.) While

I was talking to her, I asked her if she thought Dad would like to go hunting with us. She said she'd ask him, but she doubted he would.

I was quite surprised when the phone rang a half-hour later, and it was Mom telling me that Dad was excited about being invited to go hunting, and he would be ready to leave on Friday after work.

It would be quite crowded in Bob's car with three of us in the back seat.

"What are we going to do if we get a few caribou?" I asked Stan. "Bob's trunk is quite large, but with enough stuff for five days and five of us, it could get crowded."

"I think we ought to take our trailer again," Stan replied. "That way, we'll have plenty of room to haul our stuff."

Bob and Stan both got off work early on Friday, and soon we had most of the trailer and car loaded. Dad drove over in his Jeep and put his camping gear in the car. And, we were off.

The roads were excellent. Stan was right, it hadn't snowed since we were there last, and driving was first-rate. We made a beeline for the cabin that we'd stayed in before and were happy to find that it remained unclaimed. This time, Bob had brought a piece of plywood along, so he promptly covered the hole in the floor. We didn't have to worry about him falling through it ever again.

Hunting went well, and we soon had six caribou. We hung them around in various trees to keep the predators away from them and let them cool down. We decided we could go home earlier than planned. So, on Sunday night, we prepared to leave early the next morning. We were eating our Sunday evening dinner when we heard rain on the roof. We were happy to be inside where it was dry but were concerned about the roads.

The next morning when it started to get daylight, we found that the rain had turned to snow, and there was about six inches of new snow on the ground. Plus, it had rained a bit on top of the snow. When the sun started coming up, the temperature dropped into the freezing zone, and the roads were a terrible mess.

We got our caribou out of the trees and loaded in the trailer. Then, we set out on the icy roads. Bob was driving, and several times we slid going around corners. As we rounded one bend, we found a long line of stopped cars. We had no idea what might be going on ahead since we couldn't see that far and it was still snowing. The road was terrible.

Dad was riding in the front seat. "I'll go see what the problem is," he volunteered.

As he stepped out of the car, his feet slid out from under him, and the last we saw of him, he was sliding on his rear around the bend up ahead.

We were afraid to get out of the car! So, we sat there, and soon we saw Dad making his way gingerly back up the road. He was walking in the deepest snow he could find and trying to stay out of the car tracks.

"Two pickups slid off the road and are blocking it," he reported when he reached the car. "They've sent a car ahead to get a wrecker, but it'll be some time before it can get back here and be able to make the road passable."

With nothing to do, we had our sandwiches and drank some coffee. It was nearly dark when the traffic started to move. We were happy to reach the ALCAN Highway before it was completely dark.

We were pleased to find that the roads were bare, and Bob took off down the road at a speedy clip. Imagine our surprise when the brakes locked-up, and we sashayed all over the road. Stan and Bob rechecked everything and decided that it was a fluke. So, we took off again. When we were moving a little over 20 MPH, the brakes locked again. This time, the trailer came unhitched, and only the safety chain was keeping it with us. The trailer would slow down, the safety chain would give it a jerk, and the tongue would slam into the back of the car. Bob tried to speed-up so he could dodge the trailer tongue, but with the brakes locked, that didn't work very well.

Finally, we came to a stop on the road. Stan and Bob rechecked it all again, re-hooked the trailer tongue to the car hitch, and once again we started off. We had no trouble going up a hill, but once we reached the top and started down, the brakes locked again. As before, the trailer came unhooked, and this time it slammed so hard into the back of the car that the safety chain broke. Since the trailer had the caribou mostly in the back, the tongue stood straight-up in the air, the trailer turned around and raced down the hill backwards. Bob managed to evade it, and as we got to the bottom of the hill, the trailer slowed. It gently turned around and came to a stop on the right side of the road.

This time, the guys talked it over and decided that the brakes only locked-up when Bob drove over 20 miles an hour. Traveling slower than 20 miles an hour made it a very long trip! We didn't reach our house until dawn was breaking, but we unloaded the caribou and hung them up. Dad took off for his home in his Jeep, and Bob and Dee headed home.

Bob took his car into the garage the next day. The only thing they could find wrong with it was that it was low on brake fluid. However, that was the last time we ever went caribou hunting on the Taylor Highway with Bob and Dee.

LITTLE SWEDE ONCE AGAIN

Fortunately, the winter of 1961-62 was not as cold as the previous winter. We had built a garage onto our house and were able to park the car there. Stan enjoyed having a warm car without flat tires. Of course, after it sat outside at work for eight hours, it was cold and had regained its frozen tires. With the short daylight hours in Alaska, the winter always seems long. As the daylight got longer and the temperatures moderated in the spring, Stan started dreaming of once again going fishing at Little Swede Lake. Both of our fishing trips so far had not ended well. This time would be different, or so he imagined.

He was happy with the Jeep, but he couldn't haul much in it. He kept wishing that he had one of the Military Weapons Carriers. They were built like a pickup, with a box that he could haul almost anything in. He was happy when he found one that was coming up for sale at the Army/Air Force Salvage yard. He was really excited when his bid was the winning bid, and he could bring that 1953 Dodge Weapons Carrier (Weps) home.

He put the Jeep up for sale and almost immediately had a buyer. From then on, he used the Weps. "I bet I could take the Weps down there to the top of the hill overlooking Little Swede," Stan said one day. "It looked like perfectly good tundra, and that surely would make our trip a lot easier if we didn't have to haul all the supplies from the road by foot! It must be a mile closer."

"You really think that would work?" I asked. "That road we used to walk on looks like it's full of old ruts. I'm not sure that's a good idea."

Never one to give up without a fight, he set about making chains for all four wheels of the Weps. Early June saw us all packed and headed for Little Swede. Dad and Mom were coming along too, but the Weps had only one seat, and it was full of our immediate family, so Dad drove his Jeep.

We drove all night, but in Alaska during June, it never gets quite dark. We arrived at the access point to Little Swede Lake, and were plumb tuckered out, so we decided to just get out the sleeping bags, and have a nap.

We must have slept for about four hours. When

we woke up, Dad asked, "What time is it? My watch says four, but is it 4:00 a.m. or 4:00 p.m."

Rubbing his bleary eyes, Stan replied, "Darned if I know. It's kind of overcast, and I can't see the sun. It could be either."

About that time, a pickup drove into a parking spot, so Dad went over to ask him.

"Can you tell me if it is morning or afternoon?" he asked.

The guy looked at him as if he'd lost his marbles. "You don't know if it's morning or afternoon? You've got to be kidding. Of course, it's afternoon!"

We had a bite to eat, and then Stan put the chains on the Weps. It had bench seats along both sides so we could sit in the pickup box when not driving down the highway, and it had plenty of storage room on the floor. We got our supplies loaded, and with the exception of Dad, climbed into the Weps and off we went. Dad decided he could follow us in the Jeep.

We had gotten about halfway to the top of the hill, with all going smoothly, when there was a big thud, and we quit moving. Stan got out of the Weps and stood there looking puzzled.

"I can't believe what I'm seeing," he said. "Look at this, the front axle is buried in the mud! You'd better get the kids out of the Weps, and onto solid ground.

Look at this ground! When I walk on it, it jiggles like a bowl full of jelly. It's amazing that the rear wheels haven't sunk, too!"

He was right. The Weps looked like it was mired in a bowl of nasty-colored jelly. Was this why the ground was full of ruts? I gingerly got Danny and Sue out of the truck, sat them on the ground, and they walked to solid ground. Then, I got 10-month-old Sallie, carried her to safety, and set her down, only to have her immediately plop down on her behind in the mud and begin to let us know she was not one bit happy.

In the meantime, Dad had stopped a distance behind the Weps. Up to this point, the Jeep was light enough to stay on top of the tundra, but after seeing the predicament the Weps was in, he was concerned that it might sink at any minute.

"I think I'll head back to the road," he said. "We should have at least one vehicle that isn't stuck!" With that, he put the Jeep in reverse, and slowly backed towards the road.

"Any idea what you're going to do?" I asked.

"I can cut some trees, although there aren't many trees handy," Stan said. "Maybe if I get enough wood under it, I can jack it up, and corduroy the road out behind it until I find solid ground."

"I think I'll just walk back to the campground," Mom said. "Anyone want to come with me?"

A chorus of, "I do!" rang out. It was hard to get the little ones to stay upright on the rough terrain, but we finally reached the campsite. It was nearly dark when we heard the sound of the Weps. Stan's plan had worked, and he and Dad had been able to get the Weps back to solid ground.

After a good night at the campground, we decided we would NOT give up on Little Swede. The next morning, we donned our packs to walk into Little Swede. We had done it before, and could do it again! The hole that the Weps had been in was quite impressive. It had sticks poking out of it in every direction, but fortunately, the Weps was gone.

We managed to get everyone down near the lake, set up our tent, and let the "little ones" rest. They were out like lights. It wasn't long before Stan had his line in the water and was reeling in a trout. What a delicious dinner we had that night. We spent only one more night there, but the fishing was great. We each caught our limit (and yes, Dad had his fishing license!).

BEAR LAKE

Our garden produced well that summer, and we had quite an abundant supply of garden veggies in the freezer. However, our supply of moose and caribou was dwindling.

"I think we should have Bob drop us off at a lake where we can hunt moose," Stan said to me. "We could spend a week or so there, and maybe we'll even see a bear."

"Sounds like a good plan to me," I replied bravely, wondering as I said it, if it really did or not. "What lake do you have in mind?"

"Bob said he'd seen quite a few moose this summer near Bear Lake, so I thought we'd go there."

I asked Mom if she'd take care of our kids while we went hunting, and as always, she was willing. The Sunday that we were to fly in to the lake dawned bright and clear. After my last experience flying with the boys, I was a bit hesitant to get into the plane, but it looked reasonably safe. After all, its seats were all nicely bolted in-place. It was a beautiful day for flying, and we flew very low, so we could see the countryside. I was intrigued by some circular bare spots in the tundra, with a round mound in the center.

"What makes those weird looking spots?" I asked Bob.

"Those are swan's nests," he replied. "They build them up like that so they can watch closely for predators."

Of course, the swans had already migrated to the Lower 48, but their nests were fascinating. Apparently, they returned year after year to the same nests.

It didn't take long before we were circling Bear Lake. Bob asked us where we would like to camp, and after we'd surveyed the entire lake a couple of times, we settled on a spot near the intake to the lake. Bob landed and taxied to the shore. We pulled the plane up on shore and unloaded all our supplies. We had brought a small tent for sleeping, and some canvas to string between the trees in case it rained, so our folding chairs and camp supplies would not get wet.

Bob left, and we set-up our camp. Dinner that evening was easy. We'd brought some moose steak along, plus some potatoes, so fried moose steak and potatoes filled our bellies.

"Do you hear that funny plopping sound?" I asked Stan. "What do you think it is?"

"I think it's fish jumping in the lake. They're probably catching mosquitoes since there are a bunch of them around. I did bring fishing poles and my hip waders, so I may try to catch some," he told me. "It didn't seem very deep when we were unloading, so it should be a cinch to get some fish."

We went to bed that night and slept like logs. While I was cooking breakfast the next morning, Stan went out exploring. He came back, white as a sheet.

"Would you believe there are tons of fresh bear tracks between us and the lake shore?" he asked. "I sure didn't hear any bear around last night, but they could have had a tasty snack out of us if they'd wanted to. I'm going to rig up an alarm for tonight."

We had emptied a can of beans the night before, and he emptied a few more. He strung the cans with their lids on a rope around our campsite. I'm not so sure the noise from those cans would wake us, but it did make us feel more secure. Fortunately, our security system was never tested. The fish were so plentiful that the bears were happy with fishing and paid no attention to us.

After breakfast, we set about exploring our area. We climbed up a nearby hill, finding lots of cranberries growing on the hill, but no moose sign. We walked part way around the lake, seeing lots of bear signs, but not one moose track. We concluded that Bear Lake was aptly named, and decided that next time Bob took us hunting, we wanted him to take us to Moose Lake!

Bob was planning to come back on Wednesday to check on us and bring us more supplies. So, we had only a couple more days to fend off the bears. Stan mostly stayed awake that night, jumping at every noise. His nervousness rubbed off on me, and I had a restless night, too. Tuesday was a repeat of Monday, with us looking forward to the following day when our rescuer would arrive.

Wednesday dawned bright and sunny. We got most of our camping gear packed, and were ready to leave Bear Lake. So far, we had not seen one bear, but every night they left many tracks along the bank of the lake. They didn't wholly eat the pike they were catching, either; we would find fresh carcasses and partially eaten fish strewn along the lakeshore every morning.

We hoped that Bob would arrive early in the day, so we didn't even go looking for a moose. As the day dragged on and no Bob, we began to worry. What could be keeping him? When it started to get dark, we decided we needed to re-establish our camp. We took inventory of our supplies and realized that we needed to supplement our food supply if Bob didn't come soon.

Thursday morning dawned bright and sunny, just like the previous day, but still no Bob. Stan decided it was time to increase our dwindling supply of food by catching some of those pike that jumped day and night in the lake, so he put on his hip waders and headed out into the lake. The water was just about an inch from going over the top of his waders when he started fishing, and soon he had a fish. However, fighting with the fish made waves, and soon his boots were filled with water. When he got his fish back to shore, he had to hang up his waders over the campfire and try to dry them. This was almost impossible, but they did dry somewhat.

Friday there was still no Bob, but we had enjoyed the pike for dinner the night before. Stan decided he could build a fishing stand, so he cut down some trees and tied them together into a stool, using some rope to tie the branches in place. He put on his still damp boots and hauled his fishing stand out to where the water was just getting close to coming over the top of his boots. Then, he climbed up on his stand and sat down on top of it. Fishing went well. He just had to toss out his lure, and he'd have a fish. When he had six fish, he climbed back down from his stand and brought the fish to shore. He soaked some of the pike in salt water and planned on trying to figure out how to smoke it the next day. In the meantime, we ate another fish for dinner and enjoyed it.

With the fishing under control, we once again set out looking for berries and moose. We found some blueberries that had not fallen off the bushes yet, so we picked them. There were lots and lots of cranberries. There were even some bog cranberries. I'd only seen pictures of them in the brochure put out by the State of Alaska, but never in real life! It was the oddest-looking cranberry I had ever seen. The plant had only two or so leaves, but it put out a long string that was up to a foot long, and on the end of the string, was a cranberry. They were growing on the green tundra and looked so unique. It was very slow picking them, but we managed to get a couple of quarts.

We hadn't brought enough sugar to make perfect cranberry sauce, but we used what we had. It went well with our fish, and our supplies were lasting better.

"I think tomorrow is Saturday," Stan said. "There should be lots of moose hunters coming by, and maybe we can find out where Bob is."

One plane did land, but it landed at the other end of the lake, and even though we put green branches on our fire, the hunters didn't seem to see us. We were disappointed when they took off without our ever getting their attention. Maybe Sunday would bring more planes.

We were up early, trying to figure out how we could attract attention if a plane landed on the other side of the lake again. We finally decided we ought to fire three shots, in the traditional Mayday signal. We were disappointed when no planes landed that Sunday. Back to our tart cranberries, and fish. The smoked pike were delicious; fortunately, we'd brought along enough salt to last for a while.

We continued our subsisting, and hunting moose in our spare time, until Wednesday, when finally, a plane landed on our side of the lake. We didn't recognize the plane and were pleasantly surprised when we could see that Bob was the pilot.

"What happened to you?" Stan asked. "You were supposed to be back here last Wednesday, a whole week ago!"

"Well, it's a long story," Bob replied. "The day after I dropped you, I flew my plane with the wheels up north, where I was supposed to be dropping off some hunters in a few days. I wanted to scope out the landing area. As I was landing, a crazy gust of wind hit. It picked my plane up and threw it upside down on the runway. I wasn't hurt, but the airplane was severely damaged."

"I was lucky that a friend was already parked on the runway, so we got my plane pushed out of the way, and I caught a ride home with him. I decided to go the next day and see if I could get the plane turned over and repaired. So, I flew the plane that I'd flown you guys in. I started to land on a nearby lake so I could walk to the runway, and I hit a submerged log in the lake. My plane sunk! So, there I was stranded for a day or so near the lake. It wasn't very deep water, so I didn't have any trouble getting to shore. It was kind of a miserable night."

"Then, when another plane happened to come by, I sent word to my friend to come pick me up. He did, but he had just taken the floats off his plane. It took quite a while to get them back on, and then he let me borrow his plane. So, are you ready to go? Any moose?"

"No, we've never even seen a fresh track, and the next time you take us hunting, we want to go to Moose Lake, instead of Bear Lake. There are too many bears here for comfort!" Stan replied.

We gathered our belongings and were happy to see the last of Bear Lake.

ACCIDENTAL CARIBOU

"What do you think about making a quick trip down towards Paxton, and see if we can't get some more caribou for the freezer," Stan asked me.

"Well, we're getting low, and since we didn't have much luck getting a moose, it might be worth a shot," I replied.

"If we take the car, instead of the Weps" Stan said, "we can make better time getting there, and have more time to hunt."

"Where will we sleep if we take the car?" I asked. "I wasn't very comfortable when we slept in the car that one time."

"We can do it again," he replied. "It might not be so comfy, but it does work! Time is of the essence."

"I suppose so, it would be good to put more meat in the freezer."

Mom, bless her heart, was willing to watch the

kids, so we gathered together a few camping supplies and some food.

After work on Friday, we were on the road. We got to the hunting grounds just as the sun was peeking over the mountain tops. We had taken turns driving and napping on the way down, so we were not completely exhausted. We hunted up and down the highway, but never even saw a track.

Even though the car wasn't as comfy as a bed, we were tired enough that we slept like logs. Stan had the coffee on when I woke up the next morning, and we were ready to hunt as soon as daylight appeared.

Up and down the highway again, and still no tracks or caribou! It was getting on towards afternoon, and about time for us to leave the area, when Stan spotted a herd of caribou. The road we were on had been carved out of the side of a steep hill, with the hill on one side and a drop off on the lower side, and the caribou were way out in an open flat.

"I think I can shoot over their heads," Stan said. "Maybe they'll panic and run towards the road."

He got out, aimed way high, and shot. Imagine our surprise when one of the caribou dropped like a ton of bricks!

"I don't think you held quite high enough!" I told him. "Now what do we do? Would it be easier to get to the caribou by climbing down this steep bank, or by going back down to the road on the flat and trying to find it?"

"I think I'd rather chance the bank," Stan replied. "I'm sure it'd be easier to get our bearings from here. Bring the knives, and I'll get the axe. At least, we won't have to go back home empty-handed!"

We locked the car and set off sliding down the steep hill. It was a relief when we reached the flat, although the snow was about knee deep, so wading through it in the direction of the downed caribou was a chore. We finally stumbled across their tracks.

"Which way do you think we should go?" I asked. "Right or left?"

"Let's go right. From the angle of where the car's parked, I think it's that direction."

We started tracking the herd, and it wasn't long until we found an area where the tracks showed that they'd suddenly started running. Lying there, was our caribou. Stan began to clean the animal, while I just wandered around. I noticed that a black pickup stopped near our car, way up on the hill. I wondered what they were up to! I hoped they were not bent on stealing our car since that would really put us in a bind.

I walked out into a very open spot in the snow and

started waving my hands. I was quite shocked when I could see the little toy guy get out a long stick and put it up to his shoulder. He was aiming his rifle at us! I waved my hands harder and danced about in the snow like a demented person. It was a great relief when I saw him lower his rifle.

Before long, our onlookers got into their pickup and left. I was relieved that they left our car behind. Stan finished getting the caribou ready to drag out, and we were off. It took us nearly two hours to get the meat dragged to the bottom of the steep hill. Stan walked up the road to where the car was parked, turned around, and came back down to pick up our meat. It had been a very long day and was just getting dark as we started on the long road back home.

A couple of days later, Stan came home with a big grin on his face.

"I ran into a friend of mine at the base today, and guess what he told me. He said he and his hunting party were the ones that spotted us way out there in the flat with our caribou. He didn't have field glasses, so he'd used his rifle scope to see what we were up to. He was amazed to see me cleaning the caribou. He wondered how I'd made a shot like that; it must have been nearly 2,000 yards. I didn't tell him it was an accident! I just acted as though it was a common, everyday experience."

Stan never did confess to his friend that he'd only been trying to scare the herd closer to the road. Some things are best not broadcasted!

MOOSE IN THE CABBAGE PATCH

*W*e still had no moose for our freezer, although we had a fair supply of caribou meat. It was Halloween, and the kids and I made a few stops around the neighborhood trick or treating. The kids didn't quite understand about Halloween, but they were happy with the candy they'd been given and didn't want to quit!

Stan stayed home and doled the candy out to our trick or treaters. The kids and I had just returned home, when we started to run low on the candy at our house. We shut off the lights and hoped the remaining trick or treaters would not do tricks. They didn't.

We got up the next morning, and while I was putting on the coffee and starting breakfast, Stan got his shower and dressed. He kept hearing some strange sounds coming from the backyard. He was kind of afraid to look out, thinking that it might still be trick or treaters. If it was, what could they be up to? He finally got up his courage, and upon opening the drapes, he saw three large objects in our garden. They were moose. One of them had horns, and they were grunting! Who knew they did that?

November 1 was the first day of the second moose season. When he realized what day it was, he got excited. He dug out his rifle and stealthily came to the kitchen. He whispered to me "There's a bull moose out in the cabbage patch and I want you to shoot him."

He handed me his gun. My gun only had open sights, and it wasn't daylight enough to see the sights, plus he figured that his rifle with the scope would be able to pick out the bull.

"I've never shot your 30-06," I whispered back. "I've never even used a scope before. Tell me what to do!"

We eased our way to the back door of the kitchen, and Stan told me exactly how to hold the gun. He opened the door, and I looked through the scope. All I could see was fur, but I moved the scope around until I realized that I was looking at a front leg. I moved it slowly up the neck and was happy to see that the one I was aimed at had horns. I moved the scope down the animal until I was behind the front shoulder and pulled the trigger. The moose fell over in a heap, right in the cabbage patch.

Stan ran to get his knife and bled out the animal. Then, he cleaned it and tossed a rope over a pole we had set up right near the septic tank when we were moving that pesky building off our sewer line. He used the Weps to drag the moose to his makeshift rack and soon had the moose hanging from the pole to cool down.

In the meantime, I finished cooking breakfast. Stan finally had time for a cup of coffee, ate his breakfast, and still made it to work on time.

We were happy to have the meat for the freezers. This was the first moose that I'd shot, even though I'd gone moose hunting several times. I was pretty thrilled and told everyone about the moose I'd shot in the cabbage patch.

Christmas rolled around, and Stan brought out this massive package, with my name on it. I had no idea what it might be and was hardly able to contain myself until the 25th dawned and I could open that package. There were my mounted moose horns, with a beautiful plaque, saying "Shot by Rose Rybachek in the backyard." What a thoughtful present!

After we moved back to the North Pole area from our time living at the mine, we were too involved with raising our family, working, and spending our summers at the mine to go hunting (besides, we lost our babysitters, when Mom and Dad moved to Montana!).

CRITTERS

$\mathcal{I}$n June of 1963, my parents moved from Alaska back to Montana. Stan and I moved our family to the mining claims near Livengood. We never again ventured to either the Taylor Highway or the Paxson area hunting or fishing. That chapter of our lives was finished.

We got so busy with our mining that we had no time for hunting. I have written about our experiences outside normal civilization in the books: _Mining for Alaskan Adventures, Volumes I and II_, plus _Bumps in the Road_.

We did have a couple of exciting adventures that I didn't share with you in those books. Both of them involved our friend, Monte. Stan had gotten acquainted with Monte at the Air Force shop on Eielson AFB, and Monte spent quite a bit of time at the mine with us. His wife was working in Washington state, and he got very lonely living in the barracks.

Monte loved to hunt, and during hunting season,

he was a regular visitor at the mine. One day he went hunting by the river. It wasn't long before he burst through the door, all excited and breathless from running. "I saw a bear!" he shouted. "I think I wounded it, but I couldn't find it, and I think it was a grizzly bear."

"I'll go with you to see if we can find it," Stan told him, as he grabbed his gun and boots. "We can't have a wounded bear near the house, but I doubt it was a grizzly. I've not even heard of one being in this part of the country. How far away from the house was it?"

"Well, it was just upstream from the bridge," Monte replied. "It was just ambling along, eating some cranberries. I don't know how I missed it."

They soon returned empty-handed. We were very concerned about the little kids playing outside, with a wounded bear within a quarter of a mile of the cabin! I made sure that when the kids were outdoors, I went with them, and I carried my rifle. We did think the dogs would alert us if the bear approached, but could we trust them?

A couple of days later, Stan and Monte finally found the bear. Apparently, Monte's shot had wounded it seriously enough that it had crawled off into the brush and died. They were both surprised to find that it *was* a grizzly. The guys decided it had no doubt been passing through when it had the misfortune to run afoul of Monte. Anyway, we were relieved to know that there was not a wounded bear near our cabin.

Another event was when Monte came back from moose hunting and was again excited and babbling.

"I got a moose!" he shouted. "It's way up the hill past the dam, and nearly to the end of your ditch."

The ditch was over three miles long, and over tundra that was impossible to drive a vehicle on when it was not frozen. And, it was not frozen.

"There's no way we can reach it with any of our equipment," Stan told him. "We'll have to pack it out. Fortunately, I have a couple of backpacks that we can strap pieces on. We'll need to get it out before the wild critters find it, so come on!"

Monte was a big man, and so was Stan. They hiked up to the kill to begin the tedious job of hauling out the moose.

"If you grab a hind quarter, I'll take the front one," Monte told Stan.

"Are you sure?" Stan asked. "The front quarter of a moose is a lot heavier than the back quarter."

"Sure, I can do it, if you'll help me get it loaded on my backpack," Monte replied.

Stan helped load the quarter and then helped Monte

get to his feet. It was heavier than Monte had figured, but his pride would not let him recant.

They had gone a short distance when Monte missed a step as he was stepping over the ditch and fell backwards into the ditch. With that massive hunk of moose on his backpack, he couldn't move... and Stan had to come to his rescue. Stan always said Monte would have drowned if he'd been alone since there was no way he could get his head out from under the water in the ditch.

They cut that front quarter into two pieces, and Monte took only one piece from then on. They managed to get the whole moose packed to our cabin and hung up to cool. Monte was more careful where he hunted from then on.

MASS RESIGNATION AND RADIO

$\mathcal{W}$e faced a serious dilemma. Should we continue living winter and summer at the mine? We could apply for a Correspondence Course to home-school Danny for first grade, but upon discussing the issue, we decided that one of the most important things learned in school was the ability to interact with other students. So, we reluctantly packed our belongings and moved back to our house in North Pole a few days before school was to start. We were happy to find that the school also offered a half-day kindergarten for Suzie, so both kids would be able to ride the bus to school in the morning. Sallie would remain home with me until we went to get Suzie at noon. Danny would ride the bus home at night. Danny was very excited to go to school. He soon made friends with several of his classmates. Suzie, on the other hand, was a little reluctant to leave home, but she soon overcame her anxiety.

I was very excited when the kids brought home

a note informing us that a PTA meeting would be held the next week. When I was in school, my Mom was very active in the PTA, and the PTA had many exciting activities going on. I really wanted to get involved.

One of my Mom's friends had older children that were going to North Pole Elementary school. "Are you going to the PTA meeting?" Maryann asked me. "I think it will be fun, and if you'd like, I can pick you up on the way."

"Sounds like a plan," I told her. "I'm excited about getting involved in the PTA."

We found out that the meeting was to be held in the gym, so we settled ourselves in the chairs. We were surprised at the small turnout of parents. The five-member board was seated prominently on chairs in the front of the assembly. I was thrilled when the president rose and called the meeting to order.

"Since the borough has seen fit to expand the number of students at our school this year, to allow students that live outside the city limits to attend, we have decided that it would not be fair to all of you new parents for us to remain as officers. Therefore, we resign."

With that, the entire board rose and walked out the door. We all sat there with stunned looks on our faces.

My friend Maryann rose, and said, "I don't think that was very nice, but I do think this school needs an active PTA. I suggest that we elect temporary officers now and hold an election next meeting for permanent officers."

Her suggestion was met with resounding applause, and I nominated her for president. In retaliation, she nominated me as secretary. Thus, my association with the PTA was born.

We were both elected to our respective positions at the next meeting. Our first order of business was to plan and produce the Halloween Party, which was a smashing success. The North Pole PTA was back in business.

The next year, Sallie was enrolled in school, and the local radio station offered a fundraising opportunity for organizations, called the Community Club Awards. I volunteered to head up our local North Pole PTA's collection efforts. We needed to have our members collect sales receipts from the various sponsors of the Awards, turn them in to us, and once a week we had to tally all the receipts. Each club was awarded money based upon the amount of their receipts. North Pole had a great team, and we usually were near the top of the winnings.

SOFTBALL, ANYONE?

"*H*ey, did you hear about the new lady's softball league they're forming?" my friend Rosanna asked me one morning on the telephone. "They say there'll be several teams, and if we get on a team, we might even get to go to Anchorage to play. Want to come and try out?"

"Gosh, it's been a long time since I played softball," I replied. "I don't know if I even remember the first thing about it. But, what could it hurt to try?"

So, Rosanna and I went to the tryouts. We both ended up earning a spot on one team. She played first base, and I as a shortstop. I really wanted to be an outfielder, but the coach decided I should play shortstop. I sort of figured our coach was grabbing at straws, and didn't have anyone else that would take the job.

"Guess what?" I proudly told Stan when I got home. "I made the team! I'm going to be playing softball."

"What?" he asked. "Have you lost your mind? We

don't have time for you to go out there and run with all those young girls. We have important things to do."

"Well, some of us think this is important, too," I told him. "I plan on playing."

That began my three-year stint as a ball player. For a while, I actually had the highest batting average in the Fairbanks area. I loved playing. Rosanna and I would take turns driving to practice and our games.

Then, there was the one big game with an Anchorage team, and our pitcher didn't show. The coach pointed at me, and told me to pitch! Oh, my, I was not a pitcher, so I went out on the field and proved it. I was never so humiliated in my life when they hit almost every ball I pitched. Needless to say, we didn't win that game!

After three years, Rosanna's husband's hitch was up in the Air Force, so he was being stationed elsewhere, and she left. I gave up, too, and never returned to softball, but it was fun while it lasted.

DIP NETTING AT CHITINA

$\mathcal{W}$e were very happy when Mom and my siblings drove up the Alaska Highway to visit in 1967. Dad decided he'd stay in Montana. Betty was attending college, and needed to earn some money, so she wanted to work in Fairbanks for the summer. Henry and Debbie were both in high school.

Stan came home from work one night, as excited as I'd ever seen him. "Want to go dip netting?" he asked.

"I don't even know what you're talking about," I replied. "How can I know if I want to go or not?"

"I was talking to Bob, and he told me about dip netting," he said. "They've opened the Copper River near Chitina for subsistence fishing, and all you have to do is take this big net, stand near the stream, and the salmon jump into it. We can pitch a tent, and take our pressure cooker, and can the salmon as we catch it. I think he said a family is allowed to catch 50 fish."

"Hum," I replied. "What about the kids? Can they

go with us? And, Mom and Henry and Debbie? Can they come? Where do you get the dip nets?"

"Calm down," Stan said. "You're sounding as excited as I was. Yes, the whole family can go. Bob told me that if you have a resident fishing license, you can do subsistence fishing. Big Ray's sells dip nets, and we can go when they have the fisheries open for subsistence fishing.

"Count me in," I replied.

We decided to go the following weekend. We drove the Weps, since we had no idea how rough the terrain might be. Mom, Stan and Sallie rode in the front seat, while the rest of us sat on the hard benches in the back. We arrived at O'Brian Creek in the early morning, but since it didn't get dark, we had no trouble setting up our meager camp. We brought small pup-tents.

At the mouth of O'Brian Creek, we saw some folks standing out in the river, holding out their nets. This looked like the place. But there were so many fishermen, there wasn't enough room for one more, let alone four. So, we decided to drive up the steep hill on the far side of O'Brian Creek. This landed us on an old abandoned railroad bed, the same bed that we had traveled on to arrive at O'Brian Creek. At one time, the railroad had a trestle over O'Brian Creek, but it had washed away. Someone built a steep road up to the railroad bed on the far side, and the Weps had no trouble climbing up onto the old rail bed. We went a bit further down the track, and found a wide spot in the railbed. This would make an excellent camping spot, so Stan parked the Weps as close as he could get to the hill.

The other side of the railbed presented a steep drop-off down to the River. It was nearly straight up and down, and once you reached the river, it was moving swiftly through the rapids. There was a little bit of backwater, and that's where we aimed to go fishing. It was a dangerous climb, so we told Sue and Sallie that they couldn't come down the hill with us, but Henry maneuvered it quite well. Debbie stayed with the girls in our makeshift camp.

Stan was the first one to catch a fish, and it was a beauty. Soon we all had a fish or two. We laboriously hauled them back up the hill, cleaned them, put them back in the Weps, and then carefully turned around to go back to O'Brian Creek to do our canning.

"Why don't we move our camp to this spot?" Stan asked, as he turned the Weps around. "We can't can the fish here, since there isn't any water, but we could keep them in the coolers until we have enough, and then drive back and can them."

"Sounds like a good plan to me," I replied. "I'm

a little afraid of that hill, though. It's so steep that if someone slipped and fell into that river, we might never see them again."

"I have a rope, and I'll tie us to some of those scrubby trees when we're fishing," Stan said. "Once we get these fish canned, let's move!"

Move we did. The wide spot in the road was still available, so we parked the Weps in a strategic location, and set-up our pup tents a little way in the woods, up a rather steep trail. Sue, Sallie and Debbie went to bed. About that time, a young teenager came into the area, rolled up in a sleeping bag, and was out like a light.

Mom and I were getting the food stuffs ready for the next day while Stan and Henry went fishing. I was bent over in the back of the Weps, getting some food to make sandwiches for the fishermen, when I heard a strange sound.

"Mom, what's that noise?" I asked, looking around.

"Well, if I didn't know better," she replied, "I'd think it was a bear. "It sounds just like some of those bears that I had to put up with in the Park when you were a baby."

We walked around the side of the Weps, looked toward where the teen had gone to bed, and there standing over him was a fairly large black bear. It was just sniffing him, and the boy was still sound asleep.

I reached into the Weps, and dug out the .357 pistol. It wasn't needed. I was shocked when Mom grabbed a fishing pole, brandished it like a sword and ran towards the bear, hollering, "Get out of here!"

I wasn't the only one shocked. The bear took one look at Mom, and headed as fast as it could into the trees.

"Do you think that bear will come back?" I asked Mom. "And, where did you learn how to scare a bear like that?"

"Oh, they were real nuisances when we lived in the Park," Mom replied. "I used to shoo them away with my broom all the time. I think it was more effective than the fishing pole, but I guess that worked. As for whether or not it will come back, I wouldn't be surprised. I think we need to wake that boy and get him into the back of the Weps."

It was quite a job waking the youngster, but he finally dragged his sleeping bag across the opening, crawled into the back of the Weps, and was soon sleeping soundly once again.

"What about the girls?" I asked. "They're sleeping in those little tents up the hill!"

"I think we better get them into the back of the truck, too," Mom said.

We made our way to the tents, and roused the

girls, who were less than willing to stumble down the trail in the dusk. But we were insistent, and they soon were snuggled in their sleeping bags in the back of the Weps with the stranger.

"Now, what about Stan and Henry?" I asked. "Do you think the bear will go down there and eat them? They should have a bunch of fish, and the bear might be hungry."

"Maybe you should take them the pistol?" Mom suggested.

Soon I was on my way with the flashlight, trying hard not to slide on my keister down the steep trail to the river. Stan was less than enthused when I told him about the bear.

"I don't think you needed to bring me the pistol," he said. "How are you going to get back up the trail? What if you meet the bear on the way?"

He begrudgingly walked me back up the trail to the Weps before returning to fish. Stan and Henry spent most of the night fishing, and we never saw the bear again. Once they brought up their fish, it was time to move camp so we could can the salmon. We woke the boy, and he ambled down the railbed.

We had to remove the pup tents, but everything else was safely stowed in the Weps. Once we got the pressure cooker going back at O'Brien Creek, Sue got very upset.

"I didn't even get to fish," she wailed. "I came along with you guys to fish, and you wouldn't let me go down that hill. I want to go fishing here."

Stan took pity on her, grabbed a net, and said, "Here, I'll go with you. Put on your boots, we'll go to the mouth of O'Brien Creek. There are not as many fishermen there now as there were yesterday."

They set off down the creek bank. Mom and I monitored the pressure cooker, and when it was time to remove the lid, we dumped the contents in the creek to cool, and got another batch going. Every one of those cans sealed.

About an hour later, Mom yelled at me, "Come look at this!"

There was Sue making her way back up the trail. A huge fish head stuck up about a foot over her head, and its tail was dragging on the ground. Stan had strapped it to a backboard on her back, and she was bringing home her trophy!

"Where did you get that fish?" I asked her as I was helping her get the fish unstrapped.

"I caught it." She proudly said.

"You caught it? Where's your Dad? And, Henry?" I asked.

"Well, when I got the fish, they decided to keep fishing, and maybe they could catch a big one, too. Dad offered to bring this one home, but I wanted to do it myself! Do we have to can it?"

"I'm afraid we do," I told her. "We don't have any way of transporting something that size home."

About an hour later, Stan and Henry returned with empty nets.

"Tell me about that fish of Sue's," I asked Stan. "Did she really catch it by herself?"

"Oh, yes," he replied. "Once that monster got in her net, she wasn't about to let go, and if I hadn't been there right beside her to grab her and the net, they'd both been going downstream. It was a struggle for both of us to get that thing on the bank. She was not going to let it get away!"

We figured the fish weighed in at about 70 pounds. How Sue managed to carry it all the way to the camp was a miracle. I guess what they say about adrenalin kicking in is true. We had many pressure-cooker loads to get all of our salmon canned, and ended up with enough canned salmon to last us a couple of years. We never saw the bear again. However, we did read in the newspaper where the Fish and Game had killed a pesky bear near O'Brian Creek. Was it "our" bear? We will never know.

HAM RADIO?

I was enthralled when my neighbor across the street showed me their amateur radio set up. She and her husband had studied for several months, taken the test, and received their ham radio licenses. They put up an antenna, bought a radio, and were on the air.

"Come and see my radio station," Eloise said to me one morning after I had sent the kids off to school. So, Sallie and I went across the street.

"How would you like to call your mom?" she asked me.

"You can call my Mom from your radio?" I replied.

"Well, not directly, but if we find a ham that's near your mom, he can run a phone patch, which means he has this gizmo that will connect the radio to the phone. Then, your mom only has to pay for the long-distance charge from wherever he is, instead of all the way from Alaska."

She found a ham in Great Falls, and soon I was

chatting with Mom. Instead of it costing about a dollar a minute, the whole conversation ended up costing $3.00, and we talked for a long time.

"I want to get my ham license," I told Stan when he came home from work. "Eloise said it wasn't all that hard, and they'll be coming to test again in June. You should get yours, too."

We spent the winter studying. Stan was very good with theory since he worked in Teletype Maintenance. I, on the other hand, figured the books were written in Greek. Thank goodness for practice tests. We also had to learn 13 words per minute of Morse code or CW.

The day dawned that we were to take our test. We were both on the nervous side. Neither one of us had trouble with the written test, but when it came to taking the CW, both were stressed out. We both failed. We did manage to get the five words per minute to qualify for the technician type of license, but we couldn't talk with that class of license, we could only use CW.

My hands were like blocks of ice, due to stress. I approached the examiner. "Can I retake the CW?" I asked.

"Do you think it would do any good?" he replied, rather sarcastically.

I reached out and grabbed his bare arm with my cold hands. He recoiled, and said, "Sure, you can try again. Try to warm up first, though, okay?"

After a hot cup of coffee, I did pass the 13 WPM Morse code. So, I had my general class license. Stan also retook the test, but he just couldn't print fast enough. He practiced writing for the next six months, and the next time the examiner was in town, in December, he passed his code. So, at that time, he was also able to talk on the radio.

The next spring, Stan put up a tower, built a cubicle-quad antenna, and we bought a radio.

"There it is," Stan told me when he had the radio connected and ready to go. "Go ahead and make a contact!"

"Ah," I replied as I picked up the microphone. "I hear a lot of stations on there, but I'm not sure I want to try to talk to any of them!"

"Go ahead," he said again. "It can't be that hard. Just call CQ and see who comes back to you."

This reminded me of my first day at school. Talk about mike fright! However, as I was tuning around the band, I heard this melodious female voice. "This is K4ICA in Florida, and I'm looking for check-ins for the YL System. Do we have anyone out there?"

This sounded doable. I could do this! So, I replied to her, "This is KL7FQQ in Fairbanks, Alaska."

"Well, hello there, KL7FQQ," she replied. "This is V. Mayree, K4ICA, and you have checked into the Young Ladies International Single-sideband Communication System. This is a worldwide system that mostly handles emergency traffic, but when there are no emergencies, the members contact each other for a beautiful awards program. Would you like to make any calls?"

"Do you have anyone on from Montana?" I asked. I was thinking of those phone patches!

"Actually, we do. W7EOI is in Great Falls. Would you like to call him?"

"Yes, I would," I replied.

I called him, found out his name was Lyle, and he offered to move off frequency with me and make a call to my parents. That began a long association with Lyle. He made many phone calls for me.

I loved the idea of being able to talk around the world. I spent many happy hours making friends and contacts with people on the YL System.

We found out that Heathkit offered radio kits. All you had to do was to buy the kit, solder it together, and you had a radio. Stan was good at soldering, and I was good at reading directions, so we built a radio.

We took that one to the mine so we could talk back and forth when one or the other of us was there. Then, we got another kit, and built that. Finally, we got a colored television kit, and built that. Stan constructed a cabinet for it, and we had that for many years.

EARTHQUAKES

"What's that?" I asked Stan as I shook him awake in the middle of the night in June 1967. "Do you feel the house shaking? What's happening?"

"That, my dear, was no doubt an earthquake," he replied. "I got used to feeling them when I was in Iceland. We used to have them all the time, and it got so they didn't even wake me up! I must have slept through another one!"

"It's happening again," I said a few minutes later. "This one wasn't quite as strong, but I felt it, did you?"

"How could I miss that, now that I'm awake?" Stan replied. "I think it was stronger than the ones in Iceland, and I'm sure it was an earthquake."

We had just settled down to go back to our snoozing when a powerful one hit. This one nearly tossed us out of our bed.

"Yikes!" I exclaimed. "Do you think we need to

get the kids up and out of the house? How much of this can the house stand?"

"I don't think there's any danger yet, but if it gets any stronger, we better move."

One more hit during that nearly twenty-minute span. Then, peace reigned, and we could return to our slumbers.

The next morning, the newspaper carried a story about the earthquakes. Sure enough, we had four jolts during a 21-minute period. They consisted of tremors measured at 5.6, 4.3, 6.0 and 5.3. We felt them all!

Aftershocks continued for several weeks. The newspaper reported that 70 of them had occurred in an hour following the quake, and continued for several weeks at that rapid pace. We became so used to being jolted out of bed in the middle of the night, that we barely noticed them. One particular aftershock in early July, though, really had me worried. The house started shaking so badly that I decided I should probably get the kids outside just in case the house fell in.

"Come on, kids!" I yelled to them. "We need to get out of the house!"

I had heard that the safest place in case of an earthquake was in a door frame, but if the house caved in, wouldn't the door frame cave in, too? Then I looked out the back door, and the ground was undulating like ocean waves. Imagine what the power poles looked like as they rose and fell with each surge. Should we leave the relative protection of the back-door frame, and venture out onto the waving grass? Or, would it be safer just to stay where we were? After what seemed like an hour (but was only minutes), the waves subsided, and the earthquake was over. At least for the moment.

I've heard conflicting reports that the epicenter was 12 miles from Fairbanks (which was exactly what we were) or 30 miles. Wherever it was, it was too close for comfort. We were happy when the number of aftershocks dropped to 10 per hour in early July. Most of the aftershocks were so light, we didn't feel them, but read about them in the newspaper. We were all shaken up!

TRAGEDY AND FLOOD

ollowing the earthquake, it started to rain. July was a very wet month that year, and the ground in our garden became soggy. The plan was that Stan would take his vacation in August, and we planned to spend the whole month at the mine. I knew that often it frosted towards the end of August, so before we left, I decided I needed to harvest part of our garden, just in case. The kids had been going on their bikes to a nearby dam that only had about a foot of water. They loved swimming, making mud balls, and just cooling off in the pond.

"Mom, can we go swimming?" the kids asked me one morning, as I prepared to go to the garden. "I promise we'll be home for lunch!"

I could not turn down those pleading brown eyes. So, I agreed. Little did I suspect that with all the rain, the dam had filled until it was nearly five-feet deep!

I was still working with vegetables when Sallie and

Sue came racing their bikes down the street yelling, "Mom, come quick, Danny's drowned!"

I borrowed Sue's bike, told the girls to go next door and tell our neighbor Val, and set off for the pond as quickly as I could go. When I got there, there was no sign of Danny. I waded into the pond and searched for him with my feet until I finally found him. I dragged him to the shore, gave him mouth-to-mouth resuscitation, but he had swallowed an awful lot of water. Val came, told me he had an ambulance on the way, but I wouldn't quit with the mouth-to-mouth. When the ambulance arrived, they said it was too late, and they took Danny with them.

This was definitely a family tragedy. Needless to say, we didn't go to the mine. Stan went back to work after the funeral, and I kept the girls close to me.

A couple of weeks after Danny died, Fairbanks was hit with a devastating flood. When we woke on Sue's birthday, I turned on the radio to hear, "The Chena River is flooding. Reports are that Fairbanks is under several feet of water. An emergency shelter has been set up at the University of Alaska."

The other radio station was off the air. It was located in the basement of the Northward Building, so it was completely silenced. The transmitter for the one radio station was located on Farmer's Loop Road, above the flood-ravaged city. One of the announcers made his way to that transmitter and broadcast from there. Hams from across the area responded to the emergency and set up emergency communication stations, so we had some sort of communications. Outside of ham radio, we were completely cut off from the outside world.

Our home was relatively unscathed since it had been built on a manmade knoll, but we could go completely around it with our riverboat. We lost our electricity for about a week, but Stan figured out how to get our ham radio on the air, using batteries. We were happy to be able to pass messages to people in the other states that were concerned about their loved ones. It made us realize that life went on, we had to keep on living.

I spent about 24-hours straight, with only occasional breaks, on the radio passing Health and Welfare messages. The girls were very helpful, but wanted to go out on the boat!

We had experienced earthquakes and floods and we had our suspicions that the country would burn next, but apparently, we had enough water to squash all the lightning strikes, and the number of forest fires that year was at a minimum.

CCA

Our youngest daughter, Cynthia Rose (Cyndi), was born a year later, in December. It was fun having a baby around, and she was a well-behaved little girl. Mom was able to visit from Montana shortly after Cyndi was born.

The next August, the Director of the Community Club Awards resigned, and the manager of the radio station, Ted Layne, called me one morning.

"How would you like to be the Director of the Community Club Awards program?" he asked me.

"What would I have to do?" I asked.

"Well, if you're interested, you could come in, and we could talk about it. You have to keep track of all the receipts the clubs turn in, announce the winners and what their winnings are each week, and put out a newsletter, to name a few of the duties."

I met with him and decided that the job would be great, and since it was a paying job, it would be helpful to add to our family income. The program ran from

September to April. At the end of each segment, the station held a banquet for all the participating club members. I never will forget Ted introducing me to the group at my first banquet.

"I want you to meet Rose Rybachek, the Director. She's usually shy and quiet, but when you put a microphone in front of her, you can't shut her up!" he told the group.

A year later when we held the banquet, I had a lot of last-minute issues to take care of, so I dropped off my almost two-year old daughter Cyndi at my friend Betty's house. Cyndi loved her blanket, and always called it her "Drinkie." So, of course, it traveled with her.

I finally finished my prep work, and just had time to race home to change clothes and pick up the girls before the banquet. When I got home, I was quite surprised to find that Cyndi wasn't at home with the girls.

"Where's Cyndi?" I asked.

Sallie replied, "Isn't she with you?"

"Oh, good grief," I said. "She was, but I left her at Betty'!."

I called Betty to confess what I'd done, beg her forgiveness, and tell her that I'd pick Cyndi up and take her to the banquet with me.

"That's fine," Betty told me. "By the way, what does she want when she asks for her drinkie? I've tried water, milk, juice, and I can't think of anything else!"

Upon being told that Cyndi called her favorite blanket her Drinkie, Betty was able to give Cyndi what she wanted, and all was well.

This was the first time that Cyndi had been to a buffet, and the first thing she wanted on her plate was a whole lime. I tried to talk her out of it since I'm sure the lime was meant as decoration. She was adamant, so I let her have it, and she gnawed on the lime all evening. She wouldn't admit that it was sour and kept saying how good it tasted.

The banquet went off without a hitch, and the girls enjoyed themselves.

HAM RADIO CONVENTION

I checked into the YL System one morning, only to be greeted by V. Mayree. "Rose, some of us are wondering if you're going to come to the Convention next June. It's in Treasure Island, Florida, and you can fly into Tampa and take a shuttle. We'd really like to have you come."

"Gosh, I haven't even thought about coming," I replied. "but it does sound interesting. I'll see what I can do."

That night when Stan got home from work, I cooked steaks for dinner, which I thought was his favorite meal.

"Would it be okay if I went to the Convention next June in Florida?" I asked him.

He looked at me with a surprised look on his face, and said, "I guess it would be okay, if you can earn the money to go."

That sort of put a damper on my excitement. Since I was a stay-at-home Mom, how could I earn enough money to go to the Convention? My job with CCA had faded, they were not going to do that promotion any longer. I earned a little money doing leatherwork, but not enough to finance a trip to Florida! What to do?

The next day, I got a notice in the mail from the State Petit court system, telling me to appear for jury duty. So, off I went, and managed to get on a jury that lasted an entire week. I had a start for my trip!

A month or so later, another notice came in the mail, this time from the Federal Court System. Off I went again, and this time I was on a jury that lasted nearly a month! I was racking up the money.

I thought I'd reached the end of my rope, when another notice arrived. This time, it was for Grand Jury. I served on that for three months. After adding the money I'd made doing leatherwork to my jury earnings, I had enough money to pay the registration fees, hotel room, and airline ticket from Montana to Florida, with some left over for gas to get to Montana.

A few years before, we purchased a small, used travel trailer, and I decided I could probably drive our Ford down the highway, pulling the travel trailer, and not spend money on lodging. We could cook in the trailer, and the kids and I would have a memorable trip.

Stan wasn't all that keen on me taking off with the three kids, but then I talked to a couple of hams that lived in Big Lake, Alaska. They were going to drive down the highway about the same time I needed to go. They said I could travel with them. That made Stan feel a lot more comfortable (and me, too!). He put a ham radio in the car, and we planned to make contact every evening.

The kids and I met the hams, Sandy and Mary, in Delta Junction, and were off down the highway. It was an exciting trip, although I wanted to travel a lot faster than they wanted to go with their pickup camper. Often, I'd take off and leave them behind, and we'd meet at a camping space at night.

One afternoon, the kids and I stopped in a camp area for lunch. I made sandwiches for us all, and we sat at a nearby picnic area to enjoy our lunch. We hadn't been there long, when a couple of guys on motorcycles showed up, and sat at a table nearby.

"I need to go to the bathroom," three-year-old Cyndi said.

"Well, go ahead," I told her. "Sallie will go with you."

Soon Cyndi came back by herself, and let out a bellow. "Mom, those long-hairs stole my sandwich!" she screamed.

I took one look at the bikers, and sure enough, they had understood every word she said. They did look like long-haired hippies, and they didn't look very happy, either.

"Cyndi, you're at the wrong table," I told her. "Look, your sandwich is still at this table."

She was pacified, and finished off her sandwich in no time. I decided to hit the road as quickly as we could, since it looked to me like the bikers were still angry. Who wants to be called a long-hair, even if they were?

It was very nice to be able to keep in contact with Stan as we traveled down the road. Every evening when he got home from work, we had a schedule. One day conditions were such that we could not hear each other, but a very nice ham in California relayed for us.

We had just made contact when the ham said, "Stan wants to know how things are going."

"Just fine," I replied. Then there was a huge bang, and the car started wobbling. "Except that we just had a blowout on a trailer tire. Does he have any suggestions?" I asked, as I pulled to the side of the road and stopped.

Before we left Alaska, we had invested in new tires for the camp trailer, and Stan had convinced me that I didn't need the extra weight of a spare tire for it!

"He says maybe you can try the spare for the car?" the ham replied.

I got out, dug the spare out of the trunk, jacked up the trailer, and got the lug nuts off. I was amazed when the holes lined up, and the tire fit, although it was a bit smaller than the tire on the other side of the trailer. We slowly made our way about 10 miles down the road to the nearest filling station. They sold tires, and they had one that fit. Two-Hundred and Fifty Dollars ($250) later, we were once again on our way.

When we got nearer to Great Falls, Montana, I told our slow traveling companions that I was leaving them, and was just going to try to get to Mom and Dad's place before the Memorial Day weekend. So, off we went. However, we didn't quite make it. When we arrived at my parents' home on the 30th, they had already gone to the family picnic. So, we spent the day touring the town, playing in the playground, and were sound asleep in our trailer when they got home.

Of course, they had to wake us, and insisted that we move into the house, which we did. I was there for a few days before they took me to the airport, and I was off to Tampa. Florida, for the Convention.

I had never been to Florida before, so after we landed, I was excited to board the shuttle, and get whisked across a causeway to reach the hotel on

Treasure Island. What fun to see palm trees waving their stately fronds in the breeze. It looked just like a postcard. This was the first convention I'd attended, and I thoroughly enjoyed meeting people I'd only talked to. It was amazing to me that when I shut my eyes, I could recognize voices, but if I looked at a person when they were talking, I had no idea who they were! Anyway, it was a wonderful convention, until Hurricane Agnes paid us a visit.

I was enthralled with watching the palm trees as they bent in the wind, looking nothing like the picture they had presented when I'd arrived. The surf was wild as it bashed the beach near the first-floor windows of our hotel. Sitting on the balcony was an experience I'll never forget. When there was a lull, some of us walked on the beach and found some very interesting items that had washed ashore.

However, Agnes put an end to our Convention, since the hotel lost its electricity. As soon as the causeway was deemed safe to travel, we were loaded onto the shuttle, and hauled back to the airport. I looked like I'd taken a bath in baby oil. Who knew that the wind from a hurricane would have so much oil in it? Everything and everyone dripped oil.

I was a little embarrassed to show up at the Montana

airport, dripping oil, but I had memories that lasted a lifetime, and my family still claimed me.

A couple of weeks later, Stan flew down to take a vacation. We visited his family in North Dakota and Wisconsin, and then pulled the travel trailer back to Alaska. No flat tires on that leg of the journey. It was a delightful vacation, and Stan never again told me I could do something if I earned the money to do it!

NEW HOME

*D*ad and Mom's Quonset hut house had suffered badly in the flood of 1967, and the folks that bought it just moved away, leaving it to fend for itself. Stan and I bought it from my parents and spent quite a bit of time remodeling it to make it livable again. Then, we sold our house in 12 Mile Village and moved into the Quonset. It was located on the banks of the Piledriver Slough, and was a bit closer to Fairbanks than our home at 12 Mile Village had been.

We moved into the Quonset's, with our two dogs. We had a Labrador retriever named True Blue Jackson III, who we called "Troop". He loved to retrieve, and we also had a beagle named Red Dog.

It was fun living on the banks of the slough. We often tried to fish but were never very successful. We did enjoy seeing the ducks as they swam in the water, sometimes with their entire family.

"Where did this duck come from?" Stan asked me as he came through the door one day, packing a lifeless mallard duck. "I found this on the step and I don't think Troop can catch a duck! Look, it's been shot!"

"I heard some shooting early this morning," I replied. "I wonder if Troop retrieved it for some hunters, and instead of giving it to them, brought it home?"

Apparently, that was what had happened. It wasn't the only duck that miraculously appeared on our front step during duck hunting season. We enjoyed the fruits of his labors. Then, one day, he didn't come home. Probably a disgruntled hunter decided he'd had enough. We missed that old dog.

We had lived in the Quonset for about four years when Stan got the idea that we ought to build a house. We had purchased some property near North Pole, and that was his choice for a building site. We ordered a Capp Home, which was a complete house that came in a multitude of pieces. We had to prepare a foundation for the house, so Stan bought a small Cletrac dozer and dozed out a hole for a crawl space. We built forms for the foundation, and on the allotted day, the cement truck arrived. My brother Henry had moved to Alaska to work at the Pancake House and he volunteered to help us with the cement. We always laughed about the driver of the truck, since he kept yelling at Henry to do odds and ends, and kept calling him, "You, the boy in the blue shirt!"

The foundation turned out perfect, the forms were removed, and we had it sprayed with urethane foam before we filled in around it with dirt. We wanted to get the house weathered in so we could finish it during the winter. And, we did.

Cyndi was five years old and in kindergarten, so she, along with Suzie and Sallie, could ride the bus to school. Cyndi only went half-days, so another bus brought her home at noon. Every evening, the kids and I headed over to the new house to meet Stan.

Sometimes we'd stop at a neighborhood grocery store for something we needed. One time we stopped at the grocery store and I gave the kids each a quarter to spend. I was sitting in the car waiting for them to spend their money when Cyndi came out and asked for four cents.

"What for?" I asked. "Don't you have enough money for a candy bar?"

"I want to buy a can of mushroom soup," she replied. "The lady said I needed another four cents."

I gave her the money. After all, if she was buying soup instead of candy, she deserved it.

Stan met us at the new house every evening after he got off work. I cooked dinner, and we spent the evening working on the house. The kids usually fell asleep in sleeping bags, and we'd pick them up, put them in the car, and off we'd go back to the Piledriver Quonset. We were really tired by the time spring rolled around, and the house was finished enough that we could move in. It was a red-letter day when the kids first caught the bus in front of our new home, instead of having to walk a quarter of a mile to the bus stop! They loved it.

We celebrated our move by buying a new car. It was a 1975 Ford Gran Torino, which we had for many years.

BURIED IN SNOW

*W*hen spring rolled around, our first order of business was to erect our ham radio tower. We were just across the road from Bradley's Airstrip, so we decided we might need a FCC permit before erecting a tower. The permit was granted for a 70-foot tower, so Stan dug a hole for the base, then mixed cement in a box, and soon we had our tower up. We had many happy hours hamming with our tri-band beam. He left a pully attached to the top of the tower, so when Christmas rolled around, we were able to connect a long string of lights and pull them up to top of the tower. It was pretty spectacular.

It started snowing in September, and just continued to pile up. By January, we had between four and five-feet of snow on the ground.

Stan bought a snowblower on tracks and managed to keep our driveway and the sidewalk clear, but he was beginning to have trouble blowing the snow over the top of the enormous piles he'd made.

"I'm getting concerned about the roof." He said one morning after he'd been out blowing snow. "I know this house is very well built, but I came by a big warehouse in Fairbanks, and the roof had caved in. It wasn't a pretty sight!"

"What can you do about it?" I asked. "It would be an awful job to shovel!"

"I think we can hoist the snow blower up on the roof using that pully on the tower. I should be able to blow the snow off with it."

Stan went up the tower, and stepped over to the roof with the shovel, to make a space for the snowblower to land, and we hoisted it up. I stood by watching as he started the snowblower and it began eating into the snowbank, tossing snow in a huge arc. I was glad I wasn't involved.

It wasn't long before the snowblower had almost disappeared under the snow. The snowbank was nearly two-feet taller than the snowblower's intake. Soon, the undermined snow caved-in on top of the snowblower, and the blower sputtered and died.

Stan removed the spark plug and brought it to the kitchen, and placed it near the stove to dry out. He was soon back up on the roof and had the blower running again.

"Grab that shovel," Stan yelled at me. "You can go

ahead of me, and break the snow berm down, so I can blow it without it falling on the blower and killing the engine."

"Me?" I asked. "Surely you don't expect me to get up on that roof with you, and shovel? I think I have something to do in the house!"

Unfortunately, he wasn't joking. Soon I found myself decked out in my snow-machine suit, struggling to climb the tower. It is difficult to climb a tower when you were padded like the Michelin Man. I managed to get there without falling off. It was hard work keeping ahead of the snowblower and knocking down the berm. It took us two days of hard work before we finally had the roof cleared.

We didn't get much more snow that winter, but our house did slightly resemble an igloo. With all that additional snow from the roof, the snow berms were sloped off nearly to the roof. Our picture window was completely covered in snow. The kids thought it was great fun to climb up on the roof and jump off into the snowbank.

One day I was in the bedroom making the bed. I pulled the drapes open because even though the windows were covered with snow, some light still filtered through. I thought I saw something move out of the corner of my eye, so went to see what it was.

There were the front legs of a cow moose. She had apparently used our snow berm to climb up and was enjoying succulent branches from the birch tree that grew outside our window. I was happy that she didn't decide to climb on the roof!

We were very concerned that we'd have another gigantic flood when the snow melted that year, but the temperatures warmed up gradually, and the snow disappeared with no flooding. Fairbanks had dodged another bullet.

TV STATION BECKONS

*W*hen a full-time bookkeeping job opened up at the radio station, I was pleased to be asked by Ted Layne if I was interested. I was! This job led to doing some bill collecting and copywriting. I really didn't like the bill collecting and managed to pass that job off to another employee as quickly as I could.

I enjoyed the copywriting, but I was thrilled when I was asked if I'd like to become a full-time salesperson. Sales was fun, because we had full authority to work with our clients to develop TV commercials and get them produced. How interesting! One of my clients used a talking truck, and several of them used my kids in the commercials. After all, who else had such darling kids?

When Christmas rolled around, I was asked to be Mrs. Claus on TV with Sue and Sal as elves. They escorted the kids up to Mr. Claus, and I accompanied them back to their parents. It was a fun time.

Then the station manager called me into his office one day, and asked, "How would you like to host a TV talk show?"

"I don't know the first thing about doing something like that," I answered.

"Well, Norma Zimmer in Anchorage hosts a top-rated talk show at our Sister Station, KTVA, and I'd be willing to fly you down there to have her teach you the ropes!"

How could I turn down an offer like that? I enjoyed visiting with Norma and learning from her how to schedule guests and what else was required. The day of my debut approached, and I was quite petrified. What had I gotten myself into? I'd always been shy and bashful, and here I was going to be on TV?

Rose's Window aired live, so there were no retakes. The first time the cameraman pointed his finger at me, and said "You're on," I blanked out, and didn't recall anything until he said, "Clear!" I had to watch the tape to see what had happened! I must have had a good auto-pilot, though, since it didn't appear from the tape that I was at all scared, and the program had gone well. The second day was a repeat, but then I started to relax, and began to remember what had happened, and could begin to hone my skills as an interviewer. Some people were natural interviewees, but others reminded me of pulling teeth. I'd ask a big, long question, and they'd answer, "yes". With those folks, I was happy when our time was up.

During Viewer Comments, I was reading the comments one day, when one said, "How can you put that woman on the air? She doesn't know what she's doing, and should be taken off the air immediately."

"Sorry, this letter is for someone else," I told the viewing audience, and I didn't read it. See, I DID know what I was doing!

NOME

$\mathcal{I}$ remained active in the PTA, serving several years on the Statewide Board. Then, I was elected as Statewide President. This involved at least two trips to meetings held in either Chicago or in another part of the country. I enjoyed flying and often was able to take an extra week on my way home to visit with my parents in Montana.

One of the positions I held on the Alaska PTA Board was as Leadership Trainer. In that position, I traveled around to various parts of Alaska to conduct Leadership Workshops. The trip I made to Nome was no doubt my most memorable one. My hosts were teachers in Nome and had been there for quite a few years. They met me at the airport, and I was given a ride in their pickup.

"Let's stop at the terminus of the Iditarod Sled Dog Race," my hostess said to me." "You know, they've only been running the Iditarod for a couple of years.

This is where they finish! Do you know the story behind this race?"

"Well, I know it's supposed to commemorate a serum run or something. What is it exactly?" I asked.

"Well, back in 1925, the doctor thought there was an outbreak of tonsillitis in Nome, but kids started dying, and he discovered it was diphtheria. They located a lot of serum in Anchorage but had to figure out how to get it to Nome, before the whole town died. So, they put the serum on the train to Nenana, and many mushers battled the 50-below zero temperature and windy conditions to save Nome. They succeeded in getting it from Nenana to Nome in only seven days when it usually took 12 days for the trip by dogsled. So, that's what the race is all about."

I could just picture the modern-day dog teams racing down the snow-covered street after their 1,000-mile jaunt. Fortunately, the street was almost bare on this bright May day.

My leadership training went well, and after the training session, they held what I would have considered a potluck, although I believe they called it a potlatch. Most of the families brought food of one sort or another. I was introduced to muktuk and told that it was the traditional Inuit/Eskimo and Chukchi meal of whale skin and blubber. The sample I was given was pickled and was quite tasty. Also, my hosts baked a whole salmon and smothered it in a sauce made from ketchup and brown sugar. It was delicious.

Before I flew away the next day, my hostess told me, "I'm sorry that you didn't get to see them beach a whale. That's really something to see! School declares a holiday, and everyone is on the beach. They butcher the whale, and everyone gets their fill of muktuk. It will be smeared all over the faces of the little ones. I wish you were here to see it!"

Unfortunately, I did not get to see the celebration! I missed it by about a week.

TIME MARCHES ON

The girls were happy that they were able to catch the school bus right at the end of our short driveway. The borough was building a new junior/senior high school in North Pole, but it was not quite finished when Sue entered seventh grade, so she attended Main School in Fairbanks. This was the first and only time the girls were not in the same school until Sue graduated.

We bought them a horse for Christmas one year, and Stan built a barn. The barn was big enough for three horses, and had a room for chickens. It had a hip roof, with a hay mow. So, we got chickens and a couple of pigs. It was quite an experience hauling all our livestock to the mine for the summers. We didn't keep the pigs over the winter but butchered them in the fall. The chickens were a different matter. The horses put off so much heat in the barn that it kept the chicken's water from freezing, and we enjoyed fresh eggs all winter.

When in school, Sue was the studious type and enjoyed her role as Librarian Assistant. I fully expected her to go to college to learn how to be a librarian. That didn't happen. All during her high school years, Sue kept talking about running away from home. I kept telling her that I'd help her after she graduated, but that she really should stay in school and live at home until then. One day as graduation approached, she asked, "Mom, do I have to run away when I graduate?" I told her, no, and she did stick around for a while.

Sallie excelled at sports. She was awarded a scholarship to Boise College when she graduated. However, there was one requirement; her shoulders had been slipping in and out of joint when she was playing basketball, and they required that she have them operated on before the scholarship was valid. We talked to the doctor, and he told us that the success rate for that type of surgery was only about 50 percent. We opted not to have the surgery.

Upon Sallie's graduation, the girls drove to Anchorage and lived with their aunt and uncle for a while. It wasn't long until they were back in Fairbanks, and attended one semester at the University of Alaska. Neither of them decided to return for the second semester, and both got jobs in the Fairbanks area.

For a short time, they rented a mobile home in the

North Pole area. One day, they invited us for dinner. As we drove into the yard, we could see their barbeque in the backyard.

"Look at the flames shooting up from that grill," Stan said to me. "I hope they don't have the steaks on there yet!"

That was the first question we asked as they responded to our knock on the door.

"Sure," Sue said, "They should be ready in about 15 minutes."

"If you don't get them off there immediately, they'll be cremated!" Stan told her.

She raced to the grill and sure enough, the steaks were pretty well incinerated. The rest of the food was delicious, and they learned a valuable lesson about barbequing.

YOU HAVE THE JOB

On a bright sunny morning in February, 1983, the phone rang as I was doing dishes. I was surprised when the caller identified herself as one of the Editors of the <u>Fairbanks Daily News-Miner</u>.

"We're interested in starting an opinion column in the paper on natural resource development," she said. "Your name has been recommended to us as a possible columnist. Would you be interested?"

"Gee, I don't know! I've never thought of doing something like that. What would I have to do?"

"We'd figure out when the column would appear in the paper, and your deadline would be three days before. You could write about anything having to do with natural resource development, and since you are involved with mining, we would expect a heavy emphasis on mining. We're going to be interviewing prospective columnists next week. Would you like to come in for an interview?"

I decided that it would be quite challenging to see

what they had to say, so I agreed to the interview, and we scheduled a time. I sent the kids to school that day, and off I went. The editor and I hit it off very well, and the next day she called.

"We'd like you to submit a proposed article," she said. "It can be from 750 to 1,200 words. Then, if the article meets the Editorial Board's review, you have the job."

I had caught a ride with Stan to the TV station that morning, so on the way home, I told him all about my meeting. "She said I could write on anything I wanted, any suggestions on what I should write about."

"Well," Stan replied. "I have no idea, so do whatever you want!"

With that vote of confidence, I decided to write on how mining can help the fishing industry. I submitted my article, and in a couple of days, I received the call that I was now a columnist. I would have to develop an article every two weeks, and I could submit them in advance if I wanted. That began a four-year arrangement with the *Fairbanks Daily News-Miner*. I thoroughly enjoyed being able to express my opinions. I like to think that I was able to convey the views that many of the miners in Alaska held.

A CALL

S ometimes doing dishes can get a person in all sorts of trouble. I was innocently doing my dishes one morning in May of 1983 when the phone rang.

"Hello," I said.

"Hello, Rose," the man said. "This is Howard Grey, Executive Director of the Alaska Miners Association from Anchorage. I wanted to let you know that the Editor of *The Alaska Miner* has submitted her resignation. We've been brainstorming here at the Anchorage Branch of AMA, and we think you ought to consider being our next editor."

"Howard," I replied. "This is a surprise. I've been writing a column for the *Fairbanks Daily News-Miner* for about three months now, but I have no experience with editing. What would it entail?"

"Well, mostly you'd have to gather the material, do the dummies, and send it all to Carl, our publisher. He'll do the final layout and the printing. You'd have to write a monthly editorial, and come up with the cover. You'll have to attend the Convention, but you do that anyway. Besides, it's a paying job. What do you think?"

This sounded like another offer that would be hard to refuse. I was working for the local TV station, but I no doubt could find time for this job too.

Mining by the small miner was under severe attack, and some of us firmly believed that the only way for the small miners to survive was for them to band together. I discussed this offer with Stan, and we decided it would be a worthwhile endeavor. It was a monthly publication, and usually consisted of either 28 or 32 pages. The first edition I edited was the March 1983 issue. This was the beginning of a nearly 12-year career as editor.

Stan and I had been members of the Alaska Miners Association (AMA) for many years, but we'd also been active in several other mining-related organizations. There was the Placer Miners of Alaska, and the Miner's Advocacy Council, plus the Alaska Women in Mining. These organizations held fund-raisers, lobbied for the small miners, and were very active in the political field.

TRIP

*I*n July 1984, as I was once again doing dishes, the phone rang.

"Hello," I answered.

"Hello, Rose," the male voice said. "This is Howard Grey again. You know we are sponsoring that mining tour to the Northwest Territories and Greenland that leaves in a few days. We haven't quite sold all the seats. Since we have to pay for them anyway, I wonder if you'd like to go along, and report on it for *The Alaska Miner*?"

"When does it leave again?" I replied.

"It leaves July 8, so you have a few days to get ready."

"I'll be there."

Over 30 of us boarded the plane in Anchorage to take the tour. We had barely gotten strapped in when the pilot announced, "Ladies and Gentlemen, in preparation for take-off..."

Pulses raced, and hearts beat fast as the plane took

off, headed for Whitehorse, Yukon Territory. There, we cleared Canadian Customs and got a briefing on the impact that harsh regulations were having on the historic mining in the Yukon.

This was the journey of a lifetime for me, which I never forgot. I took lots of pictures and did a four-page write-up for the Alaska Miner. When I got back home, I couldn't quit talking about the experience.

"Stan," I said, "You wouldn't believe this trip. From Whitehorse, we flew to Pine Point, Northwest Territories, to tour the Pine Point mine. They say this mine is the largest open pit mine in North America. It was exciting. We spent the night at the Pine Point Hotel. Then, back on the plane for a short hop over to Yellowknife, also in the Northwest Territories. This was the Con gold mine. What a beautiful location on the shore of Yellowknife Bay, not far from the Great Slave Lake. This one became the first gold producing mine in the Northwest Territories when they poured the first gold bar in September 1938. We also got to tour the Prince of Wales Northern Heritage Center Museum and had dinner with government and industry representatives. It was an eye-opener."

"What do they mine at Pine Point?" Stan asked. "I don't think I've ever heard of that one. I have heard of the Con mine, and the gold they've produced."

"They mine lead and zinc," I replied. "We had a rather short night there, after all the festivities, but at 8:00 the next morning, we were all on the plane and heard the familiar words, 'Wheels up!' We were headed for Greenland."

"Our plane landed quite a distance from the terminal, and several of us were walking around, just looking at everything. We kept hearing this announcement from the building, saying, 'Get off the tarmac!' We didn't realize the 'tarmac' was the pavement we were walking on until finally, we saw a Mountie headed in our direction. Then, upon his orders, we skedaddled into the building!"

"You're lucky you didn't all get arrested!" Stan said. "I think they frown on people wandering down the runway!"

"Well, it really wasn't an active runway, we were way over by the fence, but still, they didn't seem to have much patience!"

"Anyway, we finally all got in our helicopters, there were several of them, and we took off for the three-hour ride to the Black Angel mine. The scenery was spectacular. Towering, snow-covered, very steep hills, beautiful blue water, and several ships. It was breathtaking."

"You were in the helicopter for three hours? That's a pretty long ride, I wonder how many miles it was?"

"You know, I wish I'd thought to ask, but I didn't. We ended up near a quaint little village called Marmorilik, and I know it was in west Greenland. We were on one side of a fiord, and there was a cable stretching across the fiord that ended in a hole in the side of the mountain. We figured that was the mine; it really did look like a black angel across the fiord. The next morning, we actually got to get in a car hanging from that cable and zipped across the water to the adit of the mine. Wow, was that something. We were able to put on hardhats, with those bright mining lights, and had a delightful tour. They also mine lead/zinc, with a little silver thrown in. When we got back, we were all starved and enjoyed a feast. They even had pickled herring and caviar. Everything was delicious."

"It's a wonder you didn't gain 10 pounds, from all the delicious meals you had," Stan said.

"Well, I haven't gotten on the scales lately, so I may have. Anyway, the mine folks had entertainment, and we were treated royally. We didn't get to bed very early again but were in the helicopters by 5:00 the next morning, so we were rather a bleary-eyed group that took off headed for our plane."

"We made it back to our plane (I think it was a

Convair 580) and took off for Thule, Greenland. We had to wait in Thule for about two hours for the weather to clear in Resolute Bay. Once we landed there, we were taken to the Narwhal Hotel, where we all crashed. The next morning, we were taken in three groups to the Polaris mine, which is located on Little Cornwallis Island. This Island is well within the Arctic Circle, and only about 75 miles from the Magnetic North Pole. You wouldn't believe the facilities they have there. They even had hydroponic veggies growing. The mine itself is below sea level, and in permafrost. What a feat to get the mine discovered and developed."

"What do they mine there?" Stan asked.

"It's another lead/zinc mine," I told him. "We had only one more stop to make before we headed home, so back to our airplane. It was another short night before we were once again headed out, and this time to Tuktoyuktuk on the Canadian Beaufort Sea. We learned all about the exploration and development that was happening near that port."

"Our final stop was to refuel at Inuvik, NWT. But on the way there we had some sort of mechanical problem with the airplane, so we got diverted to Reykjavik, Iceland. Can you believe it? Isn't that where you were stationed?"

"Well, there, and at Keflavik, too. I hope you took lots of pictures so I can see what has changed!"

"No pictures," I told him. "The Air Force wasn't all that happy to see us. They made us sit in our plane way out in the field for the longest time. Then, they finally took pity on us, and let us get off and go to the mess hall for lunch. Since it was 2:00 p.m. by then, we were all starving. They cautioned us not to take pictures, not to wander, and to get back to the waiting room as soon as we finished eating."

"I think we were all pretty happy when the announcement was made that we were free to go; the plane was fixed. The rest of our trip was uneventful."

"We were all tired but enthusiastic when we deplaned in Anchorage. The funniest thing happened, though. One of the tour participants was a State Senator. She spent quite a bit of her time digging up native plants in Canada to bring back to Alaska. When we landed at the airport in Anchorage, the entire plane ended up quarantined and parked way out on the runway. We had vegetation that we'd brought back into the U.S., without the proper documentation."

"After a couple of hours, most of us were allowed off the plane, and had no trouble getting through Customs, although it was a fairly long walk to get there."

I never did hear what happened to the senator and her plants. I always intended to ask her, but never found the right opportunity. I sort of figured that subject should not be broached without having a glass of wine in hand."

"It sounds like a wonderful trip," Stan told me. "I sort of wish I'd gone with you!"

LAWSUIT

I continued hosting *Rose's Window* on Channel 11 and selling advertising. One morning, Stan announced, "I think it's time for the mine to begin supporting us, we've been supporting it long enough. So, I'm going to turn in my resignation on May 15."

"Well, if you're going to quit your paying job, so am I." I replied. "You can't have all the fun." So, our resignations were submitted, and we started spending all our summers mining full-time. Our winters were spent selling gold nugget jewelry. We held jewelry parties, similar to Tupperware, only our company was called Gemalaska. While I did the selling and bookkeeping, Stan made the jewelry.

Sallie got married in January. She and her husband Ron stayed in the Fairbanks area. Four months later, Sue also got married, but she and her husband Jerry moved to Seward.

Stan was appointed to the Alaska Water Board to represent miners with water quality issues. He attended several meeting in various parts of the state. In November of 1985, we were in Anchorage to attend the Alaska Miners Association Annual Convention. I was the elected President of the Association when the newspapers carried the story, "Five Placer Miners Cited by EPA."

You guessed it! Our mine was one of the mines listed. We were not pleased since we had been working closely with agency personnel. We thought they understood the problems posed by the deep-frozen overburden at our mine, and that we were working as hard as we could to comply with their regulations. Apparently, they had not understood, or else, they just wanted to make an example of miners that were quite well known and respected in mining circles.

Since most of the miners cited were in Anchorage for the convention, we met with a mining attorney who was recommended as being one of the best attorneys in his field.

After listening to our problems, he said, "I recommend you all settle for the smallest amount of money that we can negotiate."

Several of the miners decided that it was in their best interest to settle, but Stan and I decided that we'd like to fight the lawsuit. Since we couldn't afford an attorney, we would have to do it on our own.

"I saw some books on pro-se litigation at the library," I told Stan. "Maybe we can learn how to defend ourselves."

"Sounds like a plan to me. It's too bad we don't have some sort of computer, it sure would make filing briefs and whatever we need easier," Stan told me.

"You know, I know a miner that has some sort of a small computer. He keeps turning in articles for the _Alaska Miner_," I replied. "Maybe he can give us pointers."

The miner had an Osborne computer, and he was more than happy to lend it to us so we could try it out. It worked so well; we soon bought our own. We used that for several years. We took depositions of several big guns in EPA (including the Region X Director, whom one of the attorneys told us had never been deposed before!) and put together a pretty vigorous defense.

GRANDS AND WRECKS

We were thrilled when Sallie announced in 1986 that she was expecting, and soon after, Sue made the same announcement. Sallie had a sweet baby girl in October, and Sue had a handsome baby boy in February. It was fun being grandparents.

The State of Alaska was very concerned with the plight of the placer miners, and passed legislation that offered grants to miners to develop innovative technology that would help other miners comply with the burdensome regulations. Stan and I applied for a grant to develop underground mining technology. Dr. Skudrzyk from the University of Alaska agreed to help with the monitoring, if the grant was issued, and he had a grad student that was interested in doing his thesis on underground mining. We were thrilled when we were awarded the grant. It was a five-year project.

When we were just getting set-up and beginning preliminary work on the grant, we had a major cave-in of ice at the mine. The state was gracious enough to give us a one-year extension to begin work. However, that winter we were involved in an auto accident.

As Stan told the police officer that responded, "we were driving down University Avenue, when there was this snowplow plowing out this side road. A car in front of us wanted to turn into the side road, but the snowplow was in its way. The car stopped in the right lane of the street, waiting to make the turn. I stopped quite a way behind the other car. When I looked in my rearview mirror, I could see a pickup come barreling down the road behind us, and it wasn't slowing down at all. There was traffic in the other lane, so I couldn't get over, so I told Rose to hang on. That pickup smacked into us really hard. When we were hit, the seat backs on our Plymouth collapsed, and we both ended up in the back of the car. Then we crashed into the car in front of us. There was no excuse for driving that fast on these slippery roads."

We were amazed to overhear the lady driver of the pickup telling the trooper her version of how the accident had happened. "I was just driving down the road minding my own business, when that car jumped out in front of me, and I couldn't do anything but hit it!" Regardless of her version, she was cited for driving too fast for conditions.

Our car was totaled. We both had whiplash, and

both required months of medical attention, but we finally recovered. We knew that we could not let the accident stop us from continuing with the grant. So, we spent most of the summer preparing to start our underground mining project.

Cyndi was a senior in high school that year. We didn't really want to leave her home alone while we did the underground mining, so were happy when a friend (Mike) volunteered to help at the mine, if we'd pay his expenses. He had been a sapphire miner in Montana, but he wanted to learn underground placer mining for gold. He and Stan worked at preparing the operation, while I ran errands for them.

About a week before we figured that Stan and Mike would move to the mine site to begin mining in earnest, we were involved in another accident. This time, we were just leaving a parking space after some Physical Therapy, and were headed towards the street, when a pickup backed out of its parking space, and smacked us in the side of the car. Again, our car was totaled, and we had to find another one quickly. Fortunately, we were not injured badly in that one.

That first year, I cooked many "TV dinners" and delivered them to the guys at the mine. They were able to toss them in the microwave and have hot meals. The project went well, and Mike was happy with all he'd learned. Cyndi won a full scholarship to New Mexico Tech, so she left us the next fall. With Cyndi away at school, I moved to the mine to try to take Mike's place.

I operated the drill, and Stan took care of hauling the ore to our winter stockpile. While he was hauling, I usually was busy with the Osborne computer, handling briefs and getting other papers ready to file. We made weekly trips to Fairbanks to keep up with the mail, since the mail was no longer delivered in Livengood. The courts kept me busy.

GRANDPARENTS AGIN

*S*allie again announced that she was expecting, and soon Sue followed suit. Sallie gave birth to a handsome baby boy in July, 1988, and Sue gave birth to a beautiful baby girl a few short months later, in December. Grandparenting had doubled.

With the underground mining project, our summers were our own to enjoy. Jerry and Sue purchased a pleasure boat in Seward, and we often traveled down the Parks and Seward Highways to visit and go fishing. It was great fun catching the large halibut. Once in a while, we overnighted on the boat. We loved being on the boat, seeing the beautiful scenery, and even once in a while watching as the killer whales cavorted, or the porpoise played their games.

Then, one year, Stan broached the subject of buying our own boat.

"I know a guy that has a boat for sale, I think we should buy it, and then we could go fishing even when

Jerry is working. I'm sure the van would tow it, so what do you think?"

"I'm not really excited about owning a boat. Sometimes even on Jerry's boat, I get to feeling queasy. But I suppose if you want to try it, we can."

The words were hardly out of my mouth when we were the proud owners of an 18.5-foot boat. On our trips to Seward, we usually stopped along the way to overnight. We had a gas stove that we cooked on and a very comfortable bed in the van. It was nice to lie in bed and look at the stars overhead through the skylight. The only item missing was a restroom, so we camped at various state-sponsored campgrounds. We had a couple of hair-raising experiences taking the boat to Seward. One time, the back wheel fell off the van. It went rolling across the ditch, and the van dropped with a thud. Fortunately, we had just left a restaurant and were barely moving.

"What caused that?" I asked Stan.

"I just had the tires rotated, and I guess they didn't tighten the lug-nuts. We'll have to have the van towed to the nearest town, and have it fixed. When we hit the ground, it knocked a hole in the gas tank, and our gas is leaking all over the ground!"

Fortunately, my brother was on a break from his job, so he was able to come from Anchorage to pick

Mom and me up, so we didn't have wait for the tow truck. The shop was not able to get it fixed until the following day, so Stan spent the night in the van. He was quite unhappy when he woke up to find a couple of smokers sauntering down the sidewalk, and watched in horror as one of them tossed his cigarette into the street. Fortunately, the gas that leaked out of the tank had evaporated and was no longer a danger, but he never forgot that close call.

Another time, our troubles didn't end after we had the boat in Seward. The first few trips out on the ocean were almost disastrous. There was no doubt a reason that Stan had gotten such a good deal on the boat. The engine ran well enough to get us out of the bay, and into the ocean itself. Then it quit. Coming in with the small emergency motor took a long time, and once in a while when the wind kicked up, it could get downright rough and dangerous.

There was a time something went wrong with the steering on the boat, and we turned in rapid circles through a bunch of other boats, until Stan could kill the engine. He soon had the problems fixed, and we enjoyed many hours in the boat, catching salmon, plus halibut.

"I really enjoy going out on the boat," I told Stan.

"But, when we get to rocking in the waves, I feel awfully queasy."

"I wonder if it would make a difference if you drove," Stan said. "Sometimes when your brain is occupied, it helps with motion sickness."

"I never drove a boat," I told him. "What do you have to do?'

"It's about like driving a car, except you don't want to make any really sharp turns," he replied.

So, from then on, I drove the boat. His solution worked; I was never queasy again.

HUNTING AGAIN

One fall, Stan and Jerry decided they would go deer hunting before we started the underground mining. It had been a long time since I'd eaten venison, so I was excited about it. Their plan was to fly to Montague Island. They rented a cabin from the Forest Service and were all set to go. We drove the van to Seward in preparation of the big day.

"Well, the weather is too bad for us to get off today," Jerry said on the morning they were supposed to depart. "I guess I'll just go to work and we'll try again tomorrow."

Stan and I played with the kids while Sue went to work. We had to laugh at our little grandson. In the afternoon, the sun came out. When it shone into the living room, he yelled, "Oh, no!" and raced over to the drapes and pulled them closed, leaving us in the semi-darkness. Apparently, the sun wasn't welcome at their house in Seward, although it was a ray of hope for the hunters. The next day the guys were able to load their equipment on the plane, and take off for Montague. They were to return in a week.

We looked forward to their return, but the clouds came back, and the plane wasn't able to get them on time. This went on for several days. If they didn't get home soon, they would miss Thanksgiving!

Finally, the plane was able to pick them up. We met the plane, and were shocked when first Jerry got off, and then Stan. Their faces were as black as could be. Only their eyeballs and teeth were white.

"What happened to you?" Sue asked.

"Well, we had a bit of a problem," Jerry replied.

"I can see that!" Sue stated.

"It started raining, and wouldn't quit. Our wood got very wet, and the chimney on the stove wouldn't draw like it should, so we ended up with a lot of smoke in the house. We got one deer, but we had to eat that, since the plane didn't come to get us when it should have. All in all, it was not a very fun trip."

Stan decided he wanted no part of Montague after that, so he never returned.

ACCIDENTS HAPPEN

Cyndi put her scholarship to good use, and graduated from New Mexico Tech with a degree in Mining Engineering. We had expected her to come back to Alaska after graduation, but instead, she got married. She married one of the professors at the school. Then she got her Master's Degree, and finally got her Law Degree.

We were excited when she called to tell us that she was expecting. She had a beautiful baby girl. A couple of years later, a son was born.

Mining continued to go well, we would remove the ore during the winter, then it would take only six weeks or so to sluice in the summer. We could devote the rest of the summer to gardening and fishing.

As we were gearing up for our last year required to complete the grant, we were involved in yet another auto accident. This one was a head-on collision. Mom was with us, and she suffered a severe injury; she had to have emergency surgery, and was hospitalized for over a week. I suffered a closed head injury when my head broke the windshield. Stan injured his knee and ended up having knee surgery. This was the third car we totaled in a five-year period, and none of the accidents were our fault. We felt persecuted!

We managed to continue mining to finish the grant but were lucky that the State was not all that concerned with the amount of our production that year since we were barely able to continue.

Our court date was rapidly approaching on that lawsuit, but my brain was so befuddled that I was having an awful time trying to cope with the various discovery requests and motions. We contacted several attorneys, but they would not touch our case. We were granted one extension before it came to trial, but once that disappeared, we were facing trial.

"I'm going to settle," Stan said to me one morning. "There is no way you can continue, and I can't type!"

He met with the attorney and settled the $1.5 million-dollar lawsuit for $15,000. Our 10-year battle with the EPA was finally over.

THE YLISSB

*D*uring and after the 1967 flood, I had been very active on the ham radio, especially with an organization called the Young Ladies' International Single Sideband Communication System (YLISSB). They had been very helpful in passing messages for me during the flood, and in helping me to keep schedules with hams that would call my folks and run phone patches.

After we'd gone mining full time, and the lawsuits loomed, I had mostly abandoned ham radio. Oh, sure, when Stan was at the mine, I'd still turn it on and talk to him, or if I was there, he'd turn it on and talk to me so we could keep in touch. Other than that, neither of us were active.

So, one day after the lawsuits were settled, I turned the radio on again and went to the frequency where the YLISSB met. I was greeted like an old friend, and I surely enjoyed talking to some of my friends from years gone by.

I found that there had been a lot of changes. When I had first joined, the Founder, V. Mayree, was in charge of everything. As she aged and had grown weaker, she'd turned management of the group over to a ham in Washington. This lady was not the President, she was the Chairman of the Board. The Board of Directors elected all the officers and were the only ones with the power to change the Bylaws. This led to several disgruntled members.

I was quite surprised one day when I received a call from the Chairman of the Board.

"Would you like to be a board member?" she asked me. "We have a vacancy coming up on the board."

"Let me think about it," I replied. "I'm not sure I'm cut out for board membership."

I talked to several of my friends, and one of them wisely said to me, "You cannot change it from the outside in. Only by being on the inside can you make changes!"

I gave it some serious thought, and soon called her back, and accepted. At the next convention, I was appointed. Shortly after that, the treasurer suffered some health setbacks and asked for a replacement.

I told the Chairman, "I could take on the job of treasurer, but I want to do it now, since its mid-July, and not wait until the first of the year."

"I have asked someone else if they'd take the job, but she wanted to wait until the end of the year to make her decision. Could you wait until the end of the year and I've received her answer?" Flo asked me.

"No," I told her. "If I'm going to be treasurer, I want to take on the job now during the slow time. I don't want to wait until the first of the year when all the dues become due. It's now or never."

"Okay," she replied, "You win. You can start immediately."

I received a box of index cards and some paper accounts from the treasurer. I decided we needed to get more modern, so began transferring data from the cards to a computer. I held the job of treasurer for several years. During that time, the Chairman's health kept failing. Another member of the board and I kept talking to her about changing the way the organization was constructed, by allowing the members to amend the bylaws, and vote for their officers.

"Okay," Flo told me one morning. "Go ahead and draft the bylaws the way you want them."

I did, and before long the board approved the new bylaws. At the election in 2006, I was elected president. Flo passed away soon after, and with her, went a lot of the history of the YLISSB.

I held the position of president until 2010 when

term limits didn't allow me to run again. However, I was elected again in 2012 and held the position until 2016. I thought I'd retire that time, but in 2018 I was elected again. Surely, this is my last term!

Now, back to my story. Once Stan had settled the lawsuits, we were never physically able to mine again, thus began the last chapter of our lives.

SECTION V

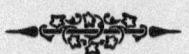

The Final Years

PERMANENT SNOW BIRDS

When I was younger, I never really believed people when they told me that the older a person got, the faster time passed. However, I'm a believer now that I've joined the Senior Generation. It seems like the final years of my life have been a blur. We were slow to recover from the effects of our automobile accidents, especially the last one. I found that the cold weather really bothered me, and there were winter days when I could hardly get out of bed.

Our jewelry making business closed since I was not up to selling, and Stan was not up to creating the jewelry.

"We have no income." Stan pointed out to me one day. "Our insurance money is soon going to vanish, and neither of us can work. Any ideas?"

"Well, we do have that 20-acre parcel of land we bought for our retirement. Maybe we can sell that. Maybe we can sell all those mammoth and wooly mammoth bones we mined… they should be worth something."

We were able to sell the land and the bones. Thus, we didn't starve, and could pay our bills.

A year or so after we sold the bones, the following article appeared:

Anchorage Daily News
Monday, November 13, 1995.

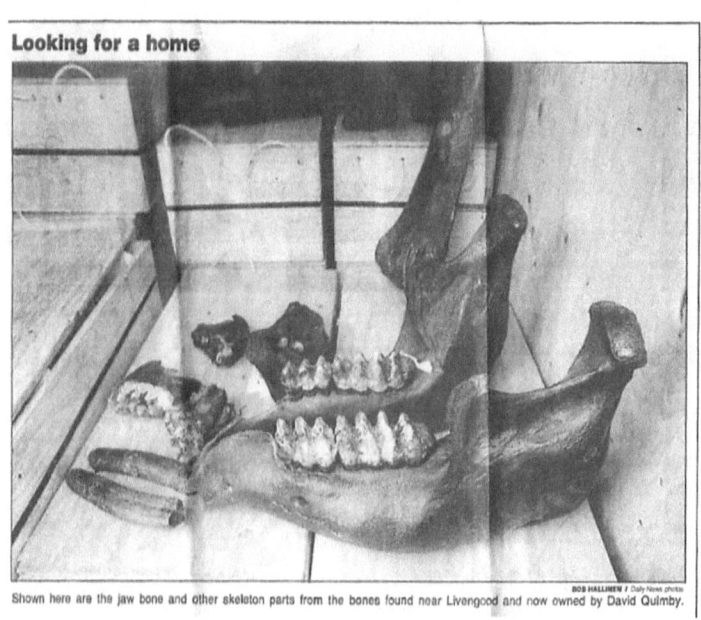

Looking for a home

Shown here are the jaw bone and other skeleton parts from the bones found near Livengood and now owned by David Quimby.

Mastodon's skeleton goes on the block
By NATALIE PHILLIPS
Daily News reporter

Growing up in the 1960s in Fairbanks, Sallie Stuvek remembers summers spent at the family mining claims and stumbling across old bones and fossils, but thinking nothing of it. The basement of the family home was full of bones.

"We tripped over them all the time," said Stuvek, now 34. "I have kids now, and my kids' fish. All the pictures of them are with fish. All the pictures of me as a kid are standing next to mastodon tusks."

Stuvek's parents... Stan and Rose Rybachek... were placer miners. One of their claims was off the Elliott Highway, just south of Livengood. In the early 1960s, that claim produced what is now being called the most complete mastodon skeleton ever found in Alaska.

Roland Gangloff, curator of the museum at the University of Alaska Fairbanks, said the American Museum of Natural History collected a lot of bones from the state from the 1930s to the 1950s, but it is not clear just what exactly the New York City-based museum has.

There are only bits and pieces of mastodons in collection around this state, Gangloff said.

"As far as we know, nothing as complete (as the Livengood bones) has been found."

"Considering it's the state fossil," he added, it would be nice to have a complete one in the state."

About two years ago, David Quimby of Anchorage bought the bones from the Rybacheks. He isn't saying how much he paid. But he preserved them with mineral oil, had them carbon-dated, and had them appraised at $425,000, and has been trying to sell them ever since. He even hauled them to the famous Tucson, Ariz., Gem, and Mineral Show in 1994 and put a $225,000 price tag on them, but got no takers.

"If you have bones to sell, that's the place to go," said Jeffrey Saunders, a curator at the Illinois State Museum.

Quimby almost lost the bones last week when he fell behind on $109-a-month payment at the storage unit where he had them stashed. He paid up and is now negotiating to sell the bones to the Southcentral Museum of Natural History in Eagle River.

Mastodons roamed the earth up to 10,000 years ago. They were browsers, not grazers, which means they preferred eating bark, berries and leaves from shrubs. They could be found across the northern United States, specifically in the Great Lakes area, and they were last found in the northeastern states, Saunders said. They like to live on the edge of forests, as opposed to grasslands that the mammoths liked.

While mastodon tusks and a molar now and then are common finds, the Livengood mastodon is 80 percent complete. What's missing is the skull and some leg bones. Most important, the complete spine was found, which helps define the size of the animal. Carbon dating suggests the Livengood mastodon is at least 20,000 years old, but other tests suggest the bones might be as old as 107,000 years.

Quimby is anxious to sell the bones because he is broke and ill. He said his preference is to see them stay in the state, so he will sell them for $175,000 unless the buyer is willing *to donate them to an in-state museum. Then the price is $125,000.*

The museum at the University of Alaska Fairbanks would like to have the bones for research and to exhibit in a new museum it is building. But the university museum does not have the money for such an acquisition.

"It's very discouraging when you figure how many millionaires have made money in this state," Gangloff said. "The big oil companies are big supporters of the arts and performing arts, but there is a strange attitude toward science."

The board of directors at the newly formed Eagle River museum would also like to have the bones. They have set up a fund at the National Bank of Alaska in Eagle River and are launching a campaign to raise the money through donations, according to Greg Hall, president of the museum's board of directors.

Mastodon

The mastodon, a browsing mammal somewhat smaller than the present-day elephant, became extinct only in the last 10,000 years.

■ **RANGE:** The mastodon belonged to a line of proboscideans, or trunk bearers, that expanded its range from the Old World, where it originated, to the New World some 15 million years ago. However, by 2 million years ago only the American mastodon survived on this continent. Mastodon remains have been found from Florida to Alaska. Frozen carcasses have been recovered here.

■ **HABITAT:** Mastodon inhabited dense, spruce-dominated forests where they browsed on course vegetation such as spruce cones, twigs, leaves and mosses.

■ **SIZE:** Up to 10 feet tall at the shoulder, with a shaggy brown coat and upward-curving tusks.

Livengood

Site where mastodon bones were found

Minto

Manley Hot Springs

Tolovana River

Wilber Creek

Chatanika

Chatanika River

Chatanika

Tanana River

Trans-Alaska Pipeline

Fox

N

0 5 10
Scale in miles

Fairbanks

North Pole

Tanana River

Nenana

Sources: Academic American Encyclopedia;
Sidney Homenstien, American Museum Department of Invertebrates

RON ENGSTROM / Anchorage Daily News

455

The sale of the bones spawned a strange story a few years later. As the article said, we sold them to a man in Anchorage who told us that his plan was to sell them to a buyer in the Far East. A couple of years later, we ran into him, and asked about the bones. He told us that shortly after he'd bought the bones, the yen tanked and his buyer backed out. So, he was stuck paying storage on the bones in Anchorage, where he'd taken them.

The man suddenly died, and of course, quit paying storage. When the storage unit owners opened the storage unit, they thought some sort of large-scale murder had occurred and called the police. The story soon came out, the bones were finally cleared, and the bones were shipped back to Fairbanks, where they have since been donated to the University of Alaska Museum.

MOVING ON

Stan launched a claim in the early '80s with the VA, regarding a service-connected injury that he suffered back in the 1950s. This was a long, drawn-out ordeal, but finally, in the mid-1990s, he was awarded 100 percent disability, and a monthly check started to arrive. It was a life-saver.

I was diagnosed with post-traumatic fibromyalgia after our last accident, and one of the symptoms was sensitivity to cold. So, we decided we would take a winter trip outside, and see if the warmer weather was helpful. We flew into Houston, rented a car, and drove through the Carolinas. We visited my grandpa's old stomping grounds in Blue Ridge, Georgia (meeting some folks that knew him), and spent Thanksgiving in Boone, North Carolina. It was amazing how much better I felt being out of the snow and cold. I hated to get back on the plane to return to Fairbanks, but we did. I spent most of the remainder of that winter in bed.

"This has been a miserable winter," I told Stan one morning. "Is there any way we can just travel all winter? Or go somewhere where it's warm, and rent a place to live?"

"I think that is doable," he replied. "Let's see if we can get a house-sitter who will pay the utilities, and that should solve that problem."

We found someone that was willing to pay the bills in lieu of rent, and got the van ready to travel.

"Where are you going when you go outside this winter?" a friend asked us.

"We really don't know. We were hoping that we'd find a place that really grabbed us when we were out last fall, but we didn't really find one."

"If you don't know where you're going, why don't you try South Texas?" he asked. "We really enjoyed it last year when we spent a couple of months there, and the cost of living is rock-bottom."

The "rock bottom" was what caught our ear. So, we headed for Texas, after making stops to visit with Mom and Henry in Montana, and Cyndi in New Mexico. We arrived in Harlingen and found an apartment to rent. We enjoyed our winter, and our health improved. We lived in a nice residential neighborhood, and it was fun to take our Yorkie, Rambo, for a walk to a nearby park, where we could turn him loose when no one was using the park. He loved to run.

"Let's walk to the grocery store," Stan said to me one morning. "We can leave Rambo home, so we can cart home the groceries. It isn't all that far, and I'm sure the exercise would do us good."

So, we set off without Rambo, and it was a good hike. On the way, we ran into some friendly folks that we visited with.

"Where are you living?" they asked us. "Well, we have a little apartment above a garage in an alley just a few blocks from here. Where do you live?" I replied.

"We're staying at an RV park, called The Farm," the lady told us. "It's located on Solis Road outside of La Feria. If you like to play Bingo, we play every Friday night, starting at seven-o'clock. You're welcome to come if you'd like."

We checked our map and found where the road was. Friday saw us at the Bingo hall. We met some charming people there, so we decided that the following year, we would try to find a place to rent closer to The Farm. Our wish was soon granted. As luck would have it, The Farm had a cottage they rented, and their long-term renters were not returning the next year, so we snatched it.

The next year, we moved into the cottage. It was a two-bedroom cottage with a family of possums living under it. Rambo had quite a time with the possums. I'm convinced he was not brave enough to discuss life with them face-to-face; he needed the floor as a buffer.

He also made us laugh when he discovered a full-length mirror in back of the rocking chair. He leaped to the top of the rocking chair, and barked at the dog in the mirror. Rambo got so excited! He fell to the seat of the chair, and then had to climb back to the chair-top to continue harassing the dog in the mirror. He never tired of this game.

"We want to return to the cottage next fall," Stan told the owner. "We know you rent it for only the winter. Do you want a deposit?"

"No," the owner replied. "You've been good tenants, and have kept things in good repair. The cottage will be waiting for you when you arrive next fall."

We did have one sad experience while living there. We took Rambo for a walk way out in a field and turned him loose so he could run. For some reason, he decided he'd run towards the highway and try to catch some of the speeding cars. He refused to pay attention to any of our shouts, and we watched in horror as he caught a car. He didn't stand a chance. We buried him on the property.

A week or so later, we drove to Houston to visit some of Stan's relatives, and while there, we saw an ad for Yorkies. We went to check them out, and when we returned to Harlingen, we had a six-week-old Yorkie, named Mr. Buddy.

RV LIVING

$\mathcal{W}$e were quite surprised when we arrived at The Farm the following fall to find that someone was living in the cottage! Stan immediately set off to find the owner!

"I'm really sorry," he said, "But this couple wanted to rent the cottage year-around, and I couldn't pass up the extra income. I'm sure you can find another place nearby."

We were suddenly homeless! We called Annie, a friend of ours that we had met at The Farm.

"Annie," I said, "Can you guess what happened? He rented the cottage! We're living in the van for a while, but it appears that we won't be at The Farm this year. Are you coming down?

"No," Annie replied. "We can't get away this winter, but I can bring our fifth-wheel down, and you and Stan can stay in that at The Farm."

"Oh, no, Annie," I told her. "We'll just find a place to rent, but it's very nice of you to offer."

"Don't you even look for a place." She told me. "We will be down in two days. You just find a place to park it."

"Knowing Annie," I told Stan. "We better find a spot to park it, she will be down." So, we did.

True to her word, she and Joe arrived with the fifth-wheel. We enjoyed living at The Farm, but I really was not fond of living in the fifth-wheel. That spring, we started looking for a permanent place to live. We found a vacant lot in the South Texas Haven Subdivision in La Feria, bought a mobile home, and had it set-up. We got the utilities hooked-up and had a couple of weeks in our new house before we were scheduled to head back to Alaska. Our friends, Annie and Joe, came to The Farm and stayed in their fifth-wheel, once we moved out. We had some wonderful visits during those two weeks.

We had scheduled our utilities to be shut off on the day we planned to leave. Annie and Joe returned home with their fifth-wheel, and we decided to go out to eat. We stopped at a restaurant in Walmart and apparently got some tainted mayonnaise on our sandwiches. We both came down with a severe case of food poisoning.

I tried to call the electric company to keep the electricity on, but our phone had already been disconnected. The water was scheduled to be shut-off in a few hours. So, I drove myself across the street to a bank of pay phones and called both the water and electric companies. Of course, I was put on hold and thought I was going to die before I finally managed to talk to a person, and keep the utilities on. I was never so happy to fall into bed as I was when I got home.

We recovered in a few days and continued our trip home.

During the following winter months, while we were in Texas, Stan worked hard at improving our place in La Feria. He added a garage that contained a second bathroom. He had a well dug and planted carpet-grass. He also planted a couple of grapefruit and orange trees, plus a lemon, a lime, and a pecan tree. He had bougainvillea growing in our front yard and planted a couple of sago palms. These are small tree-like plants that look like a miniature palm tree. And of course, we put up an amateur radio tower and antenna. Our winter home was fantastic. I began recovering from my fibromyalgia.

We saw a specialist in California on our way home one spring, and he prescribed some medication. This was somewhat effective, but I still had quite a few of the symptoms. I read about the beneficial effects of chelation on clogged arteries, so the next year both

Stan and I started taking chelation treatments. Soon, my symptoms of fibromyalgia disappeared, and I was able to stop the medication. We continued the chelation for many years. I would still be doing it if I could find a local doctor that gave it.

WINTERS IN TEXAS

*C*an you tell that we very much enjoyed our winters in Texas? We often made trips across the Mexican border to just enjoy being there and listen to the mariachis. The food was delicious, and of course, there were the numerous dentists and pharmacies that charged very reasonable rates. On one of our trips across, Henry and Mom went with us. They were preparing to go back to Montana. Mom had recently been diagnosed with myasthenia gravis, and her medication was quite expensive. So, we decided to see if the pharmacies had it in stock across the border.

They did, and the price was about one-third of what she was paying, so we stocked up with a year's worth of meds for her. Stan was worried since we'd read somewhere that we could only bring a month's supply of medicines back across the border. Maybe his concern was what led him to get himself a case of Corona beer, and a fifth of Jim Beam. We stowed all our purchases in the trunk of the car, and as we waited in line to cross back into the United States, Stan, our driver, became more and more nervous.

"I don't know why you bought so much medication," he said, in a quivery voice. "We'll probably all end up in jail."

As we neared the Customs, he started to sweat. When the Customs agent asked if we had anything to declare, he blurted out, "The booze and drugs are in the trunk!"

The agent looked a little surprised but asked him to open the trunk, which he did.

"Okay, you are good to go." The agent told him.

With a stunned look on his face, Stan put the car in gear, and drove us home. However, he never forgave us for "almost" getting us all jailed!

We also enjoyed our time on the American side of the border. When Christmas time neared, there was the living Nativity Scene to drive through. People were dressed in costumes, and they had real live animals. This was wonderful, although we had trouble trying to shut the lights off on our car. They were automatic, and apparently, those lights took that seriously. We hated to shine lights in the faces of the performers, but... what to do?

There was the Festival of Lights in Hidalgo, with over three million lights, and hundreds of lighted displays. Riding the trolley around the city was a favorite, and even better when we got the horse-drawn carriage. Plus, there was the lighted boat parade near South Padre Island. People decorated their boats with the most fantastic light displays and motored down the waterway.

We often made trips throughout the winter to South Padre Island. It was fun to picnic on the beach, watch the fishermen, and enjoy being by the ocean.

"Watch this!" Stan would holler, as he grabbed a piece of bread and stood like a statue, while the seagulls swooped down to take the bread from his hand. We went to see the Kite Festival, with kites from across the country flying. It was amazing to watch.

We went out on several fishing charters and filled our freezer with red snapper, triggerfish, and other delicacies. We made numerous trips to the Island just to sample the seafood. There is nothing like a fresh grouper to make your palate water.

Climbing the lighthouse and reading about its history was another highlight. Grabbing dinner at Louie's Back Yard restaurant or Pirate's Landing were favorites.

In the meantime, Mr. Buddy was such a sweet Yorkie, that I brought him to Companions to see if he could qualify as a therapy dog. He passed with flying colors, so he and I made weekly trips to visit with shut-ins.

I did this in Alaska and thought it would be nice to do in Texas, so I asked one of the nursing homes if it would be okay. They were a little hesitant to let us but finally agreed. The first day we went, I noticed that the manager was hovering in the hallways and keeping a close eye on our progress. We found one lady in a wheelchair and visited with her. She was captivated by Mr. Buddy and wanted to pet him. She smiled and smiled, and had a great time.

When we were leaving, I stopped by the office and asked the manager how things had gone.

"That is the first time that lady has smiled since she's been here," he replied. "You can come anytime you feel like it!"

After that, we made weekly visits to the Home. These trips really tired Mr. Buddy out, he'd sleep for hours after we got home.

TEXAS IS FUN!

I had never played Bingo until we had made that trip to The Farm. I soon became an addict. I would go at least once a week back to The Farm to try to make my fortune. Bingo cards cost fifty cents apiece, and the pots were split among the winners. One year, I cleared $83.00, but I didn't report that to Uncle Sam. Please don't tell him.

Annie and Joe sold their farm and bought a place just a couple of miles from where we lived. We had some fun-filled times, playing Skip-Bo with them, eating, and traveling around the area.

"Annie," I told her one morning when she answered the phone. "Want to go fishing with us? We're planning on going to South Padre Island, and I bet I can catch a bigger fish than you can!"

Actually, Annie was quite a good fisherman, and I was just joking. Which was a good thing, because she caught two fish for each one I caught. Good thing we hadn't bet much!

We had our radio and were active with that. Stan could spend hours outside with his garden. He dug around the citrus trees and planted several veggies. The aloe vera would grow to be three feet tall! His vegetables proliferated.

We also enjoyed the flea markets and the farmers' markets. We attended several plays and shows.

Annie called me one morning and asked if I'd like to go to the Island to see a show with the Lipizzaner Stallions performing.

"Are you sure they're on the Island? I haven't heard anything about it," I told her.

"I read all about it in the paper." She replied. "They have a show tomorrow night, and I'll drive!"

We couldn't pass up an offer like that, so we enjoyed seeing the horses. They were wonderful.

The next week, I saw in the paper where the Harlem Globetrotters were going to be at the State Farm Arena near Hidalgo, Texas. So, I grabbed the phone and called Annie.

"Want to go see the Globetrotters?" I asked.

"What are the Globetrotters?" she replied.

"They are only the best basketball team in the whole world," I told her. "They are going to be playing at that big Arena near Hidalgo tomorrow. I'll drive if you want, and we can go out to dinner in McAllen on our way."

My Dad had seen the Globetrotters when I was a little girl, and he raved about them. After watching them, I could understand his fascination. Wow, they were excellent!

TURKEYS?

"Want to go to Port Mansfield?" Stan asked me one morning while we had our coffee.

"What's Port Mansfield?" I asked.

"Well, I was talking to Joe the other day," he replied, "and he told me about this place called Port Mansfield. It isn't that far from Harlingen, only about 50 miles or so. They have fishing charters, but you don't have to go fishing. Apparently, a lot of the residents put out corn every day, and there are a lot of wild turkeys that come into town in the evening to scarf up that free corn, and also a bunch of deer. He said you could just drive around and see them. There's a BBQ place where you can get a good meal."

"That sounds like fun," I replied. "Why don't I see if Annie and Joe want to go with us?"

They did, and we were soon on the road. As we were driving down a little country road, we saw a car stopped alongside the road, and people were out staring off towards a small lake.

"Why don't you stop and let's see what they're looking at," I told Stan.

He did, and we got out to see what was so exciting. There, across the small lake, was a herd of nilgai. I had never seen one of them alive before, just pictures. We tried to take pictures, but they disappeared into the brush before we could get the camera out.

We continued on towards the town and soon found a delightful small restaurant. True to its billing, it had a barbeque, and the barbequed brisket was delicious. After we stuffed ourselves, we got back in the car to tour the town.

"Look there," I hollered. "There's a whole flock of turkeys. Good grief, they look just like tame turkeys, and look at them gobbling their corn!"

We watched the turkeys for a while, and then drove towards the ocean. What a lovely view of the dock stretching out into the ocean, and the waves rolling in. And there, along the road, was an open field with about six deer grazing. When we stopped the car, they soon spotted us and came trotting over.

"Do we have anything they can eat?" I asked.

"I brought a bag of corn," Annie replied. "Roll down the window, and see if they'll come up and eat the corn from your hand."

I soon had a small buck eating out of my hand. The

car was surrounded, and we were each busy sharing corn with the deer.

"We better get ready to leave," Annie said. "I only have a few kernels of corn left, and we don't want them to get mad at us for running out!"

Stan put the car in gear, and we made our way out of the herd.

The next time we went to Port Mansfield, we were sure to pack a larger supply of corn!

In the meantime, back in Alaska, we had a succession of house-sitters to keep our place in North Pole from freezing. Most of them were excellent, but we did have trouble with one, whose teenage son moved in with him and had sticky fingers. Fortunately, he didn't take anything too valuable. We had to look for a different house-sitter the following fall.

GENEALOGY

$\mathcal{J}$t is always exciting to track down one's ancestors. The first and last time I ever remember seeing Grandpa Bloom, he had brought Dad a copy of his Family Tree that dated back to the Revolutionary War and beyond. I had always been interested in it but never pursued it further, until the winter of 2001.

"Stan," I said. "How would you like to make a trip back to Pennsylvania this winter? I know that my ancestors came from there, and it would be thrilling to see what we can find. Besides, our friends Rosanna and Whitey live there now, and we could visit."

"Oh, I really want to paint the trim on the house this winter," he replied. "It really needs painting, and I'm not all that excited about a trip to Pennsylvania. It's a long way!"

"Not nearly as long as the trip down here, and we can take the car, instead of traveling in the van. We'd have to stay in motels, but that would be nice, too.

Just think, we don't have to make the beds that way, or sweep the floors."

"I don't have to do that anyway," he responded. "But let me think about it."

He did think about it and decided that it might be fun. Shortly after the Christmas holiday in January 2002, we set out for Pennsylvania. We had a delightful trip and enjoyed the drive. Visiting with our friends Rosanna and Whitey was a pleasure, and meeting some cousins that I'd never seen before was exciting. We spent days exploring old cemeteries, going through dusty records in the courthouses, and following leads we found in historical societies. It took us about six weeks before we had exhausted ourselves and the trails we were following. In one old cemetery, the entire hill was covered with graves of Blooms. I knew that some of them had been related to me and probably most of them, but they didn't appear in the literature.

On our way home, we visited with a ham friend in Parkersburg, WV.

"Rose," she said to me. "Why are you limping like that?"

"My knees are getting worse, and are very painful," I replied.

"Have you ever considered wearing Birkenstock sandals?" she asked. "They tip your foot differently from the way you usually walk, and sometimes they really can relieve knee pain."

I went with her to the store and bought a pair. Within a few days, my limp was gone.

Once we got home from our trip, Stan immediately got out his paint brushes and painted the trim, so he was happy, too.

The next few years saw me writing our genealogical books. I was able to reproduce the documents we'd copied from the records, plus insert many photographs that we'd come across or taken. I did one book for Dad's family, the Blooms. I did one for Mom's side of the family, the Lilley's. While I was about it, I did one for both sides of Stan's family. That kept me busy for some time, and the resulting books were full of information. I was happy!

GOODBYE ALASKA

We commuted between Alaska and Texas for several years, driving the van, and mostly enjoying the trip. Since we had the van, we could stop where we wanted. Of course, there was the spring when we decided to take the Cassiar Highway instead of going our usual way through Dawson Creek. Many of the service stations were closed for the winter, the snow was higher than our van in places, and we really couldn't see much of the beautiful scenery. Besides, it got cold.

When we finally reached the Alaska Highway, it was 40 degrees below zero, our van was nearly out of gas, and it was dark.

"We better go back into Watson Lake and get gas," Stan told me. "We're almost driving on fumes, and it's dark and cold. I really thought that service station at the junction would be open, but no luck."

"I agree, and maybe we can find a motel that's open," I suggested. "I really don't want to try to keep warm in the van with these temperatures."

We hadn't gone far when I heard a strange noise. "What's that?" I asked. "Do you hear that noise?"

"I'm afraid it's a flat tire," Stan replied. "Do you know where the jack is? We better get that tire changed before we freeze to death, we can't keep the engine running or we'll for sure run out of gas."

"Oh, the jack," I replied. "I know it's in one of the storage places under the bed, but I'm not sure which one."

We were sitting there, trying to figure out a game plan, when a truck pulled in behind us. Stan got out to go talk with the driver.

He came back, all smiles, "He says he has a jack and can change the tire for us. He has gloves and everything. I know I have gloves, too, but I'm not sure where they are. I'd hate to freeze my fingers."

Soon the tire was changed, the van started, and the good Samaritan followed us into Watson Lake to make sure we didn't run out of gas. He refused payment of any kind.

We were able to get a motel room, and it was warm inside. We plugged the head bolt heater on the van into the electricity and it started right up the next morning. Besides, it was warmer when we got up, only 20-below. We were relieved to be on the road once again.

We had one more near disaster that happened on our trip on the Alaska Highway. We were just starting to cross the Teslin River Bridge when we heard a loud bang.

"What was that?" I asked.

"I'm afraid to check," Stan replied. "I have no power anymore. Something serious happened."

We managed to slowly roll across the bridge and into the parking lot of a lodge, Unfortunately, the lodge was closed for the season!

A car stopped, and the driver asked what our trouble was. As it turned out, our driveline had come off and was lying on the road behind us.

"I think there's an outside payphone down at the lodge," the driver told us. "If you want, I can give you a lift there, and maybe you can arrange for a tow."

The payphone worked, wonder of wonders, and several hours later, the wrecker appeared to take us into Whitehorse. It was a little over a hundred miles. Since it was dark and late when we arrived, and the service place was closed, the wrecker driver dropped the van near the service station. Fortunately, right across the street was a hotel that had a vacancy, and they allowed dogs to stay. The next day, the people reattached our driveline, and we were on our way.

MOVE? US?

One year on our way home to Alaska, we went to visit my aunt and uncle in Coeur d'Alene, Idaho.

I was pretty surprised when Stan said the next morning, "How would you like to move? We could look for a place we like while we're here, and then later we could sell the house in North Pole, and move here. We'd be a lot closer to your Mom since she's only about 350 miles from here!"

"Move? From our house?" I asked. "Now? I thought that was something we were thinking about when we got older."

"Well, my dear," he replied. "I don't know if you've looked in the mirror lately, but we are older. I think it's time."

We had always said that we wanted to move back to the Spokane area of Washington when we got older, since that was where we'd met, and we wanted to return to our "roots." My uncle Chet took us around to various lots that were advertised for sale. We found one that we really liked near Newman Lake, Washington, which was about halfway between Coeur d'Alene, and Spokane. The subdivision had just come on the market, and we got the pick of the lots. So, we bought a lot and contracted with a company to build us a large garage on the property.

When we arrived at our North Pole home later that year, we began sorting and tossing things, getting ready to sell the house. We'd been living in it nearly 35 years. For a change, we were holding garage sales instead of just attending them! We finally got the house on the market in 2004, listing it with a real estate agent. We were disappointed when she hardly showed the house all summer.

That fall, when we headed for Texas, we left her in charge of the sale. Nothing happened over the winter, and when we came back in the spring, she told us that her husband was interested in buying the house, but at a reduced rate. We immediately got a different real estate agent, and the place sold in six weeks, and for more money than listed. We had three people bidding on it! We learned a valuable lesson. Never deal with a real estate agent whose husband buys homes, does a little cosmetic work on them, and doubles his money!

Once the house sold, we made arrangements with

a trucking company for a back-haul and loaded our belongings in a 52-foot van. We had lots of room in the moving van for everything we hadn't sold. We flew to Spokane, and my uncle picked us up at the airport. We stopped on our way to his house to arrange with some day-laborers to unload the van, thinking we had several days before the moving van would arrive. Wrong! The moving van almost beat us there, coming the next day. That driver made the trip from Fairbanks to Newman Lake in three days! We barely had time to get set-up for the unloading. We were thrilled when everything fit in the garage.

One of our pastimes in Alaska had been making homemade wine from wild berries, rhubarb, and fruit juices. We had shipped over 1,000 bottles of wine to store in our garage. We double wrapped the wine, hoping that it would not freeze in the garage over the winter.

Before we left for Texas, we found a contractor that we hired to build our house the next summer. We were excited.

HELLO WASHINGTON

*A*unt Edna passed away during the winter and Uncle Chet passed away in January. He didn't ask permission or anything! We had planned to stay with him while our house was being built and I had looked forward to many visits with him. His will left almost everything to charity. The executor was kind enough to let us know when she was auctioning off his household goods, and we made it to the auction. I was thrilled when I bid the highest on one of his old radios. This radio was one that I recalled listening to when I was a youngster in Montana. Another thing to pack in the garage.

We found a delightful rental cabin near Coeur d'Alene and lived in that while our house was being constructed just across the border in Washington.

We told the contractor, "We need a wine cellar. Can you make one?"

"I suppose I can, but it would be almost the same

cost to make a full basement, so why not consider that?" He told us.

"Wow, a full basement. I like that idea," I told the contractor. "We can finish it later, but be sure and plumb-in for a bathroom, and if we continue making wine, we'd need a sink in another part of the basement."

"Okay, we can do that!" he told us.

The contractor worked on our house most of the summer. He encountered a field of large rocks that had to be removed, but there was a drainage ditch that he could haul them to, and later we'd haul in dirt to cover them.

We were somewhat shocked to find that while they were working on the kitchen and bedrooms, a pigeon built a nest in the rafters of our living room and was busily sitting on her eggs. It was exciting when the chicks hatched, although having pigeon crap in our house wasn't exactly what we wanted!

One day, our contractor said, "I really need to have that pigeon gone. We need to begin working on the living room, and with her there, the men can't finish the drywall."

"Okay," Stan replied. "I'll move the nest to that tree near the garage. Hopefully, the babies are big enough now that they'll make it."

Stan borrowed a tall ladder, carefully removed the pigeon nest, and put it in a nearby bush. We were happy to see that the pigeon found her nest and continued to care for her chicks.

We moved into the house in August. Things were not quite put away when it was time to head south to Texas, but the place was secure. We enjoyed our winter in Texas. The next summer, we hired another contractor to finish the basement, so when he finished, we had a total of three bedrooms upstairs, plus two downstairs... with a bathroom, storage room, wine cellar, and a living room/kitchen complex in the basement. That year, a young family moved into our basement for the winter while they were building their house down the street. That worked out nicely for us.

We spent the next few years developing the five-acre lot, having a chain link fence put around the whole backyard, hauling in topsoil for a garden, hauling in lots of topsoil to cover our stash of large rocks, and planting grass and fruit trees. We put in an underground sprinkler system, and soon the lawn needed to be mowed. It took nearly two hours to mow with a riding lawn mower, but it was a delightful place to live.

We continued to spend our winters in South Texas and were blessed when Sue and Jerry bought a mobile home just three houses down the street from ours. This really made Texas a wonderful winter vacation. Jerry loved to golf and spent mornings on the golf courses. We played cards, took in plays, visited on South Padre Island, and generally enjoyed life in the subtropics.

Our fruit trees produced well, Stan had a small garden, and Sue also planted a garden. We enjoyed going to flea markets, and the produce stands were exceptional. Life in Texas was exciting, but it was always nice to get back to our home in Washington each spring.

We were saddened in January of 2011 when my sister Elizabeth (Betty) passed away in Montana. I was able to fly to Billings to attend her services. She had developed melanoma, and had not suffered long. I stayed in Montana for a week or so before flying back to Texas. Going to Montana was never quite the same after that.

KNEE SURGERY

*A*s we worked on the property in Washington, my knees began to give me more and more problems. I guess the Birkenstocks could only delay the inevitable, not prevent it. So that winter in Texas, I had one knee replaced one week, and the other knee replaced the following week. The surgery went well, and I was happy when Cyndi, Mariam and Kavon came to spend Christmas Vacation with us. Stan was in the beginning stages of Alzheimer's, so he was needing supervision himself. He, Cyndi and the kids tried to make a trip across the border, with Stan giving directions. Instead of turning right, he had her turn left, and soon she was headed for Brownsville! She pulled over alongside of the road, called me, and we figured out the error.

Cyndi had to go back to New Mexico, but Sue and Jerry returned, so I was in good hands. I was pleased when my recovery was over, and both knees were working well. However, I still continued to wear the Birkenstocks. They are very comfortable!

I was back to almost normal by the time we returned to Washington. We had a completely empty basement but needed some furnishings, so we started haunting estate sales. We managed to completely furnish the basement, including pictures for the walls.

"I'd really like to get a boat," Stan told me. "We had a lot of fun with the one in Alaska, and there are a lot of lakes around here."

"A boat?" I replied. "Well, you're right, we did have fun. I don't see why not. Besides, we brought the kicker down from the boat in Alaska."

A few days later as we were out looking for estate sales, he spotted a boat parked along the street with a "For Sale" sign on it. He stopped just to "check it out," and it wasn't long before the boat was being towed home.

Stan parked the boat in the large garage and installed the motor. It was fun the first time we took it out for a cruise. We even managed to catch a few fish, and they were tasty. It was difficult for either of us to back the boat into the lakes. However, we managed to launch it several times, and every time we enjoyed being on the lakes.

Life continued to be pleasant, with our house in

Washington, and our home in Texas. We had many visits at each place from my brother Henry, and Mom. It was always a pleasure when they came. Henry had moved back with Mom in her house in Montana and was staying there. He is an excellent chef, and we enjoyed his cooking every chance we got.

On one of their visits to Texas, Mom somehow got tangled up with the car and broke her hip. She recovered quite rapidly from it but used a walker to get around most of the time after that.

Stan had worked around teletype machines when he was younger, and heavy equipment when he was older. So, it was no wonder his hearing suffered. He ended up getting hearing aids. One morning in Texas, he was at the sink cleaning his hearing aid, when he dropped it down the garbage disposal. I was shocked when I saw him quickly reach up and turn on the garbage disposal!

"What did you do that for?" I asked.

"That is just what I didn't want to do!" he replied.

He did like his new hearing aids, though.

DREADFUL 2014

The year 2014 was a tough one for us. In early January, Sue was diagnosed with breast cancer. She opted to spend the summer in Texas and get treatment at M.D. Anderson in Houston. We decided we'd keep Sue and Jerry company in Texas.

Mom had become very hard of hearing once she reached her 90's, and her eyesight was failing terribly. So, I started calling her every morning and reading to her from the Bible. We both enjoyed our early morning chats. One morning in late March, I called her as usual. She was in the nursing home wing of their local hospital at the time, having had a run-in with pneumonia, and was looking forward to her 98th birthday being spent at home. She suggested that instead of reading from the Daily Bread like we usually did, we read her favorite verses in the Bible. Which we did.

After I finished reading them, we discussed the last passage I had read, and then there was silence on the phone. Mom just quit speaking. So, I hung up and called the nursing home, and asked them to check on her. Sure enough, she had passed away during our talk. Her memorial services were beautiful.

That spring, Stan began to have serious health issues, so we decided to go back to Washington and the VA doctors there. We moved back after the 4th of July. Sue had reached a plateau, and she was on the road to recovery. Stan was diagnosed with an inoperable cancer in August. The girls came home periodically and stayed with us. Shawn, Cyndi's husband was invaluable. Stan was admitted to the VA Hospice nursing home in October. I was able to move into a room with him.

For the first couple of weeks of his stay, I pushed him in a wheelchair down to where they had a piano, and played for him. As Stan grew weaker, Sallie came to spend the remaining time with us. When we could no longer wheel him to the piano, Sallie put her phone to his ear in his bed; I called her from the piano; he would smile as I played some of his favorite songs. He passed away on November 4. Services were in Fairbanks.

Then, in December, I had a hip replaced in Texas. So, it was not a good year, but I survived. The good news was that Sue was declared cancer-free after treatment.

HELLO, ALASKA

I went back to Washington that spring from Texas but soon decided there was no way I could maintain the property by myself, so I decided to put it on the market. I spent several months on E-bay selling some of our various collections, such as antique ham radios. The post office became used to seeing me deliver boxes for shipping. I was undecided as to what I might want to do once I'd sold the place, but I just couldn't face all that grass!

Then, in late June, Stan was buried at the cemetery in Fairbanks. Even though it was a sad occasion, I really enjoyed seeing my friends. Plus, grandson Brian had gotten married, and he and his wife had a tiny baby, Hazel. Hazel was so precious! I decided that once I'd sold the place in Washington, I'd move back to Fairbanks. I found a lot near Sallie and bought it. After I returned to Washington, Sallie oversaw the building of an excellent storage shed on the property.

Back in Washington, I decided it was time for me

to have a garage sale. I was vey lucky that Sallie and Jennifer, plus Cyndi and Shawn were able to come help. We were quite surprised to find that Stan had been stockpiling tools from the various sales we'd attended. Some items, like electric drills, had ten almost identical pieces. Sallie enjoyed cutting the grass with my riding mower, while the rest of us dealt with the buyers.

Once that sale was over, I contacted an estate manager, and soon we held an estate sale. I kept things I didn't want to sell in my bedroom and blocked it off from the buyers. The rest of the items were fair game. Lots of the items sold, but some didn't, and I asked the estate manager to donate them to charity. However, he was tied-up for a couple of weeks and couldn't haul away the donated items. They remained in the garage. Would you believe I found myself out there at least once a day, shopping? It was a relief when he returned and took the remaining unsold items to charity!

My son-in-law Jerry flew down from Anchorage, we rented a U-Haul, hired some guys to come load, and before long he was on the long trip to haul my stuff back to Alaska. He made good time on the road, and he and my other son-in-law Ron managed to get everything in the shed, even the extra stuff I'd snatched. We did have a few cases of wine left, and that went in Sallie's closet. I surely didn't want them to freeze!

Debbie and Henry came over to the Washington house from Montana and helped me get myself moved out of the house. I spent some time with them, then Sue flew in, and she and I drove a U-Haul to Texas, where we had a good winter.

I attended my granddaughter Stephanie's wedding in Anchorage in June of 2016, then went to stay with Sallie. I tried to get a house constructed on my lot but ran into permafrost difficulties, so I ended up buying a home in Fairbanks. I loved the location of the house, but it had a few things that I didn't like, so I decided to spend money on a remodel.

My kids thought I was nuts, but I recalled that old adage, "You can't take it with you!" I wanted to be comfortable. I had the dickens of a time trying to locate a contractor that would do what I wanted for a price I could afford. However, I cut the plans way back and finally found a contractor. The results make me very happy. I intend to live in this house as long as I possibly can. I also plan to continue spending my winters in Texas for as long as I am able to commute. It is the best of both worlds.

My family keeps expanding. Sallie's son Brian

and his wife Melisa had a handsome and smart son, Brooks. Then, her daughter Jennifer, my oldest granddaughter, gave birth to a healthy baby boy, Hudson, on Christmas Eve, and Stephanie, Sue's daughter, gave birth to a daughter, Adrianne, in May. So, I now have two great-grandsons and two great-granddaughters. How exciting!

NOODLES, ANYONE?

*L*ife with young children can be either scary or amusing, depending on your outlook. It really is fun to be a Great-Grandma or GG for short. Watching the little ones can be very entertaining. Take the following occurrence for example.

"Hello, Mom," Sallie said to me on the phone one morning. "Hazel's daycare is closed for the day, so I said I'd take time off from work and take care of her. I didn't want to play favorites, so I thought I'd also get Brooks. I think it would be fun to take them to lunch, want to come?"

"That sounds like quite a challenge, and yes, I'd like to come," I replied. "Where do you want to go? Do you want to come to get me, or should I meet you there?"

"I thought we'd go to the Noodle House, and we probably should get there around noon, since the kids are used to eating at noon," she replied. "I can come and get you. I have both car seats in the back seat so you can sit in the front seat."

All went well until we got inside the House. They didn't have a high-chair for Brooks!

"I can just hold him," Sallie said. "He really likes to eat noodles, so I'm sure it will be fine."

Brooks had just learned to walk, and he was not one bit happy with being confined to a lap.

The waiter came over and said, "You probably better move your car, since it's sticking out into that no-parking zone. I wouldn't like you to get a ticket."

I volunteered to move the car. Sallie gave me the keys, and off I went. When I came back, there was no one sitting at the table. As I suspected, they were all in the bathroom. They soon appeared, and the wait-staff found a booster chair for Hazel. She had just gotten seated, and Sallie was making her way to her chair, still struggling to carry Brooks, when Hazel said she needed to go poo!

"I'll be happy to hold Brooks while you're gone," I said. Which may have been a mistake, since he was not happy sitting on my lap, either. He was a wiggle-worm.

The upshot was that we had a rather unusual lunch, with the kids trying to slurp noodles, get down and run, blow bubbles in their water, and Brooks letting out a howl now and then when he ran out of noodles. Sallie and I both ended up wearing noodles and rice before she asked for the check and some boxes for leftovers. She mentioned something about herding cats, and I think she was right on target! By the time we were leaving, the place had filled with a couple of large groups seated at nearby tables. We got some interesting looks from the customers.

Sallie spent some time on her hands and knees trying to de-rice and de-noodle the floor. We were both relieved when the kids were once again strapped safely in their car seats. We made a quick trip by her office, to show off the noodle-laden kids, then she brought me back to the house, where I immediately had a nap. She headed home to put the kids down for a nap, and I'm sure she needed one herself! Someday we'll laugh about this. I wish I'd thought to take some pictures!

THE BIG SURPRISE!

*W*hen I had my 80th birthday in June, 2018, Sallie was out of town, and I had just returned from a ham radio convention, so I celebrated at home alone, with Tex (my Yorkie) as my company. It was a rather sad time since both Mom and Stan were gone. Our birthdays were within a five-day period of each other in June. I was the lone survivor.

Fast forward three months later. I was thrilled when Sue decided to make a quick visit to Fairbanks. Cyndi and Shawn were here, but spending most of their time at the mine. They planned to return on a Friday, and spend Saturday with Sue. We were all invited to Sallie's for a barbeque on Saturday night.

On Saturday morning, Cyndi, Shawn and I made a quick shopping trip, and then I thought it would be time to visit at Sallie's. But, no, Sue texted that they were coming to my house! They brought hot chocolate, so I was happy about that.

Then Cyndi and Shawn got a call about going to

meet some guy to look at a trailer, and Sallie got a call from the mayor and had to go talk to him. Which left me to take Sue out to the Pagoda to pick-up some take-home, so she could carry it back to Anchorage with her. We also made a quick stop at the Santa Claus house, since the Pagoda is located in North Pole, and so is the Santa Claus house.

On our way home (in the rain), the phone rang, and it was Sallie. "Mom," she said, "We're having a surprise birthday party for you in about an hour. So, if you want to go home and change, go ahead."

"What?" I asked. "Are you kidding me? You shouldn't tell me something like this when I'm driving! I knew you were planning a surprise party last week, but my surgery canceled that. Are you sure?"

"Yes," she replied. "I'm sure!"

"I can't believe Sallie caved," Sue told me as we continued towards home. "I would never have expected that from her. For my part, I was enjoying all the planning and scheming to keep you in the dark. I was surprised that I was actually pretty good at making up stories and a few lies. Actually, the whole thing kind of reminded me of when we were teenagers."

I did feel a bit on the gullible side, and wondered how many times they had pulled the wool over my eyes when they were teens!

Sue and I came home and got her food ready to travel. Then, off to the Pioneer Museum. Cyndi and Shawn had not gone to see someone about a trailer, and Sallie had not gone to see the mayor. Both of those phone calls had been from Ron, impersonating the callers. They had been busy decorating, getting the food set out, and plates on the tables. It looked lovely, including hanging decorations that said "80," and confetti that also said "80." There was a lovely bouquet of roses. Plus, a beautiful banner saying, "Happy Birthday 80," with pictures of me with the great grandkids, etc., hanging from it. Soon guests started arriving.

Our first guest was a neighbor lady that we'd had back in the 1980s. I hadn't seen her for a very long time, and we had a nice visit. Then more and more came, and I got lots of hugs.

Soon, Ron made the announcement. "We are here to celebrate my mother-in-law's 80th birthday. The food is ready, so grab your plate and dig in."

The barbequed chicken was delicious, and the salads were outstanding. Potato salad, coleslaw and Melisa's famous strawberry salad. Even the cupcakes were delightful.

Then, came the entertainment. This gentleman, Mike, played the ukulele and sang. He was an outstanding singer. Then, he took a break and made balloon art for the kids, and for me! I got a delightful hat, complete with a dachshund that would move in and out when I tipped my head. Then, he was back to singing. I may have joined him in a song or two, and might have danced a bit. Anyway, it was a lot of fun. Unfortunately, Sue had her video phone going, so that has been documented.

It was great to see people I hadn't seen in a long time. They all seemed to have a delightful time. I will never forget my 80th birthday party!

WHAT I'VE LEARNED

One of the most important things I've learned is that Life is an adventure. We only live once. I try hard to find at least one thing in each day that makes me happy. Even if the day has beaten me down, there has to be one thing that was pleasant… I try to search it out and give thanks.

I realize that if someone makes me mad, I need to forgive them right away. Staying mad and holding a grudge doesn't do a thing to the person I am mad at, they don't even know it, but it can make me miserable.

I also try to live each day as though it were my last. I don't go to bed angry with anyone, and I make peace with the world and my friends. I try to remember that this is my opportunity to get things right and to be sure that I do!

When my time comes to leave this world, I want to make sure I do it with a happy heart. I was put on this world for a purpose, and I intend to do all within my power to make sure that I've fulfilled that purpose.

Yes, Life is an adventure, and I give thanks for the day this Rose Bloomed.